I can't STOP Pushing

I can't STOP Pushing

CLAIRE BOOSEY

BOOSEY BOOKS

BOOSEY BOOKS

© 2025 Claire Boosey

All rights reserved.

No part of this publication may be reproduced, stored in a retrieval system, or transmitted in any form or by any means electronic, mechanical, photocopying, recording or otherwise without the prior written permission of the publisher, except in the case of brief quotations used in reviews or articles.

This is a work of creative nonfiction. Some names, places, and identifying details may have been changed to protect privacy.

Published by Boosey Books

ISBN: 978-1-0682310-0-1

Cover design and interior layout by Claire Boosey

A copy of this book has been deposited with the British Library in accordance with UK legal requirements.

First edition, 2025

This is for every parent, grandparent,
and carer out there. Enjoy every moment.
There's no way of knowing where
your journey will take you.

And for my mum, Glynis
Thank you for showing me what the
best mum in the world looks like.

Introduction

Hi, I'm Olivia Field. I am about 5 foot 8, with long brown hair that always seems to have a mind of its own. You'll usually find me in jeans and a T-shirt… I've never been one for keeping up with the latest fashion trends.

Oh, and did I mention? I'm also a proud mum of two beautiful boys. From the time I was a little girl, I have known deep down that my ultimate dream was to become a mum. I couldn't wait for that moment when I'd finally hear '*mummy*' for the first time.

But let's face it… parenting doesn't come with an instruction manual or step-by-step guide. And even if it did, kids would never follow it anyway. The reality of motherhood is a rollercoaster of emotions. It's constantly worrying if you're doing it right, and feeling guilty about all the ways you think you're getting it wrong. It's sleeping with one eye open… or when you are awake (well, half-awake) … feeling like you need eyes in the back of your head.

I CAN'T STOP PUSHING

Every day brings a new challenge: a new kind of tantrum, an unexpected injury from *who-knows-where*, or a mystery stain that appears on the clean laundry you *just* folded. And just when you think you've finally got the house in order, it's time to start the cleaning process all over again.

Having a family is a whole different ball game. There's absolutely no way to plan for what you might go through. The good times, the tough ones, the ones that knock the wind out of you, and the ones that make your heart burst… they're rarely what you expect.

All you can do is take each moment as it comes and do your best to navigate through it. But despite the chaos and the never-ending to-do lists, being a mum is hands down the best job in the world.

Well… except for the part where we don't get paid. Would I trade it for anything? *Absolutely not!*

I didn't know what kind of mum I'd be. I just knew I'd never stop trying. I can't stop pushing through the mess, the love, the fear, the laughter and somehow, I've made it this far. No matter how busy, confusing, or frustrating it gets, I wouldn't give it up for the world… but ask me again after I've had another glass of wine.

Chapter 1

"THERE'S NO ONE HERE TO COLLECT ME!"

Let's start from the very beginning. I was in my mid-twenties and a lot slimmer than I am now. I was still living at home in Knysna, South Africa, with my mum (Ann), dad (Malcolm), and two younger sisters (Kelly and Tash).

I'd been working at the same hotel for five years. I started as a Guest Liaison (a fancy name for receptionist), then moved up to Front of House Manager, and finally into reservations.

Even though I was happy enough in my job, I couldn't help noticing that everyone around me seemed to be off travelling or doing something exciting… and I was still in the same place. Same job. Same routine. I never did the university or college thing.

I jumped straight into work. I was 19 when I started at the hotel… no student parties or experiences and no feeling of independence. Just full-time, grown-up responsibility. Since I hadn't gone to university or done any formal hotel training, everything I knew was self-taught. I learned on the job… every shift, every awkward guest, every complaint.

I CAN'T STOP PUSHING

They say the best experience is life experience… and honestly, it's done me wonders so far. I still remember a colleague, who was halfway through hotel school, asking where I'd trained, as he was amazed at how well I dealt with a guest complaint.

I laughed and told him I hadn't trained anywhere… unless you count learning through sheer panic and a lot of polite smiling.

If you're wondering about my relationship status… well, by then, I'd had a few breakups. I'd been through enough to know what I *didn't* want. I wasn't sure what I was looking for next, but I was ready to do something for myself. I needed a change.

When a friend mentioned working on a cruise ship… a perfect mix of work and travel… I was sold. The application process was long and tedious, but totally worth it. I was accepted to join a ship in Australia as a Junior Assistant Purser (basically reception again, but this time floating at sea).

I didn't even read my contract properly. Turns out crew members were allowed two 20kg bags. I only packed one tiny bag, completely unaware of what I'd need… and totally forgetting to save space for all the shopping I'd obviously be doing.

"THERE'S NO ONE HERE TO COLLECT ME!"

♥♥♥

The day arrived. This was the first time I was travelling overseas. Excited? Absolutely. Nervous? Even more so. My parents took me to the airport. We were early, so we enjoyed one last coffee together, then it was time to say goodbye.

"We are so proud of you", they said as they each gave me a cuddle. That did not help with my emotions. So, the goodbye turned into a very emotional one with a few extra cuddles, and more tears, than planned.

I gave them one last wave, took a deep breath and then made my way through security, followed by a long walk to the gate. I didn't have to wait there long before they began the boarding process. As I boarded the plane, my heart began to race. Who would I be sitting next to? Would they be friendly? Or would I be lucky enough to be seated next to no one? Once on the plane, I got the window seat (thank goodness… always best for sleeping).

I popped my carry-on bag in the overhead locker and held onto my smaller bag which had a few essentials like hand cream, lip balm and ear plugs. I sat eagerly waiting as everyone boarded to see who I was sitting next to. Then a very kind looking older gentleman stopped next to me and put his bag in the overhead locker. He then sat down and introduced himself. Well, we did not stop talking…

which made the time fly (excuse the pun).

Talking has always been second nature to me… keeping quiet, not so much. My mum, used to joke that the only time she truly got peace and quiet was when I lost my voice.

♥♥♥

Anyway, back to my story. As this was my first flight on my own, I needed to find a way to relax… and it was on this flight that I discovered the "routine" I now use every time I travel.

Once the plane reaches altitude and the drinks service comes around, I always ask for water (to refill the bottle I'd emptied at security) and, of course, a white wine… because yes, I was in *desperate* need of alcohol.

When the meal service comes around, I choose the vegetarian option if available, or pasta… because honestly, you never quite know what the meat is meant to be. And naturally, another white wine. Just one more couldn't hurt.

Then I'd pop on a good movie, eat my dinner in peace, and once the trays were cleared, ask for a cup of tea during the final drinks run. After that, I'd head to the bathroom, brush my teeth, have a wee (obviously), and

"THERE'S NO ONE HERE TO COLLECT ME!"

do my little night-time routine before trying to get comfy enough to sleep… key word: *trying*.

When the cabin lights turn on before breakfast, I'd freshen up quickly, change out of my cosy travel clothes, pop on a little mascara, and get ready to disembark.

♥♥♥

Finally, after what felt like an eternity in the air, we touched down in Sydney, Australia. I got through passport control easily and made my way to the arrival's hall… and that's when the panic hit. There was no one there to collect me. I searched. Looked around. Checked every sign. Nothing. To make it worse, my phone didn't work yet, and I had no way to call anyone.

Thankfully, I spotted the gentleman from the flight and asked to borrow his phone. He kindly said yes. I dialled my mum's number without a second thought. It was 6 a.m. back home in South Africa, but I knew my mum would always be there when I needed her. To my surprise, she picked up on the first ring.

"Hi, Mum, it's me," I said. "I'm at the airport in Australia, and there's no one here to collect me. I'm calling from the phone of a gentleman I was sitting next to on the plane, as mine isn't working yet. Could you please contact the cruise ship company to make sure someone is on the way?"

"Don't worry. Leave it with me, and I'll give them a call," she said.

I handed the phone back to the gentleman and thanked him. Now, all I could do was wait. Ten minutes later, he tapped me on the shoulder to let me know my mum was on the phone. "I spoke to them, and someone will be there as soon as possible," she assured me.

I knew that wasn't a cheap call for her to make, but it was a relief to know everything was sorted. I thanked her for her help and then I thanked the gentleman once more before finding a place to sit and wait.

To make matters worse, I desperately needed to pee, but knowing my luck, just as I left, the person picking me up would arrive. I couldn't hold it any longer and dashed to the restroom and returned to my seat as quickly as I could.

When I returned, *luckily just in time*, I saw someone running through the doors waving a sign with my name on it. Well, at least I finally got to see the sign with my name on it. But this guy seemed mental!
Finally! I thought, feeling so relieved.

Completely out of breath he grabbed my bags, apologised for the delay, and urged me to hurry.

"THERE'S NO ONE HERE TO COLLECT ME!"

"We're running so late," he said.

Thank goodness I didn't wait to go to the toilet, I thought. In the car, and on the way there, he took this opportunity to explain, "Out of the thousands of emails I receive, I clearly must have missed the email about picking you up."

I didn't even care… I was just relieved someone had shown up.

♥♥♥

We made it to the cruise ship in record time, zooming through the security tent for my passport and bag check. I swear, I've never moved so fast in my life. The security tent seemed quiet though. There was no one around and I was about to find out why.

Finally, we made our way down the hall and back into the light again. And there it was… what an incredible sight. The ship was gorgeous. But I barely had time to admire it.

I looked around and it hit me… just how late we were. Every single passenger was already on the ship and every senior officer, including the captain, was waiting for *me*.

The moment I stepped on board, the doors closed, and the ship began to move. The sea was rough that day, and I felt *everything*. Seasick. Homesick. Completely overwhelmed. They showed me to my cabin, and

I CAN'T STOP PUSHING

within hours, I was in tears. This was the first time I'd travelled so far, all alone, to a completely new place. I felt like I'd made a huge mistake. I just wanted to go home.

My manager (the front-of-house manager) gave me an internet card so I could video call my mum. I was so grateful…until, fast forward a few weeks later, I saw it had been charged to my crew account.

Yep. She billed me for it. Thankfully, I had a lovely cabin neighbour who let me use her laptop to call home for free as I didn't have a laptop. She didn't charge me. She just helped.

That call with my mum was full of tears and "I want to come home" outbursts. But she insisted I give it a few weeks. And I'm *so* glad I did.

♥♥♥

As I settled in, life on board slowly became fun. The crew bar events. The amazing people. The totally ridiculous guest questions…like, "Do you sleep on the ship?" (Our answer: "No, a helicopter picks us up each night and drops us off again in the morning."

One guest swore they'd heard the helicopter.) One time, while walking near the pool, a couple asked me if the water came from the ocean. I said yes. The woman

"THERE'S NO ONE HERE TO COLLECT ME!"

turned to her husband and said, "See? That's why there are waves!" Let's just say there was never a dull day at work.

A month had passed, and I was feeling even more at ease...not just with ship life, but also with exploring the incredible ports we visited. Some of the islands we stopped at included Nouméa, Port Denarau, and Isle of Pines, to name a few.

During one stop in Port Denarau, a colleague and I decided to visit a local restaurant. The weather was *awful*... strong winds and heavy rain... but that didn't stop us.

Because the ship was too large to dock directly, we had to take a tender boat to shore. These boats only carried around 20 people, and the rough seas made each trip take even longer.

Once on land, we decided to spend most of our time at the restaurant...it was warm, the food was great, and we were just happy to be somewhere dry. Let's just say...we enjoyed ourselves a little more than planned.

Before we knew it, we had less than an hour before our shift started. Panic set in as we rushed back to the port...only to find a tender queue of nearly 100 passengers. And of course, they had priority over crew.

I CAN'T STOP PUSHING

As we waited (and waited…), the clock kept ticking and the storm worsened. We were soaked, cold, and mildly regretting that extra drink. The boat ride back was painfully slow, and by the time we arrived, we were late.

We sprinted to our cabins, changed in record time, and made it to the desk about 20 minutes behind schedule. Not ideal, but at least we made it.

We braced ourselves as we walked into the front-of-house manager's office. Thankfully, we got away with a warning and a raised eyebrow.

It was definitely not our most professional moment… but we survived, slightly wobbly and a whole lot wiser. Still, I won't lie… it was one of the most fun shifts I ever worked.

Chapter 2

"ENGAGED AND EXPECTING A BABY."

I had been onboard for a few months now and was thoroughly enjoying it.

One morning, as I was going about my duties, the retail manager was setting up for a fashion show, to showcase the latest outfits for the themed nights onboard. They needed some models for the show, and as luck would have it, I was just about to take my break.

"Olivia, would you mind being a model in the show?" the manager called out to me.

"Sure, why not. I've got some spare time," I replied.

And just like that, I found myself getting ready for the upcoming show… a show that would unexpectedly change my life forever. We were paired up, and I would be walking alongside another crew member named Jack. We were all dressed in our Hawaiian-themed outfits waiting for our turn. The retail manager shared hilarious tidbits about each crew member as they showed off their outfits. From being secret mimes to marrying celebrities, she had the crowd in stitches and gathering around for more. Then came my turn in the spotlight.

I CAN'T STOP PUSHING

"And now," the retail manager announced, "for James and Olivia - who are engaged and expecting a baby!" The audience could clearly see the confusion on my face and burst out laughing.

"Engaged and expecting a baby?" I said, "Who's James?" Jack couldn't contain his laughter. "I have no idea what she is talking about," I whispered to him, starting to blush. I kept looking around trying to work out who on earth James was, but still had to remember to finish doing the show.

♥♥♥

After the fashion show, I decided to do a little investigating to learn more about this mysterious James. I was curious... of course.

As part of our training, we rotated through multiple roles during our contract so that if someone fell ill, there was always someone else ready to step in. Thanks to that, I had access to crew accounts... which, as it turns out, was very handy for a little detective work. I began doing some digging... and imagine my surprise when I discovered that there weren't just one or two, but four different James's in the retail department, let alone the rest of the ship! Naturally, I called the retail manager to ask which James she was talking about.

"ENGAGED AND EXPECTING A BABY."

"Hey, it's Olivia," I said. "I couldn't help but wonder which James you were referring to during the fashion show." Without any hesitation, the retail manager replied, "Oh, it's James Bailey. The tall one with the cheeky grin."

"Thanks," I said and hung up the phone. Thinking back now, I realise she made the whole thing up...she could've picked any of them.

But there was something about her response that made me feel a sense of excitement in me - I had to meet him. So, I straightened my uniform, checked my hair, and gave my makeup a quick touch-up before making my way across the atrium... a large open area in the centre of the ship where events were held, including the fashion show.

The shop James worked in was directly across from the reception desk. As I approached, I started to get nervous. I noticed his sandy-blonde hair and towering six-foot frame straight away. Just to be sure, I checked his name badge. Yep - James. He was undeniably handsome, and the thought of striking up a conversation made my palms sweat. Trying to appear relaxed and desperately searching for an excuse to talk to him, I decided to stand by the lip balm display near where he stood. "Hey there," I said, pretending to examine the labels. "Any recommendations for a good lip balm flavour?" James turned and smiled.

I CAN'T STOP PUSHING

"Hmm… how about the strawberry one? Always a good choice." I laughed nervously.

"Thanks. By the way… you're James, right?" He nodded. "Yes, that's me. Why do you ask?" I took a deep breath and dropped the bombshell. "Well, apparently we're engaged and expecting a baby…so I thought we might as well meet."

To my surprise, he just laughed and said, "Nice to meet you."

"I'm Olivia, by the way." And just like that, the conversation flowed effortlessly. We chatted about anything and everything. That quirky encounter… over lip balm… started a wonderful friendship.

♥♥♥

One fun part of being a crew member? Parties were a regular thing. My job title meant I was a half-stripe officer (the number of stripes indicates your rank), which gave me access to the Officers' Bar…sort of an elite crew bar for certain staff only.

One evening, there was a formal dress-up party there. I wore a stunning strapless black dress and the perfect black stilettos. Drinks were flowing, and I was feeling radiant…and a little tipsy. Since the Officers'

"ENGAGED AND EXPECTING A BABY."

Bar didn't have a dance floor, we all migrated to the crew bar where the real party was.

It was exactly what I needed - to dance the night away. Before I knew it, the dance floor cleared, leaving only James and I in the centre.

It was as if fate had intervened… as I didn't even know he was in the bar that night. And then… we kissed.

Time seemed to stand still as our lips met for the first time. We were so lost in the moment; we didn't even notice the crowd of people cheering in the background.

But there was one slight complication… I was already 'seeing' Justin, an engineer onboard. It wasn't serious - what we called a 'ship relationship'. Still, I didn't want to rock the boat (excuse the pun), so I decided to wait until he left, which was only a week away. James was fully aware of Justin and that I wanted to wait. He completely agreed…thank goodness. But we couldn't help ourselves. We started seeing each other secretly during that week. I was just so drawn to him. Clearly, he felt the same way.

♥♥♥

One night, I was watching a movie with Justin, but I couldn't stop thinking about James.

I made up every excuse to go back to my cabin. The second I got there; I rang James. Only it wasn't James who answered... it was his mischievous roommate, Alex. "Well, well, well, look who's calling," he teased. "Shall I let Justin know what you're up to?"

"No! Please don't," I begged. He laughed. "Don't worry, I'm only joking." What a relief and he passed the phone to James. "Hey," James said... just that one word... and I instantly felt better.

"Want to come over? I really want to see you."

"Absolutely. I'll be there in a minute."

"Great," I said. "Can't wait."

I heard a knock at the door. I opened it...and there he was, towering over me, arms casually resting on the doorframe. There was something so sexy about the way he stood there. I didn't wait another second... I pulled him in and kissed him.

We spent the night talking and laughing (don't get too excited...it was all PG at that point).

The next few days went quickly and before we knew it... Justin left the ship. From that moment on, James and I were inseparable. Shore adventures on different islands, dinner dates onboard, spontaneous meet-ups in the crew bar and in our cabins.

Our first *official* date was on the stunning Isle of Pines,

"ENGAGED AND EXPECTING A BABY."

and the day couldn't have been more perfect. We slipped into our swimwear, packed our bags, and hopped onto the tender boat to shore. Once we arrived, we decided to try some local delicacies…fresh coconut milk straight from the coconut (just add a straw), and chicken wrapped in banana leaves. While it wasn't my favourite, we did discover something exciting about each other: we both enjoyed trying new and unique foods.

Later, we headed to the beach to snorkel and splash about. We even set the camera on a timer and got playful shots of him lifting me in his arms. We didn't want the day to end.

Our next memorable stop? Our second date - Cairns, Australia. This was the first time the ship was staying overnight, and James had planned a surprise date on shore. I love surprises!

"Where are we going?" I asked, walking off the ship hand in hand. "It's a secret," he said, smiling. He was such fun, and I couldn't wait to see what he had planned! Our evening began with a visit to an indoor market offering clothed massages. What a treat and I just felt so relaxed.

From there, we enjoyed a delicious Bali-style dinner, where we ordered loads of different dishes to try.
Our shared love for food only deepened our relationship.

I CAN'T STOP PUSHING

And of course, we had to end the night with a bit of dancing at a lively local bar. It was so much fun… and we may have had a few too many drinks. By the time midnight rolled around, we knew it was time to head home. It was quite a long walk back, and let's just say we were pretty tipsy by this point.

As we walked through the park… just the two of us… on our way back to the ship, the drinks from earlier had gone through me *very* quickly… and I *really* needed to pee. I knew I wouldn't make it back to the ship without finding somewhere to relieve myself.

I found a nice big tree to hide behind and James stood guard. So, with my skirt up and knickers down… peeing… a strange sensation began to crawl up my legs.

Squirming uncomfortably and just managing to pull up my knickers, I asked James to turn on his phone flashlight. To our horror… I was *covered* in red ants.

I danced and squirmed, frantically brushing them off. In the hurry of trying to get rid of the relentless attackers, I had completely forgotten that my skirt was still up around my waist.

Finally, ant free, I breathed a sigh of relief and redressed myself…just in time for James to spot a security camera nearby. Brilliant. I'm sure whoever was

"ENGAGED AND EXPECTING A BABY."

watching was wetting themselves laughing.

♥♥♥

As we made our way back to the ship, hand in hand, it was now the early hours of the morning. In a moment of boldness (or pure insanity), I blurted out to James, "I thought you were going to ask me to marry you tonight," he looked baffled. "What made you think that?"

Looking back, I still can't fathom why I asked this question. But then still added, "The evening just had that vibe, you know?"

And just when I thought I couldn't make it worse, I added, "If you ever do decide to ask, my dream is for you to ask my dad first."

In hindsight, maybe I should've kept my fantasies to myself. But to my surprise, James didn't seem overly bothered by this conversation.

That's a good thing…right?

Chapter 3

"JAMES, WHAT DID YOU DO?"

As James and I spent more time together, we began to understand each other's struggles - not just the obvious ones, but the unexpected challenges that come with life on a ship. Life was a bit like a never-ending rollercoaster, full of surprises and ups and downs.

Before I started working on the ship, I hadn't given much thought to the kind of injuries we might face, or the toll the environment could take on our bodies.

One thing that took me a while to adjust to was the constant movement of the ship, especially in rough seas. You quickly learn that *everything* needs to be secured…because if it isn't, it'll slide around. And trust me, you don't want to be on the wrong side of the wall when an unsecured industrial printer comes crashing down.

Walking? Let's just say you'd be strolling down the hallway one minute, and the next, the ship would tilt, and you'd find yourself thrown sideways into a wall. It was unnerving at first. I lost count of how many times I

"JAMES, WHAT DID YOU DO?"

had to grab the hallway rails just to stay upright… especially when the seas were rough. It was like trying to walk on a moving tightrope. Over time, we all adapted. You learned to stand with your legs slightly apart, like a balance board.

Dining during rough seas was another experience altogether. If you weren't careful, your food and drink would end up sliding across the table, making an already difficult meal even more complicated. This is why everything needs to be securely fastened…especially the big heavy things like cupboards and equipment.

If you were sitting in a chair with wheels, one minute you'd be sitting there enjoying your meal or working, and the next, you'd be sliding across the floor as if you were on a skate rink. It could be quite entertaining, actually, but also a little frustrating when you just want to eat in peace!

One thing that surprised me was the misconception many people had about seasickness. I'd often see guests slumped over on couches, trying to avoid the feeling of nausea by lying down, but what they didn't realise was that this only made things worse. The best way to manage it? Walk. Move with the ship. It's the only way to help your body adjust to the constant rocking.

I CAN'T STOP PUSHING

Fight the motion and you'll only feel worse. It was one of those things you had to learn the hard way... but once you got it, it made a world of difference.

One unexpected perk of the ship's movement, though, was how well I slept. While others moaned about the rocking, I found it soothing. It was like being rocked to sleep in a giant, moving cradle. I'd never slept so well in my life.

Anyway, where was I? Oh yes... One night, I had a few friends over in my cabin... including my roommate and a couple of other girls. We were having drinks, listening to music, and enjoying a good natter. The seas were rough, but we were used to it by now. Suddenly, there was a knock at the door.

When I opened it, I saw James standing there, holding a bunch of tissues to his head...they were soaked in blood.

"James! What did you do?" I gasped.

He explained he'd been in the retail storage cupboard when the ship tilted suddenly. He lost his balance and slammed his head into one of the shelves. Hard. I felt sick with worry. Thankfully, one of the girls in my cabin was a ship doctor.

"JAMES, WHAT DID YOU DO?"

She didn't hesitate… she just switched into full doctor mode. "Let's get you down to the medical centre," she said. Of course, I went with them. There was no way I was letting him go down there alone.

He ended up needing a few stitches, but thankfully he was okay. It could have been so much worse. Still, it left me shaken to realise how quickly things could change.

There were other challenges I hadn't considered: long shifts, late nights, and the constant exhaustion that comes from a lack of sleep. You don't realise how much of an impact this has on your body until you're deep into it.

A few weeks later, it was my turn. I'd spent the day enjoying one of the islands, but when I got back onboard, I started to feel really strange. Lightheaded. Weak. Like I was about to faint. I tried to sleep it off, but nothing helped. Something felt seriously off, and my gut told me I needed help.

The crew doctor was on a break, so I went straight to reception and called the emergency line… usually reserved for guests. I explained my symptoms, and they told me to head straight to the medical centre. On my way down, a colleague passed me and said, "You don't look well."

She was right. I felt awful.

I CAN'T STOP PUSHING

The doctor on duty, the same friend who'd helped James, ran some tests, then stepped out to speak with the senior doctor. I started to worry. What was wrong with me?

When she returned, she explained my potassium levels were dangerously low. I needed an IV drip, and the treatment would take ten hours. I'd never had anything like this before… but I trusted her. I agreed to the treatment. She led me to the treatment room and asked if I needed to use the bathroom before they got started. After going to the bathroom, I settled into the bed, and they hooked up the IV. As I lay there, two thoughts hit me:

One, I needed to call the front desk and let them know I wouldn't be working my shift.

Two, I needed to call James. He'd be wondering where I was… we usually saw each other on our break.

I rang the office first. They were lovely and told me to rest and keep them posted. Then I called James. As soon as I explained, I could hear the worry in his voice.

"Can you bring me a few things? I need comfy clothes… and my laptop." I asked. "Ten hours staring at a blank wall? I'd go mad."

"JAMES, WHAT DID YOU DO?"

"Of course," he said. "I'll be there as soon as I can."

Fifteen minutes later, he arrived. "I don't like seeing you like this," he said, giving me a kiss hello. I reassured him I was okay and told him he could stay a while if he wanted. So, he did. We sat and chatted, about everything and nothing.

Eventually, after he left, I managed to drift off to sleep. Time passed quicker than I expected. When the drip finished, the doctor told me I needed to up my potassium.

"Bananas are one of the best sources," she said. There was just one problem - I hate bananas. The taste wasn't so bad, because I love my mum's banana bread that she makes… YUM! But there was something about the texture that makes me gag.

Still, for the sake of my health, I forced myself to eat them for the next couple of weeks. Luckily, I never had another drop in potassium again… even when I stopped eating bananas. Getting more rest probably helped too.

It was the first time I'd seen James injured… and the first time he'd seen me really unwell. I think that's when we realised, we actually cared. Like, really cared.

Chapter 4

"I HEART YOU."

After James's head injury and my time in the medical centre on an IV drip, our relationship only grew stronger.
And yes...it was finally time for him to meet my parents.

The moment had arrived. James was about to meet my parents...well, sort of. Since we were on the cruise ship, the best we could manage was a video call from my cabin. I was nervous at first, but once the conversation started, it just flowed. It was so much easier than I expected.

After a nice long chat, James had to get back to work. Once he left, I stayed on the call with my mum...and that's when she said something that completely stopped me in my tracks.
"You're glowing," she said. "I can see it now. One day, you'll marry him." Wow. That was not what I expected.

As the weeks passed, James and I became more aware of how little time we had left together. My vacation was approaching - a standard nine-week

"I HEART YOU."

break - and we weren't scheduled to return to the same ship afterwards. The thought of being apart made everything feel uncertain. While our time together had been nothing short of amazing, we both knew that long-distance relationships weren't easy. So, we decided to take things as they came…no pressure.

♥♥♥

During my final week onboard, James's roommate left the ship, and he wasn't assigned a new one. So, what did I do? I moved in with him, of course. With my departure approaching, we were determined to spend every possible moment together.

That week, we took our relationship to a whole new level. We had sex…a lot of it! Every morning, every night, and whenever we had a free moment, we were together. On days when our shifts didn't line up, I took the chance to sleep in - but James had other plans. He'd sneak away from work for a bathroom break, dash back to the room, and surprise me with a "quickie." It was such a fun week, and neither of us wanted it to end.

But soon, it was time to pack my bags. My suitcase was small and, thanks to some serious shopping, I had way more to take home. So, I came up with a plan - a box. Yep. I boxed up the overflow. Why not?

I CAN'T STOP PUSHING

Then, the day finally came for me to leave. I didn't want to go. I couldn't hug or kiss him enough...I clung to every last second. I'd never found it so hard to say goodbye to someone...until that day.

As I walked off the ship and made my way to the airport, I cried the entire way. I already missed him so much...it honestly felt like my heart was breaking.

♥♥♥

During those weeks apart, we talked for hours on video calls. I could *feel* the distance in my chest...that heavy, physical ache when someone you love isn't nearby. With every conversation, we grew closer, and our desire for each other grew stronger. Eventually, we both knew: no matter the distance, we were going to make this work.

So, one beautiful sunny day in October, we officially committed to each other. It wasn't just a cruise ship fling...it was real.

It was something I'd never felt before.

For our next contract, James had originally been scheduled to join a different ship. But he managed to rearrange his contract, and as luck would have it, our new start dates overlapped slightly. The good news? We would be on the same ship.

"I HEART YOU."

My flight was scheduled to arrive in Australia the same day James disembarked for his nine-week holiday. I was booked to stay in a hotel for the night and then join the ship the following day.

So, James made a plan. He changed his flight so he could spend that night with me.

I was *so excited*! The end of my nine-week holiday couldn't come fast enough. I filled my days with catching up with friends, and as soon as I could, I started packing my bags.

This time, I packed *two* bags - I was going to be prepared. I even got my hair done during my final week. I wanted to look nice when I saw him again. Like, first-date kind of nice.

As it was expensive to get my hair done on the ship and ashore, my hairdresser gave me a great trick…flip your hair forward into a ponytail on top of your head, cut straight across with the amount you want removed, and voilà…instant layers. She saved me a fortune.

♥♥♥

The day finally came. My bags were packed and in the car. My dad was driving me to the airport, since he had work nearby. I hugged my mum goodbye and we were off. When we got there, I found out my flight was delayed by an hour. Thank goodness…my connecting flight had a five-hour layover anyway, so now it was shorter.

We went to check in, and I handed over my passport. The agent looked at it and asked, "Is this your only passport?" I was confused … until I looked down. I'd brought the *expired* one.

Thank goodness for that delay. My dad rushed to meet my mum halfway to grab the correct one. He made it back just in time. Bags checked. A quick coffee. Then I boarded the plane.

The flight was smooth, and I stuck to my usual routine.

♥♥♥

As soon as I landed, I had a message from James: he was already at the hotel. My heart *raced*. I rushed through passport control, grabbed my bags, and jumped on the transfer to the hotel.

When I arrived, there he was…standing in the lobby. I ran straight into his arms and held on tight. It was the happiest, longest hug after being apart for so long.

We checked in and headed up to his room.

Technically, I had a shared room booked with another crew member… not that I ever went there.

"I HEART YOU."

James and I dropped our bags and got ready for dinner. We spent the night in the bar - eating, talking, and just holding hands. That feeling of *normal*, of being together again…it was everything.

On the way back to the room, we stepped into the lift. It was empty, and we couldn't wait any longer. James pulled me close and kissed me like he hadn't kissed me in months… because, well, he hadn't. We were completely lost in the moment… until the elevator jolted to a stop. He paused and looked at me.

"Looks like we got a bit carried away." We laughed, kissed again, and practically floated back to the room. Things got a little heated…I'll just leave it there.

While we were apart, we'd agreed to save those three special words for when we were face to face. You know the ones.

Sure, we'd found creative ways to work around it…like "I heart you" or sending emojis…but nothing compared to saying it out loud and in person. So, there we were, lying side by side. We looked at each other and said it at the same time: "I love you."
Just like that, it was real. Undeniable. Unstoppable.

I CAN'T STOP PUSHING

The next morning came too quickly, and it was time to say goodbye again. Another nine weeks apart…but this time, we knew we'd be together again soon. We spoke as often as we could, counting down the days.

And then…finally…James joined the ship. I knew I wouldn't see him right away. He had training. I had work. But I was watching the clock like a hawk. I'm not usually one to wish time away, but this time, I couldn't wait.

We'd planned to meet in the crew bar that night. The second my shift ended, I was *gone*. And there he was. I ran straight into his arms. Finally…we were together on the same ship.

We explored so many incredible places together and, best of all, spent so much more time together.

Then came our first Valentine's Day - and James pulled out all the stops. He'd secretly teamed up with my cabin mate and snuck into my room to leave a surprise: Photos of us printed and mounted on A4 boards, covered in crystal stickers. I love a bit of sparkle. And a cake. A custom cake made by the chef.

Walking in after work to find all of this was an incredible surprise. And as you know…I love surprises!

"I HEART YOU."

We even had a very fancy dinner that night. James spoiled me rotten. It was perfect…one of those nights you never forget.

♥♥♥

As we got to know each other better, I learnt that behind the scenes, James was dealing with something far more serious. His mum was very unwell. She had cancer. And being miles away wasn't easy.

I could see the worry in his eyes every time he mentioned her. I only got to meet her once…over a video call. Meeting the parents is always nerve-wracking, and there were a few moments of silence, but she quickly put me at ease.

"It's so nice to finally meet you," she said. "You too," I replied. "James speaks so highly of you."

The conversation was brief, but in that short time, I could see just how much she and his dad meant to him. There was a kindness in her voice that made me feel so welcome. It was a small but meaningful moment - one I was truly grateful to have.

♥♥♥

As our time together grew, I couldn't help but feel more and more drawn to James, and it was clear he felt the same way. One day, during my break, James asked for my help.

I CAN'T STOP PUSHING

He was now working in the jewellery shop onboard. I wandered into the store, waiting for him to finish with a customer.

When he saw me standing there, his face lit up, and he made his way over, then leaned casually on the display case. "Thanks for helping me out," he said. "Of course, what do you need?" I asked.

"Well," he began, "I've got a guy looking to buy a ring for his girlfriend, but he's not sure which style to go for. Could you help me pick out a few options?"

"Absolutely," I said, "Let's see what you've got."

As we looked through the rings, he sneakily slipped in a few questions about what I liked…and my ring size. I had no idea he was setting me up.

♥♥♥

As the days went on, James's mum was getting worse and she was moved into an end-of-life care home. James made the difficult decision to leave the ship two weeks early so that he could be with her.

During these last two weeks, I worked the night shift, which gave me the opportunity to explore more of the ports during the day.

Being an officer had its perks. Like eating in the officers' mess. This is where the managers, as well as

"I HEART YOU."

the captain, ate. And… the best one… wine at breakfast. Because if you worked nights, you weren't allowed to drink beforehand.

So, naturally, I made sure to take full advantage of this! I would call ahead to order my meal, then when my shift ended, I would head down to the officer's mess and pour myself a glass of wine to enjoy with my breakfast. Why not?

The wine was cheap and looked like apple juice…but it was free. Once I finished eating, I would head back to my cabin with a top-up to watch a movie.

♥♥♥

The night shifts were far from quiet. You would assume that working on a night shift might be calmer as guests would be sleeping. Nope!
Here are three stories for you…

Story 1: The first story started with a call around 11:30 p.m. from a guest saying they could hear a child crying…constantly. I got the same call more than once.

Eventually, I sent a security guard to check it out. He knocked. No answer. But he could clearly hear crying. So, he let himself in…and found a little girl, no older than three, completely alone in the cabin.

He brought her to me at reception. I sat her in the back room with a blanket, put a cartoon on my phone, and kept

I CAN'T STOP PUSHING

her calm while we figured out where her parents were.

Now, how do you track down parents in a packed cruise ship bar? Easy. You block their cruise ship card. See, your cruise card is like your onboard credit card. Block it, and when they can't buy anything…they have to come to reception.

It only took about half an hour before a couple arrived, confused and frustrated, asking why their card had been blocked. I confirmed their cabin number…then…you can only imagine their faces when I then dropped the bombshell: "I have your daughter."

I'm pretty sure their mouths would've hit the floor if that were humanly possible. I asked them to wait, then gently explained to the little girl that her mummy and daddy were outside. I scooped her up and brought her out…and she *clung* to me.

They tried to comfort her, but she didn't want to let go of me. Turns out, they'd wanted a night off - a "date night" and left her in the care of her two older siblings…who we later discovered were in the cabin next door watching TV. Let's just say…they were in a lot of trouble.

Story 2: The second story started around midnight two days later. A man (let's call him Mr Moody)

"I HEART YOU."

stumbled up to the desk, slammed his beer down, and began giving me the mouthful of the century.

Angry, loud, slurring his words - and I was struggling to even understand what the issue was. I picked up my pen to take notes, but he was rambling so much, I had no clue what he was saying.

Eventually, I had to put my foot down...well, actually, my fist, really...I banged my fist on the counter to get his attention. He stopped. Stared at me.

"I'm so sorry Mr Moody," I said. "But I *can't* help you if you keep shouting at me."

Turns out, he'd received multiple letters about his account but hadn't read or understood them. His cruise card had been frozen because there was no proof of payment - no cash deposit, no credit card. It was simple to fix.

He told me that no one made him aware of this when he checked in. I apologised for this and explained that if he gave me either one now, I could unlock the account immediately. He did as he was asked then grumbled and groaned under his breath, grabbed his beer and walked away.

Two days later - final cruise day - I spotted Mr Moody walking by the reception desk with a trolley full of artwork. I tried to hide behind my colleague. Too late.

I CAN'T STOP PUSHING

He saw me and walked over. "Are you the lady I met the other night?" he asked. "...Yes," I said, bracing myself.

"I just wanted to say thank you. You saved my cruise." Not what I expected...but it absolutely made my day.

Story 3: The last story happened that night. I started my shift early. The desk was rammed with guests checking in for the next cruise. It was chaos!

I was in the back grabbing water when a colleague came rushing in to say a guest was kicking off about her luggage.

As you know, I was very good when it comes to complaints, so I stepped in. I introduced myself and asked how I could help. She was fired up!

Considering how busy the desk was, she did not hold back. She began shouting at me loudly, *very loudly*, that her luxury suitcase had been dropped in the mud, and she wanted housekeeping to clean it...now!

She was swearing in front of the guests, and I kept having to apologise to a poor woman trying to cover her son's ears.

"I HEART YOU."

I explained that housekeeping was busy preparing rooms and couldn't help right away…but, if she agreed, I would take the bag to my cabin and clean it myself.

She looked horrified. "But, that's not your job," she said. "We work as a team here," I said calmly, "and if you want your bag cleaned, that's the option I have for you right now." She stared at me…then walked away without another word. The people around me literally applauded me and said "Well done for handling that so well."

A few nights later, around 2 a.m., the desk had finally quieted down and I received a very unexpected call. It was James. He never called me during shifts. My heart dropped. I walked over to my manager, who already knew about James's mum. "Olivia, is everything alright?" he asked.

"It's James," I said, already shaking. "I need to take this call."

"Go ahead," he said, and got up to go man the desk for me. I picked up the phone, my fingers trembling. "James, what's wrong?"

There was a long pause. Then, his voice cracked.

"Olivia…I don't know how to say this. My mum…" There was another pause. I already knew.

"She's gone. She passed away."

I CAN'T STOP PUSHING

"I'm so sorry," I whispered, trying not to cry. "I'm so sorry James."

"I'm sorry to ruin your evening," he said quietly. "Ruin my evening?" I replied. "You've just lost your mum. I'm *glad* you called me. I just wish I could be there." I meant every word. I loved him and I hated being so far away. I never got to properly know his mum…but I knew she would have been an incredible mother-in-law.

♥♥♥

As strange as it sounds, being on the ship was an easy distraction…the busy routine helped keep my mind occupied…but my heart was still with James.

My final week onboard was a little different. The ship was being sold, and I was part of the team helping pack everything up. It was busy…but fun. Then the final night arrived. We packed our bags, got ready to leave the next morning…and headed to the crew bar for one last big party.

It was the night before my birthday…and all the leftover drinks were free. Naturally, I made the most of it.

After more shots than I'd like to admit, I was *very* drunk. My phone rang…it was James, calling to wish

"I HEART YOU."

me happy birthday. I tried to talk, but between the extremely loud music and my very intoxicated state, it was a challenge. I thanked him for calling and promised we'd chat properly tomorrow.

Not long after, I realised I wasn't feeling great. I found my friend Tim and asked if he could walk me to my cabin. He made sure I got back safely, then he returned to the party. And here's where it all went wrong…I forgot to set an alarm.

The next morning (or rather, just a few hours later), we were supposed to be packed and in the main hall by 6 a.m. before customs arrived. Instead…I was fast asleep. Until my phone rang.

"Morning! Happy Birthday!" my mum said cheerfully. "Mum, why are you calling me so early?" I groaned. "It's not that early. It's already 6 a.m."

I shot up in bed. "Mum, I have to go! I'm supposed to be downstairs already!" I said, "Customs is arriving, and I'm late!" I barely heard her say goodbye as I hung up, then started throwing everything into my bags. By some miracle, I made it down by 6:30 a.m. Customs hadn't arrived yet.

I found a manager and asked if I had time for breakfast. He said yes as customs was running late. Still half-drunk, I found the greasiest breakfast available, hoping it would soak up the hangover. Then I re-joined the group in the hall.

Shortly after, customs arrived. We said our goodbyes…then headed to the airport. And honestly? That day, I couldn't even manage my usual flight routine. The only thing going through my mind was:

I am never drinking again.

Chapter 5

"WE SHOULD PROBABLY REPORT THAT."

It felt incredible to finally be home. After fully recovering from my wild final night on the ship, I was back to feeling like myself again - and I had something exciting to look forward to…James was coming to meet my family!

James was flying into Cape Town, and from there, we planned to travel around the country before heading back to my hometown.

I drove down the night before and stayed with our family friends, Dave and Ben, who were just as excited as I was to welcome him.

The day had finally arrived. We decided to give him a proper South African welcome and greet him in style. I had a few beers chilling in the back seat for James and me, ready for when he got in the car.

We took Dave's car, with Ben in the front so that James and I could sit in the back together.

The moment James walked through the doors; my heart raced. Seeing him again felt like everything was exactly as it should be.

I CAN'T STOP PUSHING

As soon as we got to the car, I pulled out the beers with a big grin. "Welcome to South Africa!" James lit up with the biggest smile. He absolutely loved it.

We did some travelling, which, of course, included a safari - and, knowing James, an adrenaline rush was inevitable. He's a total thrill-seeker, having done everything from skydiving and bungee jumping to caving.

While exploring the country, we stopped at the world's highest commercial bungee jump - an insane 216 metres (over 700 feet) high.

Just getting to the jump platform was an adventure in itself. The path took us through a metal cage suspended beneath the bridge, and that's when I realised…I might actually be afraid of heights.

There was no solid floor beneath us…just a metal mesh and I could see everything below us. Every step felt like I might fall right through.

Gripping the side of the cage, I turned to James.

"I need to hold on to you." I placed both hands on his shoulders, closed my eyes, and didn't let go until we were safely on the bridge.

Then came the jump.

"WE SHOULD PROBABLY REPORT THAT."

Watching James hurl himself off the edge was both terrifying and exhilarating. He didn't hesitate for a second - just leaped into the open air. His face lit up with pure joy. I, on the other hand, was just relieved it wasn't me!

♥♥♥

After a week of exploring, we finally made it back to my parents' house. James instantly hit it off with my parents…it felt like he'd been part of the family for years.

One rainy afternoon, James headed to the shops with my dad. As they drove, he grew increasingly nervous, but he knew he couldn't back out now. Taking a deep breath, he finally spoke.

"Mr Field," he said nervously, "I'd like to ask Olivia to marry me." My dad smiled. "Ah, we figured this was coming. Go ask Olivia's mum," he said. It was clear who ran their house.

When they got home, James wasted no time. He asked my mum, and she was so excited she nearly hugged him to death.

♥♥♥

Then came the actual proposal…and let's just say, I didn't exactly make it easy for him. Like most women, I have those days where I'm just in a mood for no particular reason.

I CAN'T STOP PUSHING

And, unfortunately for James, this happened to be one of those days. "Have you ever tried geocaching before, Olivia?" he asked.

"Nope. No idea what that is."

"It's like a treasure hunt," he said. "People hide things in different locations, and you use GPS and clues to find them."

I wasn't exactly in the mood for a treasure hunt, but I went along with it anyway. We made our way to the first location, and as soon as we got there, I felt uneasy. "Hmm… I'm not really comfortable with this area."

"Come on," James insisted. "I'm sure it'll be fun."

We followed the clues, but I noticed a few dodgy guys hanging around nearby, and I felt more and more uncomfortable.

"I don't know about this, James. Maybe we should just call it a day and head home for lunch."

Little did I know…I was unknowingly sabotaging the biggest moment of my life.

"Why don't we find somewhere else to go?" he said. I thought for a second. "Well, there's a beautiful garden nearby that we could walk through."

"Perfect," he said.

"WE SHOULD PROBABLY REPORT THAT."

But, of course, I changed my mind and blurted out without thinking. "Actually, scratch that. There's a private beach I want to show you."

I am sure I was driving him mad, but I think he would have accepted anything to make me happy at this point.

"Sure, why not?" he said laughing and changed the direction he was driving.

♥♥♥

The road to the private beach was a long gravel road, but the views were gorgeous. We passed the back gardens of a few incredible mansions, driving slowly to admire them. Then we spotted something odd. A man hiding in the bushes, in the garden of one of the houses.

"We should probably report that," I said.

"It seems… odd," James agreed. I remembered there was always a security guard at the bottom of the hill, so we headed there and told him what we'd seen.

"We've just received reports of a burglary at that exact same house," the guard said. James and I looked at each other. "This is turning out to be one very interesting day…"

After a short walk, we reached the entrance to the beach, and James couldn't help but admire the scenery. "Wow, look at that view."

"It's stunning, isn't it?" I replied.

I CAN'T STOP PUSHING

But I had forgotten one small thing…the 116 steps down to the beach. "Come on," James laughed. "It'll be worth it."

He was clearly more determined than I was. I followed James down the stairs and complained the whole way. But James just kept finding every possible way to keep me going. Eventually, we made it to the sand. We walked along the beach and took a few pictures along the way. It was such a beautiful day.

Then we encountered yet another obstacle - a small stream blocking our path. Not deep, but wide enough that we had to take off our shoes…you guessed it, I was not in the mood.

"Do we really have to cross this?" I asked, "Can't we just turn back?"

"Yes, we do," he said firmly. "Shoes off… let's go."

With a dramatic sigh, I followed him barefoot across the cold stream. I gave him a hard time, but honestly… I was so grateful he didn't give up on me. We found a quiet spot by the rocks and sat down. Just us. No one else around. James sat behind me with his arms around me, kissing my neck and then pulling me in closer for a cuddle.

"This is perfect," I whispered, finally feeling relaxed.

"WE SHOULD PROBABLY REPORT THAT."

"It is," he said.

"So, when do you think we'll see each other again?" I asked. He shrugged. "It's hard to say… with our schedules and living so far apart."

"I just wish there was some way to guarantee it," I said. Little did I know… there was.

I became lost in a daydream, then the sound of his voice brought me back. "Olivia," he said softly.

I turned to my left, and there he was…down on one knee…holding a ring… "Will you marry me?"
My heart leapt. I gasped, put my hand over my mouth, and burst out laughing and shouting at the same time. I think I was in shock. I didn't actually hear anything else that he said to me.

"Yes. Yes, I will." I shouted.

I was in a much better mood now, that's for sure and the ring was absolutely stunning…diamonds and tanzanite sparkling in the sunlight. It was perfect. We stayed on the beach much longer than planned, taking photos and enjoying every second.

And then James told me something I'll never forget…he had bought the ring before leaving the ship…and had shown it to his mum before she passed away. She had given him her blessing. Wow…was all I could say.

I CAN'T STOP PUSHING

We made our way back, and suddenly I didn't mind the cold stream or the 116 steps. I practically floated up them. I was so excited to spread the word that nothing was going to stop me. We stopped at the shops to grab some bubbly before heading home to share the big news with my parents. The moment we walked through the door, my mum gave me *that* look…the one that said she already knew.

"Alright, alright," I laughed. "We're engaged!"

The celebrations kicked off immediately. We called every family member we could think of. Then my mum gave one piece of advice: "Don't rush into anything - maybe give it a year." Little did she know…it would be more like three.

♥♥♥

A few days later, I had to say goodbye to James again. It hurt just as much as every other time. At times, it felt like our relationship existed more over the phone than in person. But this engagement changed everything…it was a promise that no matter how many goodbyes we had to say, there would always be another hello.

Thankfully, the distance didn't last long. We decided it was time for me to visit the UK - meet his

"WE SHOULD PROBABLY REPORT THAT."

family and travel for six months. The day arrived so fast! The nerves hit me as I made my way through the arrivals section. I wasn't sure why - maybe because this time, I was meeting my fiancé
instead of just my boyfriend.

As I walked towards him, I imagined one of those movie moments - the girl runs, leaps into her guy's arms, he spins her around, and they share the world's most romantic kiss. Reality? Even better.

Our eyes met, he flashed that irresistible smile, pulled me into the biggest hug, and kissed me like the world had disappeared around us. On the drive to his house, we never let go of each other's hands. It felt surreal - I could hardly believe I had finally arrived.

We made a quick stop at the shops, to pick up some drinks and snacks, and while waiting in the queue, James whispered, "I think I know the lady in front of us."

I looked up and couldn't believe it, "Oh my goodness... that's my next-door neighbour from South Africa!" Of all the places, on that day, in that random shop...what were the chances?

We had a lovely chat, catching up before saying goodbye to her, and then we continued on our way.

I CAN'T STOP PUSHING

Before I knew it, we had arrived at James's family home. A beautiful stone cottage in a small Cotswolds village, surrounded by common land that is also a golf course. This was also my first-time meeting one of James's family members in person. As we pulled up, his dad, Steven, was already at the door waiting. He greeted me with a big hug, and made me feel instantly at home.

In South Africa, we keep important documents, like passports, locked away in a safe. I asked if I could do the same here, but both James and Steven laughed at me. It seems like that is more of a South African thing!

One thing I'd never experienced before was snow. Of course, you see it in movies and daydream about the moment you finally get to experience it. I couldn't wait for that moment to come.

After I had settled in, we headed into the lounge to enjoy our snacks and drinks. As we were chatting, James glanced out the window and noticed that it was starting to snow.

I rushed over to get a better look. This was it…I was finally seeing snow for the first time. I felt like a kid staring into a toy shop window, completely mesmerised watching the snowflakes falling.

"WE SHOULD PROBABLY REPORT THAT."

"Wow, it's really snowing!" I said, pressing my nose against the glass. James laughed.

"Trust me, you'll be waiting a while if you're hoping to see it settle," he teased. "Let's come back and check in the morning."

The following morning, we woke up to find the common land outside their house covered, with a thick layer of snow, at least a metre deep. The golf course that had once been there was completely transformed, with sand traps now resembling deep bunkers buried beneath the snow.

We bundled up and went outside, sinking with every step. We built snowmen, made snow angels, had snowball fights - and even jumped into snowdrifts we couldn't get out of. We laughed so much, which only made it harder to free ourselves.

Being together on land was different from the ships… but it felt real. Like this was what love was supposed to be.

♥♥♥

January flew by, and for the time being, we decided to stay local as James was still working. He was the sales manager at a motorbike company. This was just for now until we joined the cruise ships again. Whenever he had time off, we went on countless walks around the area, exploring all the incredible places nearby.

I CAN'T STOP PUSHING

♥♥♥

In February, Steven had planned to climb Mount Kilimanjaro. This was something James's mum wanted to do, but didn't get the chance.

While he was away, it gave James and me some extra time together. I decided to plan something special for Valentine's Day. James had made our first Valentine's Day unforgettable, so now it was my turn to top it.

I didn't have a car, so I walked 20 minutes each way to the shops - the way back was always harder uphill, especially when I'd bought too much.

I put together a full evening: a fancy dinner, a frozen triple chocolate mousse dessert, and some fun Valentine's crackers. I even created a scavenger hunt and a slightly X-rated 'spin-the-bottle' game.

When James got home, I had his pyjamas warming in the cupboard, and his favourite rum and coke waiting. I had also poured myself my usual glass of white wine.

After dinner, the scavenger hunt was a hit. Then came the bottle game…as the bottle spun around the board…I felt so nervous and I have no idea why.

The bottle landed on "remove a piece of clothing."

"WE SHOULD PROBABLY REPORT THAT."

He crawled over to me, and suddenly, I felt very hot. James knelt in front of me, leaned in, and kissed me. We'd kissed so many times before, but this one was different. It sent shivers down my spine. The kiss deepened, growing more intense, as he ran his hands down my body. Time seemed to stop as we got lost in the moment.

The game was now completely forgotten, and all we had was this overwhelming desire for each other.

As we lay together afterwards, hearts still racing, I knew this was a moment I'd never forget... I fell even more in love with him. I'm proud to say, I definitely topped our first Valentine's Day.

A few weeks later, we both applied for a new cruise-ship job, and at the interview, we were told there and then that we got it.

Everything moved so quickly. I had to cut my holiday short by two months to go home and finish the rest of the application process.

Saying goodbye again wasn't easy... but this time, we both knew it was only temporary.

We'd see each other soon.

Chapter 6

"I'M NOT GOING IN THERE."

The past three years with this company had been nothing short of incredible. I'd made lifelong friends, explored beautiful places like the Bahamas and Port Canaveral, and attended some unforgettable crew parties.

♥♥♥

Before joining my final contract, James and I had finally set a wedding date, which meant my Mum and I were in full-on wedding planning mode. With the big day scheduled for the month after my contract ended, we had to get as much done as possible while I was home.

James was happy to let me take the reins…let's be honest, wedding planning isn't exactly something most guys are dying to get involved in. It's more our thing.

First, we needed to find a venue. The moment Mum and I walked into this one, tucked away on the outskirts of Knysna, I just knew.

"I'M NOT GOING IN THERE."

It had everything: on-site accommodation, a stunning garden perfect for photos, and a spacious event room where the bar and dining area were all in one; keeping everyone together. It was absolutely perfect. We wasted no time booking it, along with our family church, which is a stone building built in the 1800s and it is stunning!

Next came the table décor. I wanted something elegant but simple, so I chose a black, white, red, and silver colour scheme. Each table would be covered with a black tablecloth, a candelabra in the centre on top of a round mirror, with small glass bowls of floating red roses on either end. Scattered tea light candles added that extra elegant touch without overfilling the tables.

As the details started coming together, I could not contain my excitement. This was really happening!

Then came the most important task…finding my wedding dress. Since I was planning to move overseas with James, it made more sense to rent than buy one (plus, transporting a huge dress sounded like a mission in itself).

Mum and I booked an appointment at a wedding boutique nearby. You could design your own dress or rent one of the gowns in-store.

The lovely thing? The rental dresses were all named after the brides who originally had them made.

I CAN'T STOP PUSHING

"I'm not sure I want to wear someone else's dress," I told Mum, "But it makes more sense to rent than to buy." She was there to help, thank goodness, because I had no idea what I wanted. I had a vague idea: strapless, lace-up back, and not too tight. But I'd never *tried* on a wedding dress before, and I was nervous about finding 'the one'.

The assistants pulled out a variety of styles to try, and each dress was so different. One had a top I loved and another had the perfect skirt…but none of them felt exactly right. I kept thinking; *I really hope I find the right one today.*

Then, one of the assistants said, "I saved this one for last." She held up a dress and smiled. "The bride who had it made changed her mind, so it's never been worn." Could this be the one?

I stepped into the gown, and felt goosebumps as she laced up the back. When I turned to look in the mirror, I couldn't believe my eyes. It was *perfect*.

"This is it," I whispered, trying to hold back my tears. The dress was strapless, with a lace-up back and a subtle ballgown skirt…but not too much. There was a small gathering in the fabric on one side of the skirt, and

"I'M NOT GOING IN THERE."

its pearly colour was beautifully decorated with white and gold glass beads. Elegant, simple, magical. I turned around slowly to show Mum. One look and she burst into tears.

"You look stunning." she said, wiping her eyes.

Her reaction set me off, and soon both of the shop assistants were crying as well.

"I'd say that's the best sign that this is your dress," one of the assistants said. "In fact, I'm going to name this dress after you."

"Really? That's amazing. Thank you so much," I said. The assistant smiled. We found the perfect veil, and just like that I had my dress. One day, one appointment. That had to be a record.

All that was left were the invitations. I'd designed them myself, with our initials on the front, red roses inside, and all the venue details. They were simple yet elegant … just as I'd envisioned.

While I headed back to the ship for my final contract, my mum happily took on the task of delivering them.

The journey back was a quick one, and wow, was I happy to be there. Walking down the halls on the day I arrived, almost felt like coming home. Seeing all those

I CAN'T STOP PUSHING

friendly, familiar faces again reminded me exactly why I loved this job.

My office was tucked away behind the scenes, as I worked as a personal assistant on this ship. I made sure to get out and about to chat with guests.

I even had access to some of the onboard prizes, and my boss gave me the freedom to use them however I liked. If there was ever a chance to make someone's cruise extra special, I took it.

As a one-stripe officer, I also joined the other officers for the evening meet-and-greet after the shows. And that's where one of the most memorable moments happened for me.

A guest came over and asked if he could take a photo of his daughter with me. I knelt down beside her, smiling for the picture, and then he said something I *never* expected:

"I want to show her this picture one day, and remind her that a woman can do anything she wants to."

It took me a second to take it in and then I got chills. I don't think I'll ever forget those words. I really was working in my dream job and I never wanted it to end.

"I'M NOT GOING IN THERE."

However, during this last contract, I faced the difficult decision to resign. James and I had done long-distance for so long, and we were ready to start our life together on land.

Resigning was harder than I expected. I sat at my desk with the letter in my hand, trying not to cry. I'd calm down... then stand up and start crying all over again. It was just a piece of paper to hand over... but to me, it felt like saying goodbye to one of the best chapters of my life.

Finally, after hours of to-ing and fro-ing, I calmed down, took a deep breath, and headed to my boss's office, which was right next door. I knocked on the door and asked if he had a few minutes to talk.

"Of course," he said. I sat down, opened my mouth... and the only thing that came out was a gut-wrenching cry as I burst into tears. I had never seen him leap up so fast. He sat down next to me, gave me a moment to breathe, then asked gently what was going on.

"I... I'm trying to resign," I finally managed to explain through my tears. "Even though I *know* it's the right thing... I love this job so much."

"I can see that," he said. "But I also know how much it matters to follow your heart." I wiped my eyes and took another deep breath.

I CAN'T STOP PUSHING

"James and I don't want to be apart anymore. I want to start building a life with him. But leaving this behind feels like leaving a piece of myself too."

"It's hard, I know. But you've got to follow what feels right for *you*. You never know… you might be back someday."

"Maybe," I said. "But for now, I just know this is the right thing."

"Then trust yourself," he said. With that, I handed him the letter. I still felt sad, but, also strangely relieved.

I'm sure we've all been there, where we have to decide on something we weren't ready for, find that our emotions just take over and we can't explain what the hell has happened.

♥♥♥

I still had a couple of months left on board, and I was determined to enjoy every second.

One random afternoon, after I finished work, I was walking down the long hallway that runs through the middle of the ship. In the distance, I noticed James, with his backpack on, running around a corner. James shouldn't have been on break now, and it was past lunchtime, so he should still have been at work.

Every possible thought raced through my head.

"I'M NOT GOING IN THERE."

What was he doing? Where was he going? Was he seeing someone else? I rushed to his cabin...he wasn't there. You couldn't exactly call someone on a ship. I had no way to contact him.

I felt unsettled, but I decided to head back to my cabin and try not to worry. That night, my roommate Meg and I had plans for a girls' night out, and I needed to start getting ready. Meg was, without a doubt, the best roommate I'd ever had - the perfect kind of crazy I never knew I needed. I adored her. We'd become best friends, and I'd asked her to be my maid of honour.

When I walked in, she was already putting on makeup. She looked up. "Are you okay?" she asked.

"I don't know. I saw James running down the hallway with his backpack and now I can't find him. It's not like him, and I'm kind of freaking out." Meg raised an eyebrow. "You're being ridiculous," she said. "You know James. He's not like that."

"I *know*," I replied. "But I can't stop thinking about it." Meg put her makeup brush down and walked over to me.

"Look, maybe he just had to run an errand or something. I'm sure it's nothing to worry about."

"I do trust him," I insisted. "It's just... I hate not knowing."

I CAN'T STOP PUSHING

"Come on, get dressed… we're going out. That will take your mind off it." Meg suggested.

"Yeah, you're right," I said. "Let's just enjoy our night." Meg poured us both a generous glass of wine and turned up the music as we got ready. She lent me one of her bodysuits which was black, slimming and made me feel *gorgeous*. With our makeup, hair, and nails done, we were ready to go. We headed to the crew bar for drinks, then to one of the restaurants on deck for dinner. As we stepped into the elevator, I didn't even notice what floor Meg had pressed, but it kept going up.

"Where are we going?" I asked, suddenly realizing we hadn't stopped yet. Meg looked at me and smiled mysteriously. "You'll see."

"Why are we going *up* there?" I asked, a gut feeling telling me exactly where we were headed, though I had no idea why. She just kept smiling, not saying a word.

We stopped on the top floor…the one with *the* room. The fancy event room with the floor-to-ceiling window and the most amazing view. The one they use for weddings and parties. The elevator doors opened and I froze.

"Come on. Let's go inside," Meg urged trying to walk me down the hallway. "I'm not going in there," I

"I'M NOT GOING IN THERE."

said, shaking my head. "You are coming in this room," she insisted, grabbing my hand and pulling me forward. She opened the door, and I instinctively closed my eyes, feeling my whole body start to shake. When I opened them... "SURPRISE!" My friends and colleagues were all there, clapping, shouting, cheering. I put my head in my hands, feeling myself starting to blush. Meg gave me a nudge. "Are you okay?"

"This is so unexpected." I replied. "You deserve it," she said. "We wanted to surprise you with a farewell and bachelorette party." I looked around the room, seeing about 40 people. Despite the initial shock, a smile slowly spread across my face.

"Thank you, everyone," I said. "This means the world to me." The music started, and Meg attached a veil to my hair. She then told me, "You need to go sit on the chair over there." In the middle of the room was a chair with a dildo on it.

"You've got to be kidding me," I said. She shook her head, smiling. "Off you go." I hesitated, feeling nervous again...but then she whispered, "By the way, James helped plan all of this. That's why you saw him earlier." I couldn't have been more excited to hear her say that. I finally felt excited to enjoy what was in front of me…the *party* I mean…not the dildo.

I carefully sat around the dildo rather than on top of it. "Now what?" I asked. The music changed, and three of the guys I worked with started walking towards me. At first, I thought they were bringing me a drink, but no…they started *dancing*.

They had rehearsed a dance just for me. At first, I thought, *this is weird. I know these guys*. I didn't know where to look…there was so much going on. And then, their shirts came off. WOW! I did not expect that.

But everyone was having so much fun, and so were they. Just when I thought it would end there, their trousers came off. Luckily, they all had boxers on. They formed a circle around me and continued dancing. This was not the type of dance I was expecting, but by the end, I was laughing and smiling along with the rest of the room.

After that, we feasted on tapas and dessert, drank a *lot*, and danced into the early hours. At one point, my boss came over to me, saying, "Please, just enjoy the evening as late as you want to. I don't want to see you in the office before 11 a.m." He knew me well…I was usually in before him and out after him. But tonight?

"I'M NOT GOING IN THERE."

Tonight, I just let go. Meg came over and wrapped her arms around me.

"See? I told you everything was fine. Aren't you glad you stayed?" I nodded. "You were right. This is exactly what I needed."

A few days later, the time came for me to leave the ship. With tears streaming down my face, I looked over my shoulder, one last time, at the place I had called home for the past three years. Then I climbed onto the bus to begin my journey home.

Chapter 7

"ARE YOU READY?"

After nearly two days of travelling, I finally made it back home. Exhausted but excited, I knew there was still so much to do before the wedding. I had wedding dress fittings and needed to sort out the final details for the big day.

A few weeks later, James and his family arrived, and my maid of honour, Meg, flew in from Australia. One evening, as Meg and I were catching up, she said, "Can you believe it? Your wedding is just around the corner."

"I know," I replied. "It feels unreal. I'm so glad you're here."

"I wouldn't miss it for the world," Meg said.

The next day, the bachelor and bachelorette parties began nice and early. We made sure they were scheduled for two days before the wedding to allow for a much-needed recovery day in between.

The morning started with the boys "kidnapping" James. They blindfolded him and tossed him into the back of a van, all while the girls and I were in another

"ARE YOU READY?"

room getting ready. The girls had organised a drinking treasure hunt for me.

We set off to various locations around town, each spot hiding a different drink that I had to find.

While we were out, the boys were up to their own mischief at a local BBQ spot - known as a 'braai' in South Africa.

They dressed James in a tutu and fairy wings, complete with a cast on his hand that held a drinks mug.

The bachelorette party was going smoothly. We stopped at a cosy tapas place for dinner and indulged in more drinks before heading to a lively local bar with music and a dance floor. We were all dancing the night away when suddenly, the boys walked in…but James was not with them. I was a little concerned and asked Meg, "Um…where's James?"

"I didn't want to worry you earlier, but James has been passed out, in bed at home, since 8 p.m." she replied. At least he was safe, sound asleep, but it was clear he had overdone it. Thank goodness we had planned a recovery day. We enjoyed the rest of the night with a few more drinks, lots of dancing, and still made it home before midnight.

The next morning, Meg and I went to check on James, who was staying next door with Steven, his dad, at some friends of ours.

I CAN'T STOP PUSHING

As we walked in, it was clear James was in rough shape. He needed to rehydrate and get as much sleep as possible before the wedding day. Luckily, I had an army of people to help me set up the venue so that James could get the rest he needed.

After helping James, we made our way over to the venue to begin setting up. For a unique wedding favour, I had shot glasses engraved with our initials and wedding date, which we placed on all the tables. After a couple of hours, we were done. We took a step back and admired our work. It was absolutely perfect.

That evening, we hosted a big family dinner at our house before turning in for an early night. Thankfully, James was feeling much better. As we said our goodbyes at the gate, he pulled me in for one last kiss and said, "I'll see you at the altar."

To which I replied, "I'll be the one in white." A little cheesy, I know, but it left us both laughing and smiling as we headed off to our separate beds for the last time.

♥♥♥

The wedding day had finally arrived, and it was time to get ready. As we enjoyed breakfast, I suddenly realised I hadn't bought any outfits or lingerie for the wedding night.

"ARE YOU READY?"

"Give me your card. I'll pick out a few outfits for you," my baby sister Tash said. I didn't hesitate…I knew I could trust her. She was the fashion expert in the family.

Soon, my makeup artist and hairstylist arrived, and she immediately began to work her magic. I asked for a more natural look, and she absolutely nailed it.

Just as she was applying my lipstick, I remembered that I hadn't brushed my teeth. Oops! Definitely not the best day to forget that.

All these little things that went wrong didn't bother me in the slightest. You can only plan so much for a day like this, and I had decided I wasn't going to let anything get to me. This day only comes around once, and I was determined to go with the flow and make the most of it.

I haven't even mentioned the wedding party yet. My bridesmaids were my sisters Tash and Kelly, plus James's sister, Jane, and, of course, Meg was my maid of honour. They all wore floor-length burgundy gowns and looked absolutely gorgeous.

For the boys, James's dad, Steven, was his best man, and the three groomsmen were friends we'd worked with on the ship. They wore Champagne-coloured waistcoats with cravat-style ties, while James wore a red tie to match the bridesmaids. I was now ready to get into my dress.

I CAN'T STOP PUSHING

We laid a sheet down on the lounge floor, giving us plenty of space for the photographer to capture a few special moments. I carefully stepped into the dress, adjusting everything to make sure I was comfortable, especially making sure the 'girls' were in place in the padded bust.

Then, the corset tightening began.

They pulled and tugged, then pulled and tugged some more. Just as they finished tying the bow, Meg suddenly gasped - she had spotted the flap under the corset ribbons still hanging open.

Without hesitation, she crawled under my dress to fix it, while the others tried to hold everything in place. The room erupted in laughter as they tried adjusting and readjusting the fabric in a desperate attempt to get it right. Before I knew it, I was doubled over, crying with laughter. My stomach ached, my eyes were watering, and I could barely breathe. There couldn't have been a better way to start the day…laughing with the best people by my side, even if it meant them quite literally holding me together.

With the dress sorted, it was time for the finishing touches. Each of my bridesmaids took turns adding something special.

"ARE YOU READY?"

Meg and Jane helped me into my shoes...my something old. They were the same white shoes I wore with my officer uniform while working on the ships. Admittedly, I had to touch them up with a little Tipp-Ex to hide the scuff marks, but we'll keep that between us!

Kelly and Tash fastened my earrings...my something new. These pearl earrings were a special find from one of the islands James and I had visited together.

Meg then attached a delicate diamond bracelet around my wrist...my something borrowed from my Mum.

Finally, Jane sprayed me with perfume before slipping on my garter...my something blue. Judging by her reaction, I'm pretty sure she found that part a little awkward!

♥♥♥

With everything in place, I was officially ready to walk down the aisle...but first it was time for photographs. We headed outside and took a variety of shots before heading out to the cars.

While we were busy with our photos, the photographer's assistant was capturing the guys next door. They had a very creative approach to their shots. All the men were half-dressed...yes, you heard that right. They were fully dressed on top, but on the bottom, they were only wearing their boxers and socks. They kept this look for all the photos, with Steven, adjusting James' tie and putting on his watch and cufflinks.

The girls were finished with their photos and made their way down to the cars. How were we getting to the wedding, you ask? Only in two stunning 1928 Cadillacs…one green and one blue. I was in the green car with my dad, while the bridesmaids and Meg followed behind in the blue car. When we arrived at the church, we realised we were actually early.

I honestly thought we were running late. So, we had to sit in the car for a bit, waiting for the rest of the guests to arrive. I'm not a fan of waiting around, and it only made me more nervous. I started to feel thirsty and asked for a glass of water… definitely didn't want to be worrying about that once the ceremony started.

After about half an hour, we received the "okay" to head inside. We stepped out of the car and made our way along the short path to the church entrance, with the photographer capturing every moment as we walked.

For the ceremony videos, one of the groomsmen, who was a videographer, set up two cameras…one at the start of the aisle and one at the end, behind the priest. This way, they could capture both my walk down the aisle and the entire ceremony.

"ARE YOU READY?"

I had originally hired a professional videographer, but as the wedding costs started to add up, I decided to cancel him… biggest mistake ever!

I stood at the church doorway, my dad by my side, watching the bridesmaids and Meg make their way down the aisle to the beautiful sound of "Canon in D," played on the old church organ.

My dad took my hand, then looked straight at me and said, "Are you ready?"

Suddenly, I felt scared. I was about to do the biggest thing I had ever done. I'd dreamed of this day since I was a little girl, and now I was finally here. The main man in my life, up until now, had always been my dad.

But I loved James so much, and I couldn't imagine life without him. So, I took a deep breath and replied, "Yes, I'm ready."

I held onto my dad as we began to walk down the aisle. As we rounded the corner and the whole church stood up, staring at me, my nerves shot up. But then I saw James. He was looking straight at me, his eyes almost glowing with excitement. In that moment, all my fears vanished and I couldn't wait to marry him. When we reached the altar, my dad lifted my veil,

I CAN'T STOP PUSHING

kissed me on the cheek, and then turned to shake James' hand. James immediately took my hand and whispered, "You look amazing." In that moment, I felt like my heart was about to burst.

The minister began to speak, welcoming everyone from near and far. He then proceeded with, "If any of you can show just cause why they may not be lawfully married, you must now declare it."

At that moment, my grandmother decided it was her time to speak up, responding with, "Is this the part where we say something?"

The whole church erupted in laughter, and we, of course, knew she was only joking.

By this stage, I had completely forgotten about my nerves and was simply enjoying every single moment of the ceremony.

The part I had been waiting for had finally arrived. The minister announced, "I now pronounce you husband and wife. James, you may now kiss your bride."

James pulled me into his arms, and we kissed. I couldn't have cared less that all our family and friends were watching. We then did a quick run to the back of

"ARE YOU READY?"

the church and snuck into the back room, waiting for everyone to head outside before we followed.

In that brief moment alone, we shared a private kiss. I couldn't believe we were finally married.

♥♥♥

After about 10 minutes, there was a knock at the door signalling that everyone was outside. We made our way out to cheers and rose petals being thrown over our heads. We spent some time taking group photos with family and friends before climbing back into the cars to head over to the reception.

While the guests waited for us, we had arranged for sherry to be served as an arrival drink and set up a picture frame with a fingerprint tree for a bit of fun. I had designed a cartoon tree on my computer, and guests were invited to choose a colour from the fingerprint pads provided, stamping their fingerprint as the tree's leaves. They also wrote their names beside their prints so we could remember everyone. It was a fun idea to create a unique keepsake that we could have on our wall at home.

While all of this was going on, James and I took some private photos together. There were so many stunning spots to capture. We strolled through a giant chessboard, sat on a little bridge overlooking a small stream and we even took a variety of poolside shots.

One of the most fun moments was when we placed an orange life-saving float around James's neck, and I pretended to hold onto him to keep him from falling into the water. It was a fun idea, and a nice reminder of how we first met on the cruise ships.

After the photos, we spent a few quiet moments alone, just the two of us. Meg noticed and came over with two glasses of bubbly for us to enjoy together in the moment.

Before we knew it, it was time to head into the hall. We stood at the door, and then heard our MC announce, "Please stand and help me welcome the new Mr. and Mrs. Bailey."

With the music playing, we danced our way in, savouring the moment…just for a little while…before finally making our way to our table.

During the reception, we indulged in a delicious buffet with a selection of amazing dishes. Just to name a few, we enjoyed a mezze platter as one of the starters, whole roasted beef sirloin drizzled with a rich French-style shallot and red wine sauce for the main course, and a wonderful strawberry pavlova to finish off the meal.

"ARE YOU READY?"

After dinner, the speeches began. I suddenly realised no one was recording them. Every instinct told me to ask someone to start filming, but I hesitated…and didn't.

The one thing I had truly wanted on video was now just a memory, never to be replayed. The day went by so fast, and if there's one thing I learnt, it's that hiring a videographer is absolutely worth it. Moments come and go, but the ones we capture stay with us forever. Don't make the same mistake I did.

♥♥♥

As the speeches went on, there was one thing that took my mind off the no camera stress swirling in my head…a little game the bridesmaids and groomsmen had secretly started. Every time someone said 'Olivia' or 'James,' they had to take a drink.

No one caught on at first, but pretty soon, their attempts to laugh quietly had the whole room giggling.

It definitely helped lighten the mood and made the speeches even more fun. Plus, it totally took the pressure off whoever was speaking!

Next came the cake…or rather, the cupcakes! I thought they'd be a more fun alternative to a traditional wedding cake, and they turned out beautifully. Sticking to our colour scheme, some were topped with red icing, while the rest had white, all wrapped in black cupcake wrappers. They were vanilla-flavoured with a marshmallow cream filling ... YUM! To display them, I got creative and made a stand using round pieces of

glass and upside-down martini glasses. It looked so elegant. Then, of course, it was time for the dancing. James isn't much of a dancer, but he didn't have a choice when it came to our first dance.

It wasn't anything fancy... just the two of us... arms wrapped around each other, enjoying our favourite song.

Then came the father-daughter dance. After about a minute of dancing with my dad, who is also not a dancer, I decided to pull my sisters in. We all wrapped our arms around each other, and I don't think I've ever seen my dad smile so much.

As soon as that song ended, the party music kicked in, and I did not move off the dance floor for the rest of the night - only stepping away for a drink at the bar or, well, when I needed to pee.

One thing about wearing a big dress? You definitely need help going to the bathroom. Every time I headed for the toilet, Meg was right there, following me in to help lift my dress over my head so I could, you know,

"ARE YOU READY?"

actually go. After about an hour of dancing, our MC announced it was time for the bouquet and garter toss. I stood on a chair and threw the bouquet, and my sister Tash caught it. Then came the garter toss.

Suddenly, the groomsmen blindfolded James and guided him towards me. They instructed me to stay standing on the chair, which confused me at first, but I did as I was told. James was then instructed to remove my garter - *using his teeth*. I wasn't expecting this at all.

With all of our family and friends watching, James crawled under my dress and, after a bit of a struggle, managed to pull my garter down my leg. He threw it across the room, and Kelly's boyfriend Rick caught it. Rick and Tash shared the traditional dance, but Kelly didn't seem too worried about this idea as it was all in good fun.

We danced the night away to an incredible DJ. I could not have asked for this day to go any better if I tried, except for the videographer of course.

Someone once gave me a great piece of wedding advice: make sure the food, music, and photography are outstanding, and the rest will fall into place. I'd add a videographer to that list because the day goes by so fast…and the more memories you have to look back on, the better.

I CAN'T STOP PUSHING

After everyone left, James and I headed to our room. On the walk there, James told me a funny story…he had completely forgotten to decorate our room for the wedding night. Apparently, that's the groom's job! Luckily, one of the groomsmen's wives had kindly gone shopping and made sure everything was set up perfectly.

I laughed and shared my own story about forgetting to buy a wedding night outfit and how my sister had to rush out and save the day. Turns out, we had more in common than I thought!

When we walked in, we both just stopped and smiled. The room was filled with bottles of bubbly, flowers, chocolates, and even a bottle of bubble bath waiting for us.

As it was our wedding night, you'd assume as soon as we got to the room, clothes would come off for an intimate evening together…well, clothes did come off…but we both headed straight for the bubble bath. We hadn't felt this relaxed in days.

Don't worry, though…after the bath, things heated up, just as you'd expect and we spent our very first night together as husband and wife.

A few days later, everyone made their way home, and I

"ARE YOU READY?"

began the daunting process of moving to the UK. Moving to another country turned out to be harder than I had anticipated. The mission to apply for a visa, coupled with the infamous waiting game, was painful, to say the least. Form after form after form needed to be completed.

To pass the time during the endless waiting, I decided to do some part-time work managing a guest house. It was a good distraction, but the visa process was always at the back of my mind.

One day, while I was at the guest house, James called. "Hey my love. I've got some bad news I'm afraid," he said. I immediately felt worried. "What is it?"

"You know the two weeks I took off for the wedding?" he began. "Well, they were unpaid, and it's affected the visa requirements. Your visa will need to be delayed for another six months." I couldn't believe it. "Six months? James, that's so long."

"I know," he said. The months dragged on, each day feeling longer than the last.

♥♥♥

One unexpected day in October though, I was in my bedroom watching TV when my dad suddenly called.

"Olivia. Quick, come down. Someone is breaking into your car." he shouted. Heart pounding, I flew down the stairs to look over the balcony. But just as I reached it, he stopped me. "No, go downstairs and open the front door," he insisted. Confused, I stared at him. "Why on earth would you tell me someone's breaking into my car and then ask me to go investigate?" I asked.

"Just go downstairs and look," he said, with a very cheeky smile.

Realising he was joking - because my dad would never put me in danger - I nervously went down the stairs, wondering who might be at the door. A million thoughts raced through my head, but James was the furthest from my mind.

I opened the door, and there he was, standing right in front of me. I was in such shock that I actually turned around and started walking back up the stairs. I sat down, looked at him again, and realised he was really there. "You're here." I finally shouted, running back down to hug him.

He laughed. "Surprise. I wanted to do something special. I told no one except your boss to make sure you had a few days off."

"This is incredible." I said, starting to cry. "How did you manage to keep it a secret?"

"I know how much you love surprises," he replied.

"ARE YOU READY?"

"And I thought, what better way to make the wait shorter. Also, this is not unpaid leave, so it will not affect your visa."

"Thank goodness." I said, hugging him again. He stayed for two amazing weeks with lots of date nights (we even stayed a night away at a hotel) and some beautiful day trips exploring. Then we said our goodbyes.

The few months didn't seem so long anymore, and time flew by quickly.

♥♥♥

Over the last few months, I had packed up my room, made sure my documents were ready, and spent some lovely evenings with my family.

The day finally came for me to leave. It was surreal but incredibly exciting. Saying goodbye to my parents was bittersweet. I hugged them tightly at the departures gate, trying to hold back my tears. "Please make sure to let us know when you are there." my Mum said, wiping her eyes. I nodded, smiling through my tears. "I will."

As I turned to give them one last wave before going through the gate, I saw my dad climbing under the ropes to give me one more hug.

"Take care, I'll miss you," he whispered. "We're so proud of you." That did it for me - I couldn't hold back the tears any longer.

"I love you both so much," I said, hugging my dad one more time. As I walked towards the gate, I felt a mix of emotions. It was hard to leave, but I was ready for the new chapter that awaited me.

♥♥♥

After a long flight, I finally arrived in the UK. Exhausted but excited. James greeted me at the airport with a big hug and a kiss. "Welcome home," he said, with a big smile on his face.

"I can't believe I'm finally here," I said. We made our way to Steven's house, which would be our new home for the time being. We did not stop talking the whole way there. A few months later, we moved into our very first two-bedroom apartment.

Over the next few weeks, we picked out furniture and added personal touches that made it feel like home. Of course, it wasn't all smooth sailing. There were dramas along the way too.

♥♥♥

One day, when I arrived home from work, I opened the door and was immediately hit by a wave of heat. It felt like a sauna. As I stepped inside, I looked down and saw that the floor was flooded with boiling hot water.

"ARE YOU READY?"

The boiler had burst, and to make matters worse, our entire apartment was carpeted. "Seriously?" I muttered to myself.

I quickly called the onsite maintenance guy, Jim, to get him on his way and then dialled James's number.

"Hey, what's up?" he answered.

"James, the boiler burst. The apartment is flooded with boiling hot water," I said, feeling a little panicked. There was a moment of silence.

"You're joking, right?" he finally said.

"No, I'm serious. You'll see when you get here," I replied. Jim arrived in no time and started fixing the boiler. "Thanks for coming so quickly," I said. "We really appreciate it."

"No problem," he replied.

When James got home, the look on his face said it all. His eyes widened, and his mouth dropped open as he looked over the damage. "Oh, my goodness, this is unbelievable," James said, shaking his head.

"You guys really dodged a bullet," said Jim. "This could have been a lot worse."

"I know, we're lucky we didn't have much on the floor that got damaged. Only the vacuum cleaner was in the boiler cupboard, so it took the worst hit," I said. "That's still not great. But at least it wasn't anything more valuable." James groaned.

We spent the next few hours moving furniture and trying to clean up the water. By the end of the evening, we were exhausted but relieved. Thank goodness insurance covered the repairs and replaced our vacuum cleaner.

♥♥♥

Two years later, we were finally ready to buy a house. We chose a new build, which meant we got to pick out all the colours and finishes - a fun but daunting task with so many options. The process felt like it took forever. We spent days in their office surrounded by tiles and carpet samples trying to decide on what we wanted.

It was incredible to watch our house gradually take shape. We visited the site as often as we could, and each time, something new had been added. The day we saw the roof in place, was so exciting. We just couldn't wait to move in.

In the meantime, our apartment needed to be repainted before we moved out. Instead of hiring professionals, we decided to do it ourselves to save some money. "It'll be a fun project," James said, rolling up his sleeves.

"ARE YOU READY?"

"I guess it could be," I replied. "But you know something always goes wrong when we try DIY."

James laughed. "What could possibly go wrong with a bit of painting?"

I handled the deep cleaning while James and Steven tackled the painting. Everything seemed to be going smoothly until Steven moved from one room to the next. He didn't notice that paint was pouring off the tray the entire way - from the main bedroom, down the hallway, and into the lounge area. Three different carpets were now streaked with paint. When I saw the mess, I gasped. "James, come look at this." I shouted. James rushed over and his jaw dropped. "Oh no. Dad, did you see this?" Steven looked mortified.

"I'm so sorry. I didn't even notice." The carpets needed to be replaced and thank goodness our insurance covered it. We finished the painting and cleaning and we locked the door to the apartment for the very last time. We headed over to Steven's house where we would be staying until our house was complete.

The next day, we drove to our nearly completed house for another viewing. Standing in front of our future home, felt so surreal yet so exciting at the same time. We could not wait to move in.

Chapter 8

"I THOUGHT YOU WERE BEING BRAVE."

More than anything, I wanted to be a mum. Even back in school, despite being teased (that's a story for another day), I was always the gentle and honest one. I'd always take care of the people around me. One of my friends once said, "You're going to be a brilliant mum one day." That stuck with me. I think deep down, I always knew it too.

♥♥♥

But first, I needed to find a job. I applied for a few places, looking specifically for reception positions. The one I really wanted was Assistant Reception Manager at a local hotel. James suggested I go in and speak to someone directly, to show how much I wanted the job.

On Saturday morning, I plucked up the courage to head over there. But I got lost. I'd completely forgotten to charge my phone before I left home. The battery was on 10%, and I didn't know the area at all. Somehow, I ended up driving into a wooded area - the navigator was taking me on a wild goose chase!

I started to feel nervous and anxious, which

"I THOUGHT YOU WERE BEING BRAVE."

definitely didn't help, considering I was about to speak to someone about a job I really wanted. In that moment, I just wanted to cry. Every road looked the same... Where the hell was I?

I decided to pull over and breathe for a minute. I zoomed out on the navigator, trying to work out where I was. After finally calming myself down, I realised I was only five minutes away. *Phew.* Not as bad as I thought.

It's amazing how a moment can completely transform your mood and make you feel like it's worse than it is. I think I was just so nervous about going into the hotel that the whole thing had stressed me out more than I realised.

I finally made it to the hotel, took a moment to breathe... and then walked through the front door. I wandered around the lounge and restaurant areas. It was absolutely gorgeous.

I had no idea who the best person was to speak to, so I approached a lovely-looking lady who was chatting with one of the bar staff. She looked like management, so I took a chance. I introduced myself and explained that I'd applied for the Assistant front-of-house manager position and wanted to speak to someone about it. Would you believe it? She was actually the front-of-house manager? We didn't stop talking!

I CAN'T STOP PUSHING

She showed me around and told me more about the role. Then she said she'd contact HR and have my CV moved to the top of the pile. I ended up getting the job and she also became one of my best friends... and that's how I met Jen.

♥♥♥

By July, I was feeling more and more comfortable in my new position - settling into the job, getting to know my colleagues, and finding my way around the area too.

However, the feeling of wanting a baby had intensified into full-blown baby fever. I was so broody and wanted a baby so badly. I was on the pill and would never dream of coming off it without speaking to James first...but I won't lie...I was tempted. Every time I was a day or two late, felt a little nauseous, or had that weird butterfly sensation in my stomach, I'd find myself wondering ...*could I be pregnant?*

So, what did I do? Buy a pregnancy test...again and again and AGAIN! I must have gone through at least twenty, hoping that just one would show a positive. Even though I had no real symptoms beyond that gut-wrenching longing of *I want this so badly.* It started to feel like an obsession.

"I THOUGHT YOU WERE BEING BRAVE."

Apparently, this is completely normal for women when they're ready for a baby. I wish I had known that back then because honestly, I thought I was losing my mind.

One evening, James noticed me looking a bit down.

"Are you okay?" He asked.

"I just really want to be a mum. It's been on my mind a lot lately, and I can't stop thinking about it."

"I know you want a baby and I want one too… but I feel like it would be best if we wait until we are more financially stable," James replied. Every person I told this to just laughed. "If you wait to be financially stable, you'll never have kids," they would say.

It took a lot of convincing before James even considered the idea. And to make it even harder, all my friends started having babies. The waiting… the arguments… the tears… and of course, the endless pregnancy tests. I waited and waited.

One November evening, after dinner, James looked into my eyes for a long moment before nodding slowly. "Okay," he said at last. "Let's stop the birth control and see what happens." I threw my arms around him.

"Thank you, James! I'm so excited." He hugged me tightly and whispered, "I'm excited too."

I CAN'T STOP PUSHING

And so, the fun began - trying for a baby... which, of course, meant a lot of sex. Just to be sure.

Afterwards, I tried every trick in the book to increase our chances... including lying in bed with my hips elevated for as long as possible. James found it hilarious. "Is this really going to work?" he'd say laughing. "Well, it's worth a try," I'd reply.

♥♥♥

February arrived, and we were visiting my family in South Africa. On the flight over, I noticed that my period hadn't started yet. I thought I'd give it another week, figuring it might just be stress-related...but still, no period. I decided it was time to take a pregnancy test. The tricky part was buying one without my mum noticing - I didn't want to say anything until I was sure.

This was nearly impossible.

One afternoon, while my mum was busy in the kitchen, I snuck out to buy a pregnancy test. When I arrived back, I locked myself in the bathroom. My heart pounded as I waited for the result. Finally, the five-minute timer was up. I glanced over...Two lines.

It was positive! I nearly screamed...but caught myself. I wanted to tell my family in person, and this was the perfect opportunity.

"I THOUGHT YOU WERE BEING BRAVE."

I popped into the bedroom and gave James the good news. "James," I said, barely able to contain my excitement, "it's positive. We're going to have a baby."

His face lit up. "Really? That's amazing!" He wrapped me in the biggest cuddle. As soon as we walked downstairs, my mum noticed right away that something was up.

"Is everything alright?" she asked. I glanced at James, who gave me a small nod. Taking a deep breath, I smiled from ear to ear. "Actually…we have some news. You're going to be grandparents."

Her eyes instantly filled with tears and dad had the biggest smile on his face. This was their first grandchild. Everyone was over the moon.

My mum, always the practical one, insisted I take a blood test to confirm the pregnancy. "I hate needles," I moaned. She laughed. "You'll be getting so many that by the end of your pregnancy, you'll hold your arm out saying…just get it over with."

♥♥♥

We were leaving the next day, and the results would take 24 hours, so it was a mad rush to get them in time. When we picked up the results, I stared at the paper, baffled. "Why can't they just say 'pregnant' or 'not pregnant'? All these codes and medical terms make no sense to me."

I CAN'T STOP PUSHING

Mum put her glasses on and tried to read it. "I think this means you're pregnant…," she said, a little uncertainly. "Let's just call the lab," I said, already dialling the number. The woman on the phone confirmed, "Yes, you're about 1-2 weeks pregnant." Then I paused. "Wait…you said 1-2 weeks?"

"That's correct," she replied. I thanked her, hung up and turned to Mum. "That doesn't seem right. I just have a gut feeling something's not right with that."

"If you're worried, just speak to the doctor when you get home," she said. Call it mother's instinct, but something just didn't feel right. Still, I wasn't going to let that ruin the moment - after all, I was going to be a mum.

♥♥♥

A couple of weeks later, on a very snowy Friday back at Steven's house, I experienced every pregnant woman's fear: there was blood. "James." I called out, my voice trembling with panic.

He rushed into the room. "What's wrong?"

"I… there's blood," I whispered, with tears in my eyes. To make matters worse, we were completely snowed in and unable to get to a doctor. I was an emotional wreck. James immediately called the doctor

"I THOUGHT YOU WERE BEING BRAVE."

to ask for advice. The doctor booked us in for a scan on Sunday…which was two days later. "I can't believe this is happening," I said.

"We're going to get through this," James tried to reassure me. "We'll get the scan on Sunday, and we'll know more then."

Feeling too distraught to face anyone, I decided to stay in bed. With a hot water bottle glued to my stomach, and James constantly bringing me whatever I needed, I tried to get through the day I wished would end as soon as possible.

Around mid-morning, my phone rang. It was a midwife from the doctor's surgery, checking in on me.

"Hello, is this Olivia?" she asked. "Yes," I replied.

"This is June, I am one of the midwives at the doctor's surgery. Tell me what's happening." she said.

"I've never felt anything like this before," I cried. "My period pains were never this bad. It feels like my stomach is on fire." The midwife's voice was calm and reassuring.

"I know this is incredibly difficult but try to stay calm. It's okay to feel scared. Let's talk through what you're experiencing."

I had never met this midwife before, but she felt like a lifeline. She patiently explained what might be happening and tried to keep me calm and relaxed.

I CAN'T STOP PUSHING

"It sounds like you might be experiencing a miscarriage. I'll be here for you," she said. "Just take it one step at a time." Using the time in bed, I started researching miscarriages, something I had never experienced before. I was surprised to learn how common they are, though they're rarely talked about openly.

James sat next to me, reading over my shoulder. "I had no idea this was so common," he said. "Neither did I," I replied. We sat in silence for a moment.

As they say, everything happens for a reason, and as much as it hurts, physically and emotionally, it was nature's way of saying this wasn't the right time. There could have been something wrong and this was the best possible scenario for this little one. Yet again, call it mother's instinct, I just knew, this was it.

James wrapped his arms around me, holding me close. "We'll get through this," he whispered. It was a painful reminder of how fragile life can be, but also a testament to the strength we had as a couple.

♥♥♥

Scan day arrived all too quickly. I was absolutely terrified and the waiting room felt like torture. Every

"I THOUGHT YOU WERE BEING BRAVE."

time someone walked past, I thought they were coming to call us, and my heart would skip a beat.

James held my hand, trying to comfort me.

"It'll be okay," he whispered, but I could see it in his eyes, he was worried too. There was still that little voice in my head hoping this was all a bad dream. Maybe the nurse would tell me there was a heartbeat and that everything was going to be alright. You hear about moments like this in books and movies, but you never really think about how you'll react when it happens to you.

Finally, it was our turn. The nurse led us into the exam room. She tried to make small talk, sensing my anxiety, but my mind was elsewhere. "Alright, let's get started," she said, applying the cold gel.

I shivered at the sensation, unable to decide if it felt good or just plain weird. I find it so funny that they use a condom as the protective cover on the ultrasound probe, but it also makes so much sense.

James squeezed my hand tighter as the nurse began the scan. The room was silent. Each second felt like an hour. She moved the probe slowly, while her colleague took notes. The nurse started giving her colleague measurement after measurement, and I could feel my heart pounding in my chest. James's grip tightened even more.

I CAN'T STOP PUSHING

Finally, she stopped, and the silence was deafening.

The nurse looked over at me, her eyes filled with compassion. "I'm afraid there's no sign of a heartbeat or a baby. I am so sorry."

I tried my hardest to stay strong, to fight back the tears. The nurse watched me, waiting for my reaction.

"Thank you," I managed to whisper. She nodded and asked us to wait outside while she finalised the paperwork.

As soon as I sat down with James, I immediately felt emotional. This time, I couldn't hold it in. James tried to comfort me, but the nurse came back. She knelt next to me, gently placed her hand on my lap, and said softly, "I thought you were being brave."

She handed me a box of tissues and waited patiently as I composed myself. "Take your time," she said.

The nurse explained everything. "This happens more often than people think," she said gently. "It's important to give yourselves some time, and when you feel ready, you can try again." James nodded. "Thank you," he said. "We appreciate your help."

♥♥♥

The journey home was quiet. James reached over and held my hand.

"I THOUGHT YOU WERE BEING BRAVE."

"I think the nurse is right," he said. "We need some time to heal." I nodded, staring out the window at the snowy landscape.

"Yeah, I think so too. It's just… hard."

He pulled into the driveway of Steven's house and turned off the engine. "We'll get through this," he said. "When the time is right, we'll try again." I looked over at him, with tears in my eyes. "Okay," I whispered.

We walked inside.

"How did it go?" Steven asked softly.

James shook his head, and Steven pulled us both into a hug. "I'm so sorry."

I stayed in bed, for the rest of the evening, with a hot water bottle and James brought me anything I needed… including wine. I definitely needed it.

As much as it hurt, I knew this wasn't the end of our journey. It just wasn't the right time, and we'd have another chance soon.

Chapter 9

"JAMES PROBABLY KNOWS I'M HERE."

Well, it didn't take long. Finally, after nearly a year of waiting, our house was ready for us to move in.

They say things happen in threes, and on the day, we moved in, we had a new house, a new car, and I had an exciting secret - I was expecting a baby.

It was a little scary this time. Having miscarried before, I didn't want to tell anyone until I knew everything was fine.

However, I was still beside myself with excitement. I planned to tell James on our anniversary, which was just two days away. But clearly, my head and my body were not on the same page. The moment I heard him arrive home, I leapt off the couch and ran to the door. Poor guy hadn't even made it through the door, and I was shoving the pregnancy-test stick in his face.

"James, look." I shouted. His hands were filled with bags and his laptop. "Hold on a sec, babe," he said, laughing. "Let me put this stuff down. I could hardly stand still, bouncing on the balls of my feet as I waited.

"JAMES PROBABLY KNOWS I'M HERE."

Finally, he looked at me and realised what I was holding. "Is that…?" he started, reaching for the test.

"Don't!" I said, pulling it away. "I peed all over that. And yes… we're having a baby." James's face lit up and he gave me the biggest cuddle. "This is the best news ever," he said excitedly. "I was going to tell you on our anniversary," I admitted. "But I just couldn't wait."

"I don't care when you tell me," He said kissing me, "this is wonderful news to arrive home to."

Thinking back to the time on the ship when the shop manager jokingly announced that James and I were engaged and expecting a baby… who would have thought that would actually happen?

And here we were… married and expecting a baby.

Things seemed to be going well this time around. Surprisingly, I had no morning sickness. Just a little nausea when driving in the car… nothing a few ginger biscuits couldn't fix. Well, there's one other thing I noticed during pregnancy, other than being exhausted. While I may have escaped the dreaded morning sickness, I was not so lucky in the wind department.

I'm talking farts: Not the polite, under-your-breath kind. No, these were the kind of farts that could evacuate a room.

I CAN'T STOP PUSHING

At least with morning sickness, you can hide in the bathroom. But these stealthy little stink bombs gave no warning. Silent? Yes. Deadly? Absolutely. And they always struck at the worst possible times. I couldn't stop them… and poor James couldn't escape them. Honestly, I should've carried a warning label.

♥♥♥

Finally, I had the chance to meet with a midwife named Lily. I hadn't made it to this point the first time. She was calm and very quickly put me at ease, though she definitely wasn't as chatty as I was. I kept thinking I was going to drive her mad with all my questions.

During our first meeting, we had a good chat to get to know each other. Lily listened patiently as I babbled on.

"You're doing great," she reassured me. "It's completely normal to have questions and concerns. That's what I'm here for. Also, I would estimate that your due date will be around the middle of January."

"Thanks, Lily," I said. "I just want to make sure everything goes smoothly this time." She nodded, jotting down some notes. "Everything looks good so far. We'll keep an eye on things, but unless there are any

"JAMES PROBABLY KNOWS I'M HERE."

problems, you won't need to see me regularly. Just keep doing what you're doing."

James, who had been quiet for most of the appointment (probably because he couldn't get a word in…) spoke up, or should I say, got a word in. "What concerns should we be looking out for?"

"Just the usual…if Olivia experiences any severe pain, bleeding, or anything that feels off, give me a call immediately. But otherwise, just take it day by day."

"Everything's going to be fine this time," James said.

I nodded. "Yeah, I think so too." As the weeks went by, things continued to go smoothly.

Just before I found out I was pregnant, I had accepted a position at the hotel where I met Jen - you know - the one where I got lost on the way there…I had left to gain more experience in a different company but couldn't resist returning.

This meant the staff already knew me very well. This new role involved running events, which meant lots of time on my feet and a fair bit of heavy lifting…tasks I enjoyed, but I knew they'd get trickier as my pregnancy progressed.

On my first day, I met with HR to fill out paperwork, which included a safety questionnaire. That meant I

I CAN'T STOP PUSHING

couldn't keep my little secret for long. I confided in the HR assistant that I was newly pregnant and promised I'd tell my manager once we finished.

But as soon as I sat down in his office and opened my mouth, he smiled and said, "Congratulations. HR already told me."

Feeling a bit surprised, yet relieved I didn't have to tell him myself, I replied, "Oh, thank you."

Throughout my pregnancy, the company was amazing. Every time I had an appointment or a scan, they made sure I had time off without stress. As the months passed, my responsibilities were gradually adjusted to be less physically demanding. I was still involved in everything, just in ways that worked better for me.

It felt incredible to work somewhere so genuinely supportive. Their understanding allowed me to enjoy both my job and the pregnancy without unnecessary pressure.

James, meanwhile, was working for a drone company - a dream job for someone who loved being outdoors and playing with high-tech toys. Who wouldn't want to fly drones and get paid for it?

But, of course, there was a catch: the boss.

"JAMES PROBABLY KNOWS I'M HERE."

He was difficult. Always swearing, always barking orders. It was his way or no way at all. Still, James stuck with it because he truly loved the work.

♥♥♥

We finally made it to the weekend. James and his best friend, Mark, had tickets to see a show in London. Mark's wife, Charlotte, was heavily pregnant...due any day, in fact...but this was the boys' last chance to have a night out before baby arrived. One night should be fine, right?

I told Charlotte I was just relaxing at home and asked her to call me if she needed anything.

I made a quick, easy dinner and then curled up on the sofa with a movie. James had messaged to say their seats had been upgraded...they were now right up front. They were watching an orchestra perform music from well-known movies and it wasn't due to finish until 11 p.m., so I decided to get an early night.

Even though I was still in the early weeks of pregnancy, I was exhausted. Just as I started drifting off, my phone rang. Charlotte's name flashed on the screen. I knew exactly what that meant.

"Hello, Charlotte, are you alright?" I asked quickly. "I was just sitting on the lounge floor and my waters broke," she said, her voice calm but shaky. "The midwife is on her way, but maybe you could come over, just in case." Of course! The one night the guys decide to have a boys' night out, their little man chooses to make an entrance. "No problem, I'm leaving now."

I threw on some comfy clothes, grabbed my water bottle and car keys, and headed to the car. I climbed in, started the engine, tried to go forward and… nothing. The car wouldn't move. What on earth? I tried again. Still nothing. You've got to be kidding me. What am I going to do? Charlotte needed me. I had to get there. I couldn't let her down. I stood there for a moment, trying to think. I didn't know how to change a tyre…and being eight weeks pregnant, I wasn't sure I should even try.

Then I remembered our neighbours. We'd only met them a few times, but they seemed lovely. I ran to their door and knocked. Nick answered quickly. "Everything okay?"

"My friend's gone into labour, and I've got a flat tyre. I need to get to her." They'd been drinking, so they couldn't drive me, but they kindly offered to lend me their car. I was so grateful…until I remembered my insurance only covered me to drive my own car.

"Would you be able to help me change the tyre instead?" I asked. Without hesitation, they said,

"JAMES PROBABLY KNOWS I'M HERE."

"Absolutely." They were more than happy to help. What I hadn't warned them about was the jack. It was ancient, manual and quite possibly the most frustrating jack known to mankind. You had to crank it, endlessly. It was horrible.

But Nick was a hero. Despite being a bit tipsy, he changed that tyre like a pro. I could not thank him enough.

♥♥♥

Meanwhile, Charlotte kept messaging. The midwife was getting annoyed I hadn't arrived. That wound me up. Charlotte didn't need any extra stress. I apologised and promised I was nearly there. Twenty minutes later, tyre changed, I was finally on the road.

There's one thing I haven't mentioned. When I first moved to the UK, James and I installed an app on our phones that showed each other's locations.

Not stalker-y…just peace of mind. Especially when I was still getting used to things…like the time I got lost trying to find the hotel.

But tonight, I knew it was going to give the game away. Charlotte hadn't told Mark what was happening yet as she wanted to wait and see how things played out. But the second I left the house; James would've seen I was out. The app notifies us whenever either of us leaves or returns home, so it wouldn't take long for him to realise something was going on. I suppose the obvious thing would have been to turn off the location settings... but honestly, with everything going on, that didn't even cross my mind.

I finally arrived at Charlotte's house, and just as I was about to walk in, I saw the midwife walking outside towards me. She immediately had a go at me.

"Oh, you finally made it," she snapped. Seriously?

I bit my tongue, but inside I was fuming. She had absolutely no idea what I'd just gone through to get there. And Charlotte definitely didn't need that kind of attitude right now. I was here, willing to do whatever was needed... and also, by the way... eight weeks pregnant. So no, I didn't need her judgement.

I explained the situation and told her I was pregnant too. As soon as she heard everything, she apologised and suggested we start fresh. Fair enough.

We made our way inside to be with Charlotte, because she was the only thing that mattered right now. The midwife told Charlotte she wanted to check her maternity pad in the bathroom, since Charlotte had mentioned she was concerned about the colour.

Apparently, if a baby is in distress, your waters can show a greenish tinge - a sign the baby has passed

"JAMES PROBABLY KNOWS I'M HERE."

meconium (basically, their first poo). I had no idea that was even a thing. And that's exactly what had happened.

The midwife told us we needed to get to Westmere General Hospital immediately. Since there was now a concern with the baby, it was no longer something she could handle at home - only doctors could oversee a delivery under those circumstances.

While I helped gather Charlotte's things, I quietly said, "Just so you know…James probably knows I'm here."

She looked up at me, confused. "Why? Did you call him?"

I explained about the app and said, "he has already messaged me, asking what's going on." She sighed. "Do you know if he's said anything to Mark yet?"

"I'm afraid so. He has just said that I'm at your house."

The last thing she needed right now was her husband panicking while she was trying to stay calm. Then again, this might actually be a blessing in disguise - a softer way of breaking the news to him, rather than him getting an unexpected phone call from her.

Not a moment later and Charlotte's phone was ringing and it was Mark. So, she took a moment to update him. While they chatted on the phone, I took the opportunity to pack up the car with everything Charlotte needed: her

I CAN'T STOP PUSHING

hospital bag, the car seat, and the baby's bag as well. I also grabbed a few towels and laid them across the passenger's seat… just in case.

Charlotte and I climbed into the car, and at last, we were on our way. I had to take it slower than usual, because driving on a spare tyre doesn't leave much room for speed. Getting there safely was all that mattered. Not long into the drive, Charlotte started having contractions.

I eased over every bump and took corners as gently as I could, trying not to add to her discomfort. We chatted in between, just enough to keep her distracted, but each time a contraction hit, she'd pause mid-sentence to breathe through it. I kept my focus on the road whilst also doing everything I could to keep her calm and comfortable.

We parked just across from the after-hours hospital entrance, thankfully not far for Charlotte to walk. We rang the buzzer. A voice answered and told us we needed to call the maternity triage department to be let in. So, we did…but no one picked up. We called again. And again. Charlotte was standing outside, in pain, in the cold, soaked leggings and all. It was beyond frustrating.

"JAMES PROBABLY KNOWS I'M HERE."

Eventually, I gave up on the maternity line and buzzed the general hospital number, explaining (politely but firmly) that we'd been calling, Charlotte was in labour, and we needed help now. Finally, someone opened the door.

We made our way up and found the maternity triage. Charlotte was assessed quickly and hooked up to monitors.

That's when I realised, I didn't have my phone. What if I'd dropped it next to the car? James was probably trying to message me, and now, of course, I wasn't replying. Brilliant!

I told Charlotte I'd head to the car to look for it and grab her bag as well. I got back to the door we'd come in…only to see a "No Exit" sign.

You've got to be kidding me. The car was right outside. I was so close. Instead, I had to wander through endless hospital corridors, buzzing through each set of doors, trying to find an exit. Eventually, I got outside - on the complete opposite side of the hospital.

I stood there, turning in circles, trying to figure out which way to go. It was pitch dark, I had no phone, and I had no idea where I was. Not worth the risk.

I turned around and headed back inside. When I got back to Charlotte, I told her I'd wait for James. He could help me later.

I CAN'T STOP PUSHING

♥♥♥

Mark and James arrived not long after. They'd been two hours away in London, and understandably, Mark was panicking at the thought of missing the birth of his first child. Mark rushed straight to Charlotte, and then came over to thank me with the biggest hug.

Thankfully, James had travelled with Mark in his car, which made the logistics a little easier. James and I decided to go find the car and move all the baby stuff to Mark's.

We headed back to the same hospital door we'd originally come through earlier, hoping we might be able to sneak out when someone else came in. It was frustrating knowing our car was parked right outside that door… and yet, it felt impossible to get to. No one seemed to be coming in, and we didn't want to wait around forever. Especially as it was already so late and we still needed to drive home.

So, once again, I rang the bell at every door along the way to navigate us out of the hospital. At least I'd done that route once! Finally, we made it outside. And so, our journey began. We were in a city, navigating around the outside of a hospital at 11p.m.

I'm not going to lie; I was a bit nervous. It was

"JAMES PROBABLY KNOWS I'M HERE."

freezing, pitch black, and eerily quiet. But I felt completely safe with James. It took about 25 minutes to reach the car, but we were deep in conversation the whole way… talking about everything that happened that evening.

We transferred everything into Mark's car. Then drove ours around to the front entrance, so we could go check in with Charlotte and Mark and see how things were progressing. Charlotte had been booked in for an emergency C-section. The baby was showing signs of distress, and the doctors weren't taking any chances. We said our goodbyes, gave them our love, and made our way home.

It was an unexpected and utterly exhausting night - but it just goes to show, every labour is different. Honestly, the best thing you can do is be ready for anything.
In case you're wondering… Mum and baby did brilliantly. And he really is the cutest little man.

Chapter 10

"ARE WE LEARNING TO PUT OUT FIRES?"

Even though it was still early in my pregnancy, I decided it was time to start preparing my hospital bag. After what happened to Charlotte, I was not taking any chances. I also love to be organised, and I knew this would help me feel more relaxed. One evening, while James and I were relaxing on the couch, I brought out my notepad. "Alright, I'm making a list for the hospital bag." I said, smiling. James laughed, putting down his phone. "A list, huh? What's on the list?" I started jotting down items, thinking out loud as I wrote. "Let's see… comfy clothes for me, a couple of nursing bras, maternity pads, toiletries, phone charger…" James interrupted, "Don't forget snacks."

I laughed. "Good point. Snacks for both of us and a water bottle." He leaned over, peeking at my list. "How about stuff for the baby?"

"I was getting to that," I said. "A few onesies, a hat, mittens, blankets, nappies, wipes. Oh, and the car seat. We can't forget that."

"ARE WE LEARNING TO PUT OUT FIRES?"

Over the next few weeks, I slowly gathered everything on my list and researched anything I might have missed. This is what my crazy list looked like. Don't laugh…

LABOUR / HOSPITAL LIST

MUM CLOTHING:

- Slippers & Gown
- Shower Flip flops
- James's T-shirts
- Soft jumper
- Breast-feeding tops
- Maternity Bra
- Comfy clothes
- Going-home outfit
- Nightdress or pyjamas
- disposable knickers
- Breast-feeding bra
- Socks

MUM TOILETRIES:

- Absorbent towels
- Tissues
- Hairbrush
- Deodorant
- Toothbrush
- Toothpaste
- Body wash
- Shampoo
- Conditioner
- Face cream
- Antiseptic wipes
- Toilet wipes
- Lip Balm
- Hand cream
- Hairdryer & Hair ties
- Breast pads
- Maternity pads
- Eye mask & Ear plugs
- Flannel (Washcloth)
- Nibble cream

MUM AFTER LABOUR RECOVERY SUPPLIES:

- Soft Wet Wipes
- Haemorrhoid cream
- Stool Softener
- Soothing Breast wipes
- Paracetamol
- Cleansing cloths
- Mouth Wash
- Nursing pads

I CAN'T STOP PUSHING

FOR BABY

- ❏ Infant car seat
- ❏ Baby Change bag
- ❏ Change mat
- ❏ Baby Wipes
- ❏ Bottles
- ❏ Vests and hats
- ❏ Baby Grows (3 sizes)
- ❏ Going home outfit
- ❏ Baby blanket
- ❏ Nappies (about 20)
- ❏ Socks and mittens
- ❏ Coat or snowsuit.
- ❏ Muslin squares

FOR DAD

- ❏ Comfortable shoes
- ❏ Changes of clothes
- ❏ Blanket and Pillow
- ❏ Toothbrush
- ❏ Swimwear (birth pool)
- ❏ Deodorant
- ❏ Toothpaste
- ❏ Phone and charger
- ❏ Snacks and drinks
- ❏ Cash and change

EXTRAS

- ❏ Birth plan and Hospital yellow notebook
- ❏ Comfortable Pillow and a hot water bottle
- ❏ Entertainment: Earphones, book or magazine
- ❏ 2 Plastic bags for Laundry and for rubbish
- ❏ Back-up phone chargers
- ❏ Water spray, soft sponge and a hand-held fan
- ❏ Bottles of water, energy drinks and sugary sweets

Yes, I know, I probably overdid it... but would I forget anything? Absolutely not.

♥♥♥

Our 12-week scan day finally arrived, and I was so nervous. I sat in the waiting room biting my nails... which I never do (anymore)...and desperately trying not

"ARE WE LEARNING TO PUT OUT FIRES?"

to wet myself with how full my bladder was.

For the scan to be done properly, your bladder needs to be full, but the discomfort was almost unbearable. I think I had a bit too much water. The minutes felt like hours until the nurse finally called us in.

As I lay on the bed, I squeezed James's hand so tightly I was sure I was cutting off his circulation. He gave me a reassuring smile, but I could see the tension in his eyes too. The nurse applied the cold gel to my stomach and began the scan. The room was filled with a tense silence until, finally, the nurse broke it with the words I'd been so desperate to hear: "There's the heartbeat, and everything looks perfect. Baby is due in January as expected."

"Oh, my goodness, really?" I said, nearly leaping off the bed in excitement. James leaned in to kiss my forehead.

"We're really having a baby," he whispered. The nurse smiled at us. "Yes, everything looks great. You can start relaxing a bit now. Would you like the very first picture of your baby?"

"Yes please!" we both said at the same time, followed by all of us bursting out laughing.

"While I print that, you can go to the toilet and then wait in the waiting area," The nurse said. As we walked out, I felt so excited I could finally empty my overfull bladder.

I CAN'T STOP PUSHING

"I'll be right back," I told James, hurrying to the restroom. The sheer relief was indescribable…and I'll admit, a fair amount of wind followed. Silent, but deadly. I honestly felt bad for the next poor person who walked in.

When I returned to the waiting area - fairly quickly, I might add, just in case anyone got suspicious of the, erm… lingering atmosphere - James was holding the very first picture of baby.

He handed it to me with the biggest smile. I looked at the tiny image and felt like my heart was going to burst.

♥♥♥

As we walked back to the car, James turned to me. "It's so real now," he said. "I mean, I knew you were pregnant, but seeing this… it makes it all so much more real."

I nodded. "I get it. I've felt all the changes, but seeing that little heartbeat made it real for me too." A complete sense of relief washed over me. I felt like I could breathe again. This was it; we were going to have a baby. I knew things could still go wrong but we made it to the first scan, and that alone was a reason to celebrate. On the drive home, I couldn't contain my

"ARE WE LEARNING TO PUT OUT FIRES?"

excitement. "I can't wait to tell everyone." James laughed. "It's been hard keeping this secret. Let's make some calls when we get home."

The first call, I knew I needed to make, was to my mum and dad. I had already told them when we found out, but they were sworn to secrecy until our 12-week scan. I'd received nearly daily messages or calls from Mum asking when she could tell everyone.

I honestly couldn't tell who was more excited...her about becoming a grandmother, or me about becoming a mum. As soon as we walked through the door, I grabbed my phone and called her.

"Mum, we had our 12-week scan today, and everything looks perfect. I can now confirm...you are going to be a grandma." She was absolutely delighted.

"That's wonderful news. What a relief that everything is alright. I'm so happy for you and James." James smiled at me from across the room. "I know she's been dying to tell everyone", he said laughing. "She has," I replied, still on the phone with Mum.

"Mum, I know you're excited, but can you give us a few more days to call all the family before you spread the news? We want to make sure everyone hears it from us before it gets on social media."

I CAN'T STOP PUSHING

"Of course," she said. "I promise I'll keep it quiet a little longer. But I can't wait to tell my friends. They're going to be thrilled."

"Thanks, Mum. I knew you'd understand." After I hung up, I felt so much more relaxed.

James came over to give me a big cuddle. "This is really happening. We're going to be parents." He whispered. "Yes, we are," I said, smiling up at him. We spent the rest of the evening making phone calls. Each conversation making us feel so much more excited. Our siblings couldn't stop congratulating us, and our friends were thrilled. James's dad was equally excited when we called him. "This is wonderful news. Congratulations."

By the end of the night, our cheeks ached from smiling so much.

♥♥♥

As the days passed, my mum wasted no time in sharing advice. "When the time comes to give birth," she said one morning, "just go for the epidural early…don't wait until it's too late."

"Thanks, Mum," I replied. "I'll keep it in mind. But I'm hoping to go without painkillers unless absolutely necessary. Women have been doing this forever, right?"

"Trust me," she insisted. "I had an epidural with you

"ARE WE LEARNING TO PUT OUT FIRES?"

and both your sisters. It made all the difference."

"If it gets too intense, I'll consider it," I said. Over the next few weeks, advice poured in from all directions. Jen, my best friend, called to tell me about her water birth.

"You must try for a water birth if you get the chance...it was incredible. I can't recommend it enough." she insisted. James's friend, Karen, dropped by a stack of parenting books. "These were my lifesavers," she said. "And don't hesitate to ask for help. You'll need it." Even James's best friend shared his tips.

"Make sure you pack loads of snacks for the hospital. You'll both need the energy."

Our mail started filling up with baby catalogues, and our phones buzzed non-stop with excited relatives offering their two cents. It was overwhelming, but also incredibly touching to see how much everyone cared.

One evening over dinner, James said to me, "You know, it's a bit overwhelming, but I'm really grateful for all this support from our family and friends."

"Me too," I agreed. "We're lucky to be so loved. But let's take all the advice with a pinch of salt and do what works best for us." James nodded. "That's a great idea."

I CAN'T STOP PUSHING

I kept thinking more and more about my mum's advice on the epidural. I knew she was only trying to help, drawing from her own experiences. And though I was determined to try for a natural birth, I appreciated knowing all my options. At our next midwife appointment, I brought it up with Lily.

"My mum keeps insisting on an epidural," I said, "but I'm hoping to go as natural as possible. What do you think?"

Lily smiled. "It's great that you're thinking about your birth plan. Every woman's experience is unique. It's good to be open to all possibilities and to listen to your body. If you need pain relief, there's no shame in that. There is also gas and air as another option."

James nodded. "We'll play it by ear. We just want Olivia and the baby to be safe." As we walked to the car afterwards, I felt so much calmer. Talking to Lily helped. I knew in my gut I wanted a natural birth…but it was reassuring to know I had options.

♥♥♥

Since we didn't know the gender yet, we gave the baby a nickname: Baby B - since our surname started with B. Everyone uses nicknames like Peanut or Bean, but we wanted something that felt more personal.

"ARE WE LEARNING TO PUT OUT FIRES?"

The second trimester was surprisingly smooth. Still no nausea, no morning sickness, but still fully loaded with gas, though. Sometimes I had to remind myself I was even pregnant. If not for my growing tummy, I might've forgotten altogether. As my tummy grew bigger, sleeping comfortably became harder; pillows were no longer doing the trick.

One evening, struggling to sleep, I groaned, "I can't get comfortable, James. My back's killing me. These pillows are useless."

He looked up from his phone. "I've noticed you tossing and turning. Let me see what I can find."

The next day, James surprised me with a giant U-shaped pregnancy pillow. "Give this a try," he said, dragging the enormous thing into the bedroom. "Wow, that's huge. I hope it fits on the bed." That night, I snuggled into the pillow.

"This is amazing, James. Thank you." James smiled and climbed into bed. "I'm glad you like it. It's like a cosy cocoon."

Because it was U-shaped, I could turn over and still have the same pillow on the other side. But there was one small problem. I woke up to find James curled up with the other side of the pillow.

"Hey, are you stealing my pillow?" I whispered.

I CAN'T STOP PUSHING

James laughed. "It's just so comfortable. I couldn't resist." I shook my head, laughing. "Alright, but don't get too used to it. This pillow is supposed to be for me and Baby B."

"I know, I know. But maybe we can share sometimes?"

"Deal," I said. While James occasionally borrowed a corner, we both knew it was making a big difference for me.

♥♥♥

The day of our 20-week scan had finally arrived. We decided we wanted to do a gender reveal, to find out with all of our family and friends, and planned to ask the nurse at the scan. James and I were buzzing with excitement as we made our way to Westmere General Hospital.

As we waited to be called in, I said, "Do you think it's a boy or a girl?" James smiled. "Honestly, I have no idea. I think I would be more than happy with either."

Once inside, the nurse greeted us and began the scan. As she moved the ultrasound probe over my belly, the image of Baby B appeared on the screen. "Everything looks great," she said. "Would you like to know the gender?"

"ARE WE LEARNING TO PUT OUT FIRES?"

"Actually," I said, "could you write it down for us? We want to do a gender reveal."

She frowned. "I'm afraid I can't. We're not allowed to write it down in case it's wrong. I can either tell you now or you will need to wait until the baby is born."

James and I looked at each other in confusion. "How is writing it down any different from saying it?" he said.

"Trust me, I wish I could, but those are the rules." She replied. Clearly there was no changing her mind.

We took a moment to discuss. "What do you think?" I asked James. James thought for a moment. "Let's find out now. We can still have a gender reveal party; it'll just be our secret for a little while." I nodded. "Okay, let's do it."

We turned back to the nurse. "Okay, please can you tell us," I said, my heart pounding.

"Congratulations," she smiled. "You're having a baby boy." In that moment, I felt a little disappointed…I'd always imagined having a girl. But it didn't take long to pass and for excitement to take over. A boy! Our baby boy.

On the way home, I said to James, "You know, this might actually be perfect. I love that we have this little secret just between us and no one else knows."

He nodded. "I agree, our little secret." As we drove, we began brainstorming ideas for the gender reveal party.

I CAN'T STOP PUSHING

It was fun knowing we had this little secret, and we were more excited than ever to share the news with our family and friends. The initial hiccup with the nurse turned into a blessing in disguise.

♥♥♥

With our bag packing underway and the gender reveal planned, I was starting to feel ready. Baby B was doing well, and I was almost at 30 weeks. James then surprised me one evening. "Guess what?" he said.

"What?" I replied, intrigued. "I've signed us up for an expectant parents' course. It's a weekly class where we'll meet other expecting parents and learn everything, we need to know about having a baby." I laughed. "That sounds great, but no pregnancy or birth is the same. How are we supposed to prepare for that?"

"Well, I suppose we'll find out soon." James laughed. When we arrived at the first class the following week, we were surprised to see it was being held at a fire station.

"Why on earth would it be here?" I wondered aloud. "Are we learning to put out fires? Though…parenting might feel like that." James laughed.

Inside, chairs were laid out in a circle. A few people were making tea and grabbing biscuits. We took our

"ARE WE LEARNING TO PUT OUT FIRES?"

seats, trying not to make eye contact, as everyone seemed too nervous to be the first to speak.

There were four other couples, although one lovely lady was on her own as her husband was working.

The class began with introductions. Everyone had a turn to say their name, where they were from and their babies due date. Then we were asked to pick someone to talk to, other than our partner, and find something we had in common.

"Hi, I'm Olivia," I said to the woman next to me.

"Nice to meet you, Olivia. I'm Ally."

Turns out, she lived nearby, worked in hospitality, and even had a family member who'd worked on the same cruise ship as me. We hit it off immediately and didn't stop talking the entire class. James and I absolutely loved these classes. We covered everything from breathing exercises to birth positions, feeding tips, and dealing with crying babies. There were definitely some awkward moments, like when we practiced random birthing positions and breathing noises.

The most memorable session involved our instructor using sandwich spreads on nappies to signify different stages of a baby's poo. Marmite and mustard were among them. "I'm never eating Marmite again," James muttered, making a face. "Me neither," I agreed.

We formed incredible friendships in this group. Sharing laughs and experiences, we all became so close. We even started our own messaging group to plan coffee dates, playdates, and share tips and advice. It was comforting to have a group of friends going through the same thing.

♥♥♥

October arrived, and it was finally time for our gender reveal. As much as I was looking forward to it, I felt a bit sad. James and I had known the gender for so long, and I loved just being in our own little bubble.

To celebrate, we decided to theme the reveal around bees, as it worked perfectly with the "Baby B" nickname. I found the cutest little fondant bees to put on top of the cupcakes, which I decorated with pink and blue icing.

Despite the adorable setup, the day was a nightmare. It was hot, humid, and pouring with rain. This meant we had to cram 30 people into our lounge, which was definitely not designed for this many people. We also had family all over the world who wanted to join in, so we connected them via a live video stream on my

"ARE WE LEARNING TO PUT OUT FIRES?"

laptop. Of course, we ran into technical issues, delaying the reveal by about half an hour, as the video just didn't seem to want to work. Finally, everything was set. I wore a tie-dye pink and blue shirt, while James wore a t-shirt, I had designed for him.

It read "Boy or Girl" with little boxes next to each option, so we could tick the correct one afterwards.

Corny, I know, but it was all in good fun. We decided to have some fun and got two confetti cannons, one pink and one blue, to wind everyone up a bit.

"Ready?" James asked.

"Ready," I replied, holding my cannon.

We counted down. "Three, two, one..." and James's cannon went off before mine. Pink confetti exploded into the air, and everyone cheered. Three seconds later, my blue cannon went off, and the room was silent. The confused looks on everyone's faces were priceless.

"Wait, what?" my friend asked. "Are you having twins? James and I were in stitches.

"No, no twins," I laughed. "We just wanted to mess with you all."

We then revealed the truth: the actual gender was inside a helium balloon behind us and that we had known all along.

"Okay, for real this time," James said, holding a pin.

I CAN'T STOP PUSHING

"Three, two, one…" James popped the balloon… and blue confetti filled the air.

"It's a boy!" we shouted. Everyone cheered and took it in turns to hug us. It was a wonderful moment, but as the excitement died down, we looked around the room. Confetti was everywhere.

"I guess we didn't think this through," I said, laughing. "I'm sure we will be finding confetti, in the strangest places, for years to come."

Chapter 11

"I CAN LEAVE IF YOU PREFER?"

The next exciting part of having a baby was choosing the name. There were a few factors to consider.

If you're one of the lucky ones, you've known your whole life the name or names you'd give your children. I had a girl's name already picked out…of course…but this was a boy.

When you don't have a name in mind and there are a few million names to choose from, it gets complicated.

To complicate things even more, James and I needed to agree on the chosen name.

Both of us were also teased a lot when we were younger, we wanted to make sure the name we chose would avoid any teasing.

Every night, we would go through name after name, trying not to overcomplicate it. We picked our favourite five to compare. And thankfully, we had one mutual favourite: Alexander. It was also James's middle name, which made it even more special. Choosing the middle name took a little longer.

I CAN'T STOP PUSHING

Like many families, our first thought was to use a family member's name. We both wanted to honour our fathers, but I felt having two middle names was a bit much.

One night, as I lay awake, the perfect idea came to me - joining our fathers' names, Malcolm and Steven, to create Malven. The next morning, I couldn't wait to share my idea with James. "James, I've got it," I said as he came into the kitchen. "Got what?" he asked, pouring himself a cup of coffee. "The perfect middle name. What if we combine our dads' names - to make Malven?" James took a moment to think about it, then a smile spread across his face. "Malven... I love it. Alexander Malven Bailey. It has a nice ring to it."

"We finally decided on a name," I said. James nodded. "But let's keep it a secret until he's born?"

"Agreed."

♥♥♥

Since I was due in January, I decided to book a month off work, to have a break, before Alexander was born, and to relax over Christmas. I'd be heavily pregnant and wouldn't be much use at work. The Saturday before I was due to go on leave, I decided to

"I CAN LEAVE IF YOU PREFER?"

treat myself to a little "me time." I rarely go to a hairdresser to get my hair cut, maybe once a year as a real treat, otherwise, I just do it myself, just like the hair dresser taught me while I was working on the cruise ship.

But there's something lovely about getting your hair washed, enjoying a good head massage, and sipping coffee while someone else styles your hair.

The day arrived for my much-needed pampering. I completely lost track of time and was running very late. Mummy-brain had truly kicked in. I hate being late. I'm one of those people who is always early. But when you have kids, that all changes…and this baby wasn't even born yet!

I rushed out the door, flew into the car, and as I went to pop my bag onto the passenger seat, I knocked my hand against the steering wheel. I didn't think much of it at the time. I buckled up and grabbed my phone to set the sat-nav. That's when I noticed it…the gaping hole where the tanzanite stone in my engagement ring should have been.

"Shit!" I whispered, leaping out of the car and frantically searching the ground. Had the stone fallen outside? Inside? What was I going to do?

I ran back inside to find James, tears streaming down my face. "What's wrong, Olivia? What happened? And why are you still here?"

I CAN'T STOP PUSHING

The words just poured out as I explained what happened. James grabbed my shoulders gently and looked me in the eyes. "Don't worry. We'll find it."

We headed outside and searched the car. Less than a minute later, James stood up with the stone in his hand. Thank heavens. I felt like I was having a mild panic attack. James took my ring and the stone and safely stored them until we could get to a jeweller for repairs.

I finally got back into the car, calling the hairdresser to let them know I was running late. Thankfully, it wasn't a problem. As they say, better late than never.

In my final week at work, I began preparing my handover. Fortunately, I'm the type of person who likes to be prepared, so everything was pretty much up to date. Tuesday came along quickly and we had another meeting with our midwife, Lily, to check how things were going.

As the baby was growing bigger, she could now feel him through my tummy and wanted to make sure he was facing the right way. Lily smiled as she warmed her hands up before placing them on my belly. "Let's see how he's positioned today. We want his head to be down," Lily explained. "That's the best position for

"I CAN LEAVE IF YOU PREFER?"

delivery." She pressed and prodded gently, then paused. "Hmm, let me double-check."

After a few more moments, she looked up at us. "I can feel that he's breech. This means his feet or bum would come out first rather than his head."

"Is that bad?" James asked. "It's not ideal," Lily said, "but we've got time, and there are things we can try. If he doesn't turn, we'll plan for a C-section." I felt a little anxious but it's better to know now than during labour.

"What can we do to help him turn?" Lily explained a few exercises and positions that might encourage him to move. "We'll check again next week. Sometimes babies turn on their own."

"Okay, we'll do everything we can," I said. Lily smiled. "You're doing great." That afternoon, I decided it was time to do another bag check. "James, can you come here for a minute?" I called. He walked in, spotting the nearly overflowing bag. "Wow, do we really need all that?"

"Yes! And I just want to double-check everything." James picked up a tiny onesie. "Can you believe Alexander will be wearing this soon?" I felt a lump in my throat.

"I know. It's hard to imagine, but I'm so ready for him to be here." He hugged me. "You're going to be an amazing mum."

I CAN'T STOP PUSHING

"Thanks," I whispered. "And you're going to be the best dad."

♥♥♥

Just to keep me on my toes, James came down with a horrible cold, two days later, and it kept getting worse. As I was 37 weeks pregnant, I decided to sleep in the guest bedroom, to ensure I didn't get sick too.

By Wednesday morning, he was really unwell. He hadn't slept and felt terrible. I tried everything to convince him not to go to work, but being a typical stubborn man, I lost that battle and off he drove.

On his way to work, I called him. "James, you're really not well. You need to come back home and rest." He insisted, "I just have to deal with it and try to work. My boss will make me feel awful if I take the day off." I mentioned before about this boss being hard to work with, but this is ridiculous. I could hear the exhaustion in his voice and knew this wasn't right.

"James, it's not worth it. Your health is more important. Please come home." There was a pause, he sighed and then burst into tears.

"Alright… I'll turn around. I just hate feeling like this. My boss is going to be such a pain about it."

"I CAN LEAVE IF YOU PREFER?"

I didn't care about what his boss thought, I was just happy he was coming home. "Thank you. I just want you to get better." When James walked back through the door, he looked defeated.

"I just can't believe my boss… how can anyone make their employees feel this way?"

I gave him a big cuddle. "I know… but what matters now is that you're home and safe. We'll deal with everything else later."

"You're right. Thanks for convincing me," he said.

"Always," I said, leading him to the couch. "Now, get some rest. I'll make you some tea."

As he settled down, I headed off to work. I couldn't stop thinking about what had happened and feeling so grateful that James was home and taking care of himself.

♥♥♥

As James was now taking time off, he needed a doctor's note to prove he was unwell. He called the doctor and made an appointment. However, his boss made our lives difficult again by refusing to let James use the company car to drive to the doctor's surgery. I spoke to my boss, who kindly let me take a few hours off work to drive James to the doctor.

When we arrived at the doctor's office, James was worn out and so emotional.

I CAN'T STOP PUSHING

The doctor greeted us, and we followed her to her room. The doctor looked at James and then at me. "Do you want Olivia to leave the room so we can talk in private?" she asked. I started to stand up. "Of course, I can leave if you prefer," I said.

James quickly grabbed my hand. "Please don't leave the room. I want you here with me," he said, with tears rolling down his cheeks. My heart ached for him. "I'm here, James," I said, fighting back my own tears.

"Alright...let's talk about what's been going on," she said, focusing back on James. "Tell me about your symptoms and what you've been experiencing."

James took a deep breath. "I've been really stressed at work. My boss is constantly on my back, and it's just been getting worse. I can't sleep, and I feel exhausted all the time."

I chipped in, "He's been under so much pressure, and it's affecting his health. This morning, he barely had the strength to get out of bed, but still felt like he couldn't take the day off work." The doctor listened attentively, taking notes.

"This isn't just a cold. It's stress-induced, and you need to take care of yourself," she said. "Especially as you have a baby on the way."

"I CAN LEAVE IF YOU PREFER?"

"I just want to feel better," James said. The doctor gave us a sympathetic smile. "I'm going to write you a note to take the rest of the week off. You need to rest and recuperate." What a relief. That's exactly what I wanted to hear. "Thank you so much, doctor," I said. "We really appreciate it."

As we left the doctor's office, James grabbed my hand. "Thank you for being there with me," he said. "Always, James," I replied. "Now let's get you home. You need to get better before this little man arrives. Luckily, you'll have next week off for Christmas, so this will give you more time to recover."

He managed a small smile. "I'm so lucky to have you," he said. "We're in this together," I replied.

With the doctor's note in hand, James finally had the time he needed to heal and prepare for the exciting changes ahead.

As expected, his boss was furious, but there was nothing he could do about it. And honestly? I couldn't care less. We were having a baby, and James needed to get better - that was all that mattered.

♥♥♥

The next day was my work Christmas lunch and my second last day at work. It was a festive, yet busy day, as I was completing my handover to a colleague who wouldn't be there on my last day. My emails were almost done, and I had only a few tasks left to finish.

When lunchtime finally arrived, the team had prepared a roast feast for us to enjoy together in one of our event rooms. As we headed upstairs, I struck up a conversation with a colleague, and we started talking about birthdays near Christmas.

"I feel so sorry for anyone who has their birthday so close to Christmas," I said sympathetically.

He smiled and replied, "My birthday is actually three days before Christmas. Every year, my mum would celebrate my birthday at the beginning of December to make sure it felt special."

"That's such an amazing idea." I replied. "It makes me rethink how I view birthdays around Christmas. After all, it's a very special time of year."

We continued chatting as we made our way to the event room. The room was beautifully decorated, and the food smelled incredible. We enjoyed a full roast meal with all the trimmings.

I felt so calm. James was at home resting, and it was nearly my final day at work… well… so I thought.

Chapter 12

"HAVE YOU SEEN MY PYJAMAS?"

At 5 a.m. the next morning, I woke up with a strange sensation down below. My pyjama shorts were soaked.

What on earth was going on? I was sure I hadn't peed myself. Throughout my pregnancy, I'd never once felt like I couldn't make it to the toilet…but just to be certain, I smelled it. Nope…definitely not urine.

I decided to change my pyjamas and see how things went. But as soon as I got back into bed, I was wet *again*.

Something was definitely happening. Oh dear. Could this be my waters starting to break? For a moment, I panicked, unsure of what to do. I was only just over 37 weeks pregnant. Then I took a deep breath and thought, *right, let's get it together*.

First, I put on a maternity pad, then went to call the maternity unit for advice. But before I could dial, I heard James coughing in the other room. He was still so unwell, and we were still sleeping in separate rooms so I wouldn't catch his cold. I poked my head into his room.

"Morning James, I think my waters might be breaking.

I CAN'T STOP PUSHING

I'm going to call the maternity unit," I said. He responded with a groggy, "Okay," clearly not processing what I had said. As soon as I started speaking to the midwife, James appeared around the corner, now looking much more awake.

The midwife ran through some questions and then concluded, "It sounds like your waters are breaking gradually. Since you still have a month to go, you need to see a doctor." Westmere General Hospital was 40 minutes away, so we needed to get our things ready as soon as possible.

Thankfully, as you know, I like to be prepared - I'd already done all the Christmas shopping, wrapped the presents (except mine, of course, as that was James's one job), and both the baby's bag and mine were packed, aside from a clothing wash I'd put on the night before.

All of my underwear was in there. While James quickly threw a few bits into his bag, I popped my underwear in the tumble dryer. Then, I was so busy double-checking everything in my hospital bag... I completely forgot about the underwear. After loading the car, we were off.

"HAVE YOU SEEN MY PYJAMAS?"

♥♥♥

On the way to the hospital, I tried to call work. It was supposed to be my last day. The general manager was on his morning walkabout, so I spoke to a colleague at reception. "Hi, it's Olivia. I won't be in today," I said. "Is everything alright?" she asked.

"Well... I think my waters have broken, so I'm heading to the hospital. Can you please let my manager know and keep it quiet? We haven't told family and friends yet." I explained. "Of course, Olivia. I'll pass it on and keep it confidential. Good luck."

♥♥♥

Once we arrived, we were shown to a corner cubicle by a window. Thank goodness we had some natural light and fresh air. This makes a big difference in stuffy hospitals.

A male doctor arrived to ask the usual questions, then requested to do an examination.

Could it get any more awkward? My husband on one side and another man with his fingers inside me. And *no*, I hadn't remembered to give *down there* a clean-up, making it ten times worse.

After his examination, the doctor wasn't convinced that my waters had broken. "Just excess discharge," he said.

I CAN'T STOP PUSHING

I pulled out my soaked pyjamas and held them up. "Have you seen my pyjamas? This isn't discharge. They are soaked." He decided to try a method called 'pooling', which involved placing a pillow under my bum, to stop any liquid from coming out. After an hour, he returned and removed the pillow, and sure enough, I soaked the bed. That convinced him. A consultant joined and said I'd need steroid injections over two days and antibiotics, plus check-ups every two weeks.

"Everything else looks good and baby's head is down," she said. I looked at them, confused. "No, he's breech." They looked surprised. The doctor turned to the consultant and admitted he wasn't aware of this. Thank goodness I spoke up.

"How do you know he's breech?" the consultant asked. "I was due a follow-up appointment with our midwife, Lily, next week to check if he'd turned," I explained. The fact that neither the doctor nor the consultant was aware of this was concerning. They took me for a scan, and there it was, clear as day on the screen: he was bum down. This changed everything. Ten minutes later, they returned. "You'll need a C-section in two weeks. How do you feel about New Year's Eve?"

"HAVE YOU SEEN MY PYJAMAS?"

James and I looked at each other. "Well, that's certainly one way to bring in the new year." I said, laughing. We agreed, and with that settled, we headed back to our cubicle.

♥♥♥

As the doctor prepared my discharge paperwork, a midwife walked in, to let us know, they were getting everything ready for me to stay overnight. Confused, I said, "The doctor and consultant said I was going home."

She looked horrified. "Why would they send you home when the next 24 to 48 hours are the most likely time for you to go into labour?" And we lived 40 minutes away.

"We're prepared either way," I said. She dashed off and returned moments later, smiling. "They've agreed. You're staying." She asked about my birth preferences.

"I know you hoped for a water birth, but if baby comes early, that's not possible."

"I'd prefer to avoid an epidural, but I'm open to whatever's needed to keep us both safe," I replied.

"That's all we want to hear." She smiled.

♥♥♥

Being in hospital isn't fun. Luckily, I'd brought my laptop, so we could watch some movies, to pass the time. The hours ticked by slowly, and still nothing was

I CAN'T STOP PUSHING

happening.

We tried to do some walking around to get the labour started and to get out of the room for a bit. We heard women coming in and out *all day*, screaming and shouting, which was a bit daunting for a first-time mum. James kept checking in. "Are you okay?"

I nodded. "It's a bit overwhelming, but I'm glad we're here and not at home. How are you feeling?"

"Surviving," he replied. James was still so unwell. The chair he was sitting in was not the most comfortable. I felt so guilty being the one lying down and I was absolutely fine. But he was such a trooper and just kept going so he could be there to support me.

The midwife then came in to check on us. "Sometimes it's slow, but you're doing great," she said.

By 8 p.m., still no change. James was really struggling. He didn't want to leave me…well…it was more that I didn't want him to leave, but I knew he needed sleep. "Babes, go home and rest," I insisted, pulling on my big girl pants. "This could take days, and you need your strength for both the baby and me." He looked torn, but he nodded. "Are you sure?" he asked.

"HAVE YOU SEEN MY PYJAMAS?"

"I'll be fine," I assured him, even though I felt so nervous at the thought of him leaving. He gave me a kiss and reluctantly left. I decided to close my eyes and try to get some rest too. It had been a very long day, and I knew I would need my strength. But sleep in hospital? Not a chance. Beeping monitors. OBS checks. Moaning. Breathing. Contractions. It was impossible!

Around 11 p.m., a bit of pain started. It was unlike anything I had ever felt before. I decided to use an app on my phone to start timing, in case it was contractions, because they kept coming, slowly and inconsistently. I also constantly felt like I needed to pee. By my sixth bathroom attempt, the door was locked. I sat on the chair outside breathing through a contraction. A midwife walking past didn't even see me because it was so dark, and she nearly jumped out of her shoes. "Oh my gosh. You scared me," she said. "Are you okay?"

"Just waiting to go to the loo," I said. She tugged the door and it opened. "Sometimes it sticks. You've been sitting out here for no reason!" we both laughed.

By 2 a.m., the contractions were getting more intense. I called James. "I think it's happening. You'd better start heading over soon."

I CAN'T STOP PUSHING

"Okay, I'll shower and pack the car…"

"Wait…PACK THE CAR? You unpacked it?!"

"Uh… yeah."

"James, honestly…"

"I know. I know. I'll be quick."

By 3 a.m., I had made my tenth trip to the bathroom. I returned to my bed and decided to sit at the end for a bit. I had been lying down for hours, and these contractions were becoming increasingly uncomfortable.

♥♥♥

Just as I got comfortable, the woman across from me suddenly started screaming at the top of her lungs. With the privacy curtains drawn, I couldn't see much but I could hear the sound of midwives rushing in to check on her. "You're 10cm!" I heard a midwife shout. "We need to get you downstairs, NOW!" I heard her curtains being opened, and just as they started wheeling her bed out, she shouted, "*BABY'S COMING! BABY'S COMING!*"

About five seconds later, we heard her baby crying. Under the curtain, I could just see people running. "Wow, that was fast." her husband said. "Anyone have the time?" a midwife called. "We need a birth time."

"HAVE YOU SEEN MY PYJAMAS?"

That baby's cry triggered something in me. My next contraction hit and then a pain, so intense, shot through my back and around my stomach. I grabbed the cold pole of the bed, oddly enough, this helped, and for the first time, I screamed, "HELP ME!"

Perfect timing, right after a baby was born and staff were limited. "We're coming as quickly as we can," someone shouted back. I was still sitting at the bottom of the bed, so mid-contraction, I turned and crawled up the bed... bad idea!

I finally made it and managed to make myself comfortable before the next one started. Then I messaged James, "*Hurry*." After about five minutes, a midwife came running in, and within seconds, three of them surrounded me - one on either side and the other at my bottom end doing an examination.

"Do you mind if I hold your hand?" I asked the midwife on my left. She gave me a little giggle and said, "Of course you can." In between contractions, I tried to explain, "My husband went home because he was not well, but he's hopefully on his way now."

"You're 6cm dilated," the midwife said. "We need to get you downstairs now."

I CAN'T STOP PUSHING

"I was supposed to have a C-section on New Year's Eve. Baby is breech." I added. The other midwife said, "I haven't read your notes yet, but I promise you're in safe hands." They popped my phone and water on my lap and started wheeling me downstairs.

This was it. I was about to have a baby.

There was no turning back now.

Chapter 13

"GRANNY PANTIES IT IS."

On the way down, I quickly sent James another message: "I'm being wheeled downstairs. You need to get here now." He replied that he was leaving now and would get to me as quickly as he could.

As we sped through the hallways, the midwives kept talking to me, trying to keep me calm. "You're doing great," one said. "I can't believe this is happening so fast," I replied.

I still don't know why, but again, I found comfort in gripping the cold metal poles on the bed during each contraction. What I didn't realise was that the poles would keep banging into the doors and walls. The midwives had to repeatedly tell me to keep my hands inside the bed, but when those contractions hit, it was easy to forget.

We finally made it into one of the birthing rooms. They wheeled me next to another bed and asked, "Do you want to be lifted, or would you prefer to slide over?" I was in the middle of a contraction, so I asked them to wait. Once it passed, I managed to slide across by myself.

I CAN'T STOP PUSHING

The lights were bright. Everything felt surreal. The midwife on my left side said, "Alright, we're all set. Just breathe and focus. Your baby is coming soon."

I nodded, gripping her hand tighter as another contraction hit. James, please hurry, I thought. "Any special requests for the birth?" one midwife asked. "Just get my baby here safely," I replied, as I tried to breathe through each contraction.

I was so excited when they brought in the gas and air. I had completely forgotten about it. At first, I took quick little breaths...probably what everyone does the first time. It didn't seem to do *anything*. A midwife showed me how to breathe slowly... in and out... in and out... and suddenly, I felt like I was floating. It was *amazing*! I've never taken anything to make me high, but this must be what it feels like.

A few minutes later, a woman tapped on my shoulder, and said, "Olivia? Are you with me?"

I looked at her, feeling like I was very dazed, and said, "I think so."

"My name is Sally. I'm the on-duty doctor, and I will be helping you through this," she said. The gas and air had eased slightly, and I was feeling a little more

"GRANNY PANTIES IT IS."

aware of my surroundings. "I'm supposed to be going in for a C-section in two weeks because my baby is breech."

"You're too far along now," Sally said gently. "There's no time. You're going to deliver naturally. But you're in great hands, and we'll guide you every step of the way." I took another deep breath of the gas and air. "Okay, I trust you."

"You're doing great, Olivia," a midwife said. "We're right here."

"Thank you," I whispered.

Then Sally said she needed to put a cannula in my hand. As you know I HATE needles. I took a few more puffs of gas and air. I didn't even notice how tightly I was holding onto the bed until she started tapping my hand.

"You'll need to relax your hand," she said. I took a deep breath, forced myself to let go of the bed, and relaxed my hand as much as I could. A few moments later, she said, "All done."

"That's it?" She smiled. "Didn't feel a thing, did you?"

"Nope. Why am I more afraid of a needle than pushing out a breech baby?" She laughed. "You're doing brilliantly.

Just so you know, the neonatal team is standing by to check him over immediately after he's born. Are you ok with that?" I nodded. "Of course."

I CAN'T STOP PUSHING

All I could think was that I needed to focus and get this baby out safely. I took another deep breath, knowing I needed to concentrate fully on what I was doing and what the midwives were telling me.

Gas and air in one hand and the doctor's hand in the other, a strange sensation suddenly came over me - I needed to *push*. They say it feels like needing to do a giant poo. Yep. E*xactly* like that.

The midwife noticed me squirming and asked, "Do you need to push?"

"Yes," I squeaked. And off came my trousers.

As they began setting up the leg supports, I was already lifting my legs into position. One of the midwives giggled and said, "You know exactly what to do." Another contraction hit, and I *pushed*. "Keep going, Olivia! You're doing amazing," someone called.

In all the craziness, I hadn't even noticed how many people were in the room with me. There must've been about eight in total. The doctor was on my right, monitoring me closely, the midwife on my left was still holding my hand and a few other staff members were dressed and ready for the delivery.

I kept hearing them shout, "Come on, Olivia. You can do it." It really helped. I pushed. Again. And again.

"GRANNY PANTIES IT IS."

Then I heard the midwives whisper among themselves, "Still nothing." I threw my head back, feeling breathless and frustrated.

I don't believe it, I thought. *Are you serious?*

A midwife offered me a tiny cup of water. Before she could say "sip it," I'd already downed the whole thing. Oops. Apparently not ideal during active labour.

I pushed again. The pressure quickly intensified. It built and built until...WHOOSH. My remaining waters exploded *everywhere*! Two of the midwives jumped back so fast...I think I just missed them.

Thankfully, the gas and air was working wonders. I felt no pain, just an overwhelming amount of pressure, and I was completely out of breath.

Then I felt a strange tightening down there. The weirdest sensation. The midwives started to gather around me, and that's when I knew... something was happening.

"We have the legs, bum, and shoulders," the doctor said. "Now we just need the head. Congratulations - it's a boy! I need you to give me the biggest push you can."

I couldn't believe it. All I had to do was give the biggest push of my life, and I'd have my baby. I took a few breaths, rested for a few seconds, and then went for it.

I CAN'T STOP PUSHING

I pushed so hard I started screaming - not from pain, but from the sheer pressure, like a tennis player shouting as they hit the ball, but way more intense. The room seemed to blur around me as I focused all my energy on that final push.

Then...the pressure went...I watched the midwives lay him on my tummy and I heard the most beautiful sound: *my baby's first cry.*

At 4 a.m., my tiny baby was born. Tears streamed down my face as he looked straight at me with his beautiful big black eyes...though he looked somewhat like an alien. Then it hit me...I'm a mum.

I'll never forget that moment. All I could think about was how I wished James was here to cut the cord.

But they cut the cord, and as quickly as they had placed him on my tummy, they whisked him off to another section of the room, to be checked over by the neonatal team.

Just then, James walked in. He rushed over and kissed my head. He looked overwhelmed. I could tell it was a lot to take in, walking into a room full of strangers after waiting outside, knowing I was in there having our baby without him. "Are you okay?" he asked.

"GRANNY PANTIES IT IS."

"Yeah, I'm fine," I said, smiling.

He told me about how much he'd struggled to get to me. First, the boom gate to the parking lot wouldn't open. Then, because it was the middle of the night, all the doors to each section of the hospital were shut, and he had to ring the bell for each one to let him in. To top it off, when he finally asked where he needed to go, they didn't know it was me in that room because I had been brought down so quickly. That's why they kept him outside. "I'm so sorry," he said.

"It's okay," I reassured him. "Either you needed to be with me from the beginning or at the end. I was so focused on listening to what the midwives were telling me, that it would have completely thrown me off if you had walked in during." James nodded. "I'm just glad I'm here now."

One of the midwives came over to James and said, "Would you like to go meet your baby?" James looked at me, his eyes wide.

"I completely forgot about him for a moment there." That moment showed me how much he loves me. For so long it had just been the two of us, and now we needed to adjust to having our little man around. James hesitated, not wanting to leave my side, but I insisted. "Go on."

He kissed me again and went over. I watched as he looked down at our son.

I CAN'T STOP PUSHING

After that announcement on the ship, when they said James and Olivia would be having a baby... and now, here we are, with our baby.

James glanced back at me, a tearful smile on his face as he looked down at our son for the first time.

James then came straight back to be with me. Since our baby had come out bum first, with his feet over his head, I had torn a little down there...OUCH!

The midwife needed to put in a few stitches...even more OUCH! But first, we had to deliver the placenta.

"Take a few more puffs on the gas and air," she instructed. "With the next contraction, we should be able to get it out." A few more puffs, and she was right. The next contraction came, I pushed, she tugged, and out it came. It felt...weird. Like pushing out a warm, jelly pillow.

Now came the dreaded stitches. She needed to give me an injection to help take away the pain.

As you know, I *hate* injections. I'm not kidding when I say the injection felt more painful than pushing him out. Thankfully, I was still on gas and air, which helped ease the discomfort. While she was doing the stitches, the neonatal team needed to come past us to move our little man to the neonatal unit.

"GRANNY PANTIES IT IS."

The midwife looked at me and said, "I'm going to cover you up while they walk past to give you your privacy."

I just looked at her and said, "My dignity went out the window with my legs spread wide open for everyone in here." She giggled but still covered me.

Just as they were about to leave, James and I asked if we could have a cuddle and a photo. The midwife smiled and nodded. "Of course. He will still need to have the tube in his nose and a mask over his face."

He was all wrapped up in a swaddle, as well as the tube and mask, looking very different than when they put him on my tummy. The midwife held him in front of us, and we did manage to get one photograph of all three of us. It wasn't the picture I had expected, but it was still such a special moment…our special moment.

James leaned in and whispered, "He's perfect." I nodded, with tears filling my eyes. Despite knowing it was necessary for them to take him to neonatal, watching them walk away with him was one of the hardest things I've ever done.

The midwife finally finished the stitches.

"All done, you did great." she said. Another midwife smiled at me. "You did amazing. That breech birth was textbook perfect."

I CAN'T STOP PUSHING

I was so relieved that the worst was over. "Thank you," I said. James kissed my forehead. "I'm so proud of you," he whispered. The exhaustion then hit me all at once. All the pushing and adrenaline had now worn off, and I fell asleep without even realising.

♥♥♥

I woke up to the sound of shuffling as one of the midwives was cleaning up. I glanced around, still feeling what was left from the birth.

"How long was I out?" I asked.

"Just a little while," the midwife replied. "You needed the rest." I decided to try and sit up, wanting to start feeling a bit more normal. My body felt heavy and strange, and I was nervous to sit up. James noticed and came over to help. "Take it slow," he said gently, offering his arm for support. With his help, I managed to sit up a bit. "This feels so weird," I admitted. The midwife finished cleaning and came over to check on me. "It's perfectly normal to feel that way. You've been through a lot."

"Thank you for everything," I said sincerely. As I sat forward and sipped a little water, a sudden wave of nausea hit me. I barely had a two-second warning before… BLARGHHHH.

"GRANNY PANTIES IT IS."

It all came straight out onto the floor. I didn't even have time to grab a bowl, it happened so fast. The midwife was amazing, though. She came running over and immediately sprang into action.

"It's okay, it happens," she said reassuringly, handing me a bowl just in case. I shook my head. "I don't think I need it now… it's all already out," I managed to say, feeling embarrassed. She gave me a smile. "That's the effects of the gas and air, plus all that water you were supposed to sip," she explained. "You've been through a lot. Your body is just reacting."

"Well, that was definitely unexpected," James added. "Just one more glamorous moment to add to the day, right?" I laughed. This just added to my discomfort since I was still wrapped in the same sheets from when I gave birth. The midwife laughed softly. "It's all part of the process. Let's get you cleaned up and more comfortable."

She quickly cleaned up the mess and helped me settle back down. "Try to take it easy," she advised. "Small sips of water and let us know if you feel unwell again."

"Thank you," I said, leaning back against the pillows.

♥♥♥

As I was feeling a lot better, we decided it was time to share the news with our parents. First, we called, Steven,

I CAN'T STOP PUSHING

James's dad, he already knew we'd gone to the hospital. It was 5 a.m. in South Africa, so we waited a bit before calling my parents. Steven answered on the first ring. "How's it going?" he asked. "Great news, Dad," James said. "You have another grandson."

James's brother has two boys, so this was the third grandson. "Congratulations. That's wonderful news."

After sharing a few more details, we hung up, and it was finally time to call my parents. We decided to do a video call to see their reaction. When my mum answered, she immediately noticed the hospital bed behind me.

"Are you in labour?" she asked. I shook my head, smiling. Her eyes widened, and she burst into tears.

"He's born. He's born." she shouted. My dad, Malcolm, came running over, hearing the commotion. "What's happening?" he asked. "He's here." Mum shouted, tears streaming down her face. "Congratulations.", dad said, with a huge smile on his face. We chatted for a while, sharing details and savouring the moment. "I'm so grateful we can video call," I said. "It means a lot to see your reactions."

"We're so proud of you," Mum said. "Can't wait to meet him. And his name? What have you decided?"

"GRANNY PANTIES IT IS."

"Alexander Malven Bailey," I said. They both looked at each other and then back at us, "That is the perfect name. You couldn't have chosen better." What a relief to know they love it too…not that they had a choice now.

I still couldn't believe we were parents. The realisation hit me again when I remembered that our little man was born on the same day as my colleague, you know…the one who had been born three days before Christmas.

Alexander was born 29 days early, natural birth, breech, bum first and no epidural.

I couldn't help but feel proud of myself.

After a quick bath, which made me feel a little more like myself, the midwife came over and asked, "Would you like to move your things to your room, or do you want to go and see Alexander first?"

Knowing there was no time limit on visiting him, we decided to get our things settled in the room first and then spend as much time with him as possible.

"I'm absolutely starving," I admitted to James. "Let's grab a quick breakfast after we move our things," he suggested. "Then we can head down to neonatal."

"Sounds like a plan," I agreed.

I CAN'T STOP PUSHING

Once we had popped our belongings in our new room and grabbed a quick breakfast, we made our way to neonatal. As we were still in the hospital, I wandered down to neonatal in my robe and slippers. It felt a little strange, but comfort was the priority.

Entering the neonatal unit was overwhelming at first. There were so many incubators. "This way," the nurse at the door said, showing us to our little man. I still couldn't believe he was ours. This tiny little alien was our baby. The nurse smiled and said, "He's only on oxygen as a precaution. And did you know, he's the biggest baby in here."

"Really? He looks so small to me." I replied. She nodded, "Yes, really."

Holding him for the first time was terrifying and exhilarating all at once. He had so many cables connected to him, and he felt so small and delicate in my arms. James looked at him and then at me.

"I can't believe he's here. He's so cute." he whispered. I nodded, with tears in my eyes. "I can't believe he's ours."

The nurse gently reassured us, "You'll get used to the cables and the monitors. The most important thing is that you're here with him." Then she gave me two

"GRANNY PANTIES IT IS."

little fabric pads, one to keep near my bra, and one to place next to him. Every time we visited, we'd swap them over. It's something they do for babies who can't be with their mum all the time at first, so he could start to get used to my smell, even when I wasn't there. James reached over and touched his tiny hand, "Welcome to the world, little man. We're so happy you're here."

Suddenly, I remembered, "Oh no, I left all my underwear in the tumble drier at home." James looked at me, puzzled. "What are you talking about?"

"I did a wash and dry before we left for the hospital, and now all my underwear is sitting at home. The only pair I have is the ones I'm wearing," I explained, feeling a bit embarrassed. James couldn't help but laugh. "Don't worry, I'll pop out to the shops nearby and get you some new ones later."

"Thanks," I said. "I really don't want to wear the same pair for who knows how many days."

After James had a turn to hold him, we headed upstairs for lunch and then James went to the shops to find me some underwear. He also bought some tiny baby sized clothing. Obviously, we did not expect him to be so tiny, so all those clothes that I had packed, were far too big.

I CAN'T STOP PUSHING

A little while later, James returned with a shopping bag and an amused expression. "The only ones they had were these 'granny panties'," he said, pulling out a pack of large, comfy-looking underwear.

I laughed. "Granny panties it is. They're definitely better than nothing." James grinned, handing them over. I hugged him tightly. "Thank you. You're the best," and I proceeded to put on my new, oversized, underwear. And honestly? They were super comfy.
Which was exactly what I needed.

Chapter 14

"I'VE JUST BEEN FIRED."

The one thing we hadn't done yet was tell all our friends from the expectant parents' course that Alexander had arrived. Because Alexander had arrived so early, we knew it would send a few shockwaves through the group.

We chose the perfect photo and sent a message in the group chat: "We'd like to introduce you to the newest member of our family."

We got a variety of responses, ranging from: "Eeeeeek!" to: "Amazing!! Bloody hell, they're not meant to come early! They can't come early, can they? CAN THEY?!"

We giggled at all the replies and loved sharing the moment with them. The funniest response was from a couple who said the rest of their car journey was spent in total silence… clearly still in shock.

Everyone reacts in their own way, but when it comes to babies, there are no guarantees about when they'll decide to make their grand entrance. After that message, we had the whole group frantically packing their bags in case of another early arrival.

I CAN'T STOP PUSHING

♥♥♥

With everything going on, I'd completely forgotten that my sister, Kelly, was flying in to spend Christmas with us. She was supposed to stay at ours, but now that we were in hospital, she had the whole place… and all the food I'd bought… to herself!

On that flight over, she had no idea she was going to be meeting her new nephew. Steven, James's dad, kindly collected her from the airport and brought her straight to the hospital. When they arrived, James and I were in our room, trying to express milk for little man.

It was quite a task, literally having to squeeze it out of my boobs. We were so focused that we didn't hear the door open, and suddenly Kelly and Steven walked in. I quickly covered up. "Oh my gosh, sorry. We'll be out in a minute," I said, feeling a bit embarrassed. Kelly laughed and said, "No worries. We'll wait outside."

♥♥♥

Once we managed to get a few millilitres… yes, *only a few*, as my milk hadn't come in properly yet… we went to find them in the waiting area. Kelly stood up when she saw us. "Oh, my goodness, you guys. Congratulations." She said, rushing over to give me a hug. "We're so proud of you both," Steven said.

"I'VE JUST BEEN FIRED."

"I can't wait to meet my nephew. This is the best Christmas surprise *ever*." We all laughed and shared hugs. As the first of the three siblings to have a baby, I could see how much it meant to her, to be the first in our family, to meet him.

Since we were only allowed a maximum of three people in neonatal at a time, we decided to go in pairs. I took Kelly down first. When she held him for the first time, she started crying. "He's so perfect," she whispered, as she gently inspected each of his tiny fingers and toes.

I took a second to capture this beautiful moment on my phone. In the photo, he was looking straight at her. "I can't believe how much I love him already," she said.

We didn't want the moment to end, but Steven was also excited to meet his new grandson, so we popped Alexander back in his incubator and made our way back upstairs.

James then took his dad down to meet Alexander while Kelly and I stayed in the room to do a video call with the rest of the family.

♥♥♥

However, exhaustion caught up with me fast. "Kelly, I'm absolutely shattered. I think I'm going to have a nap," I said, as I could barely keep my eyes open. Just then, James and Steven walked back in. "Of course," she replied. "I'll head home with Steven. You get some rest."

We said our goodbyes and they made their way home.

James decided to take this opportunity to pop out for some food, since the hospital only provided meals for mums. "I'll be back soon," he said, kissing my forehead before heading out.

I had a good hour-long nap. I felt so much better when I woke up. Just as I was sitting up, James returned with a variety of snacks and easy meals including pot noodles, chocolates, sandwiches, yogurts, and juices. "I raided the shop," he said, laughing.

"But we don't have a fridge in the room," I said, looking around. James paused for a moment, then walked over to the window. "It's winter and freezing outside. I'll just hang the bag out the window to keep everything cold," he said. "You're a genius," I said as I snuggled back under the covers.

The only other downside to our room was that it only had one bed and a very uncomfortable chair for James to sit in. Some hospitals have those fancy reclining chairs for partners… ours did not.

"I'VE JUST BEEN FIRED."

Since there was no other option, James had been squeezing into my bed with me so he could stay close.

The hospital did have a few spare mattresses, but they were all in use…until today. Finally, one became available. Now we could both stretch out a bit and get some much-needed rest.

Our days were filled with visitors coming to meet Alexander, sneaking in naps whenever we could, and enjoying those quiet one-on-one moments… even if it was just curling up in James's arms to watch a movie.

Every time we visited Alexander, something had changed. Two days after he was born, we walked in to neonatal and the nurse told us he had developed a bit of jaundice, which is very common.

"It means his skin turns yellow," she explained, "don't worry, we'll use a mask and light therapy to treat it."

As long as it helped him, we were happy.

The next day brought good news: "He no longer needs oxygen," she said, gently removing his head cover. For the first time, James got to see his little face, "Wow."

"I know right?" I whispered.

The nurse then showed us how to change his nappy. "Since he's in neonatal, you might not experience all the different stages of poo you learned about in your parenting classes," she said. "Not devastated," James said. We all laughed.

♥♥♥

The following day was Christmas Eve. After a nice long afternoon nap, I woke up to James coming back from a walk. He had the biggest smile on his face. "What are you so happy about?" I asked. "The hospital food shop's closed, but as I was heading back, I saw a guy with a pizza and he said it was delivered here."

"So, did you order one?"

"Of course, I did!" he said. "It should be here in about half an hour." After eating shop-bought sandwiches and pot noodles for the past few days... I could see how excited he was. When the pizza finally arrived, James looked like a kid on Christmas morning. "This is the best meal I've had in days," he said. This was such a well-deserved treat. I couldn't help but smile. I had one very happy guy.

♥♥♥

Before we knew it, it was Christmas Day. When we walked into neonatal, we found Alexander dressed in his very first outfit...a turquoise blue vest with the words 'Good Vibes' on the front. He was also wearing a knitted Christmas pudding hat! So cute!

"I'VE JUST BEEN FIRED."

A Christmas stocking was hanging on his incubator filled with a blanket, hat, jumper, and a teddy bear, all donated to the hospital by locals who love to knit. Then Father Christmas arrived, handing out gifts to each incubator. He handed us a gift bag with a Christmas book inside. "This is so kind," I said, "Thank you so much."

As Father Christmas was about to leave, we couldn't resist asking, "Would it be possible to have a photograph with you and our little man?"

Father Christmas smiled. "Of course."

A nurse kindly took the photo of us all beside the incubator.

The cherry on top of our emotions came when we heard the Salvation Army Band playing carols in the hallway. Those familiar tunes filled the air, adding to the magical atmosphere of the day. I leaned into James, tears streaming down my face. "This is incredible," I said.

James nodded, wiping away his own tears. "There isn't a dry eye in the hallway," he said, looking around. We stayed there for a while listening to the music.

I then overheard a woman behind me crying, because she had just been told they could leave the hospital after being there for six weeks. This really was the most incredible Christmas.

I CAN'T STOP PUSHING

After visiting the neonatal unit, we headed back up to our room. I loved seeing all the hospital staff in the halls. They had all dressed up in fun, holiday-themed outfits.

As soon as we walked through the door, Kelly and Steven were there waiting. "Merry Christmas," they both said at the same time. They had brought all of the Christmas presents from home. We all got comfortable and passed around the gifts. Each person had their turn to open their gift as we were in no hurry for this day to end.

Later, after presents had been opened, and both Kelly and Steven had their turn to see Alexander in neonatal, we said our goodbyes so I could have a much-needed rest before dinner time.

The Christmas dinner was an absolute treat. And because it was Christmas, the hospital had made an exception to feed dad as well. "I think this might be the best Christmas dinner I've ever had," James said. I laughed. "Same."

♥♥♥

Boxing Day came, and we were still in the same room at the hospital. One of the head nurses, Mary, came in to speak with me. She pulled up a chair beside

"I'VE JUST BEEN FIRED."

my bed and sat down. "I've been thinking", she began, "I really want you to get out of the hospital for a few hours today. You're not being discharged, but you need some time outside these four walls and to get some fresh air."

"I think you're right." I agreed.

We decided to go home for a few hours and have our Christmas lunch. I had already bought everything; we just needed to cook it. Leaving the hospital felt surreal.

As I stepped through the doors and into the fresh air, I burst into tears. It felt so good, but at the same time, I felt an overwhelming sense of guilt for leaving Alexander behind. James wrapped his arm around me. "It's okay," he whispered. "We will see him later."

"I know. It's just harder than I thought."

Back home, as soon as we walked through the door, the familiar comfort of being at our own home hit me, and I cried again. Kelly gave me a huge hug. "Let it out," she said. "You need this." After I had calmed down a bit, we got cooking. The house smelt amazing, and we couldn't wait to dig in. There's no good Christmas meal without a bit of bubbly…non-alcoholic of course. As we sat down to eat, I started to feel a bit more normal. We laughed, shared stories, and enjoyed the family time.

I CAN'T STOP PUSHING

James and I headed back to the hospital around 5 p.m. We didn't want to take advantage by staying out too long. After all, our little man was waiting for us. I felt a sense of relief as we made our way back, eager to see Alexander. The time away had done wonders. It's incredible what a good cry and some fresh air can do for you.

We made our way through the corridors and finally reached the neonatal unit. We scrubbed our hands, as we do every time we go in, and the sight of him immediately made me feel so happy. I picked him up gently and held him close.

"Hi, baby," I whispered, "Mummy and daddy are back."

♥♥♥

The next day, we decided to take it easy. We sat in our room, watched movies, had lunch and then enjoyed plenty of snacks. It was nice to have a more chilled day, with nothing planned… well so I thought. Just as we got comfortable with a new movie, James got a call.

"It's my boss," he said, stepping out of the room.

A few minutes later, he returned and sat on the chair next to the bed. He was still on the phone and the expression on his face didn't look good.

"I'VE JUST BEEN FIRED."

I was only catching snippets of his conversation, like: "Sorry you feel that way…that wasn't my intention…"

I wasn't quite sure what was going on, but I could feel the tension building. I sat there, getting more and more worried as I waited for the call to end. After about half an hour, James finally hung up and looked at me with a blank stare. "I've just been fired," he said.

We had a baby less than five days ago, it was Christmas time, and we were still in hospital. How could his boss possibly think this was a good time to make that call? James was also still on sick leave… because of the stress caused by this exact boss.

I was speechless.

I was shocked.

I was angry.

I was… relieved.

"It was all a misunderstanding," James explained. "But honestly? I'm relieved. The micromanaging, the verbal abuse… it's finally over."

"I never thought I'd be happy about you losing a job," I said. "But this really does feel like a blessing in disguise." He nodded, clearly deep in thought, still trying to process everything.

I CAN'T STOP PUSHING

Now that he didn't have to go back to that awful place, he could focus on us. And I had no doubt he'd find another job. One where he was actually appreciated.

♥♥♥

With everything going on, I'd completely forgotten the dreaded postpartum poo. One of the midwives reminded me, "Have you had a bowel movement yet?"

"No." I said nervously. "Don't worry," she said. "It's perfectly normal to be nervous, but you will need to do it at some point." My bowels must have heard her and suddenly I felt like I needed to go. I rushed to the bathroom. My thoughts going crazy. Would it hurt? Would it be easy? Would everything work normally?

In the bathroom, I took a deep breath and braced myself. I sat down and… phew. It was so much easier than I had expected. I felt so relieved… in more ways than one. I opened the bathroom door, and the midwife was waiting there. "All done?" she asked. "All done," I smiled.

♥♥♥

A few days later, we were moved to the neonatal ward… but James wasn't allowed to stay overnight. I hated the thought.

"I'VE JUST BEEN FIRED."

"Is there any way we can stay together?" I asked a nurse. "We completely understand if it's not possible, but if you don't ask, you don't get."

"Leave it with me," she said. "I'll see what I can do." We packed our bags and headed downstairs... hoping.

"The family rooms are full," the nurse said.

"But we cleared another room and added a second bed so you can stay together."

"Thank you so much," I said. This made me so happy!

"There's just one thing," she continued. "This room doesn't have an en suite bathroom. It'll be up to the nurse on duty whether James can shower. The shower is in the main ward which is for mums only."

"That's no problem," James said. "We're just grateful to be able to stay together."

The past week had been crazy, to say the least... unexpected birth, hospital life, visitors, Christmas, James losing his job... and somehow, we were still standing.

Tired, emotional, slightly traumatised, and with no idea what we were doing... but still standing.

Chapter 15

"I HAVE FAILED MY BABY!"

During our parenting classes, we learned a lot about breastfeeding. But nothing really prepares you for the reality of it. So, let's talk about everything they *don't* tell you about breastfeeding.

It felt like my milk was taking forever to come in… most likely because Alexander was born so early, and my body just wasn't ready.

So, I had to try to get things going myself. James and I had already been squeezing - yes, *squeezing* - milk from my boobs a few times a day, to help get them used to the idea. The more we did it, the more it seemed to help.

I was hoping I was finally getting enough to try breastfeeding, so we made our way across the hall to see him. But when we walked into the room, his incubator was gone. I instantly felt myself starting to panic.

We quickly asked a nurse where he was, and she explained that he had been moved next door into the

"I HAVE FAILED MY BABY!"

room for babies who no longer required constant care. He was now off the breathing tubes.

Phew! Panic over!

My sister Kelly came in to visit, and while she was there, a nurse suggested I try breastfeeding him if I wanted. I'll be honest…I was struggling. I couldn't get him to latch, and it was stressing me out.

What amazes me is that even at a few days old, when they've only just arrived into the world, these tiny humans already know exactly what to do with their mouths.

So naturally, I thought…what's wrong with *me*? What's wrong with my boobs? Why was I struggling when he clearly knew what to do?

What I didn't realise at the time was that Kelly had experience helping breastfeeding mums. She knew exactly what she was doing, but with me being a stubborn new mom, I kept insisting we get a nurse to help. I think deep down, I was scared of messing up, especially in front of my sister.

Eventually, I gave in and let Kelly guide me. With her help, I finally managed to get him to latch on my left side. It was my very first successful feeding, and I couldn't hold back the tears. That overwhelming sense of relief, with his tiny eyes looking up at me, was so special.

I CAN'T STOP PUSHING

For some reason he struggled on the right. Was it my nipple? Was it just a weird shape and it wouldn't work?

Breastfeeding is anything but easy. But I was determined to get this right. A nurse then came in with a shield. This amazing little plastic thing that goes over your nipple and allows baby to latch more easily. This was a game changer. Finally, a happy baby and a very happy mummy.

The more I breastfed, the faster my milk came in. It came in quickly. But because Alexander was still so small, he wasn't needing as much as I was producing.

The nurse showed me into the expressing room. There was already a mum in there with two pumps on, sitting like it was completely normal. She looked at me and softly said, "Hi." I tried to smile at her as I stood there holding my bottles, feeling slightly terrified.

The nurse helped me get set up, and before I knew it, I had two pumps stuck to my boobs. Honestly, I felt like a cow in a milking parlour. Every now and then, I'd check to see if anything was coming out, and when it did, I'm not going to lie, I was pretty proud of myself. Who knew I'd be this excited about filling a tiny bottle with boob juice?

"I HAVE FAILED MY BABY!"

By the end, I had a few bottles ready for the freezer. This wasn't exactly how I pictured motherhood... but here we are.

♥♥♥

Fast forward a few days to New Year's Eve. Alexander had been moved into our room, two days earlier, so we could start getting used to waking up with him. The two nights weren't too bad, and I really enjoyed those special moments with him. But I was exhausted.

As a new parent, getting that balance is hard...well life in general really. You want to be with your baby all the time, but you also need to sleep and look after yourself.

We were lucky, in a way... because he was in neonatal, we had the option of getting some proper rest. But we weren't taking advantage of it, as we didn't know any different... until now.

On New Year's Eve, I sat in the chair, struggling to feed Alexander. He kept coming off and crying. I also noticed a small bump on the side of his neck. Just then, the consultant walked in during his rounds. After a quick check, he explained it was nothing serious. Just a knot caused by the strain of being born breech and he would be booked for physiotherapy.

I CAN'T STOP PUSHING

As soon as the consultant left, I burst into tears. It was the final straw. My emotions were all over the place… and the baby blues, which usually hit around three to five days after birth…had officially arrived. One of the nurses, Wendy, who we'd gotten to know really well, rushed in as soon as her shift started.

She'd heard during handover that I was in tears and gave me the biggest cuddle, telling me everything was going to be okay. All I could manage to say was, "I have failed my baby." Wendy reassured me this was completely normal. I was just exhausted.

Before Alexander was born, I was determined to exclusively breastfeed. All I'd ever heard was "breast is best," so I wanted to avoid bottles for as long as possible. But now, the nurses were suggesting the exact thing I'd been trying to avoid…letting them bottle-feed him with my milk so I could rest. I was no use to anyone as a tired, emotional wreck.

Finally, I agreed and let them feed him breast milk, from a bottle, so I could get a good night's sleep.

I curled up next to James on his single bed and cried myself to sleep in his arms. We were out by 11 p.m. and didn't wake up until 8 a.m.

♥♥♥

"I HAVE FAILED MY BABY!"

When I opened my eyes, I immediately felt like a completely different person. I practically jumped out of bed. All I wanted was to see Alexander, but I took my time, had a shower, grabbed some breakfast, then we went to see him.

New year, new start. I was ready to get this right. That goodnight sleep was exactly what my body needed and YES, I was now able to feed him properly.

They also told us Alexander had a tongue tie. This means that the skin under his tongue was too tight, making it harder for him to feed. This explained why he was struggling to latch. The procedure to fix it was simple and quick, so we agreed to book it.

Later that day, we found out Alexander was strong enough to come out of the incubator and into a regular baby bed. The family room had also become available, giving us a couple of days to stay together, as a family, before heading home. It was also so nice to have an on-suite bathroom, rather than having to rush down a cold hallway. And it was reassuring to know that the nurses were still close by if we needed help.

♥♥♥

Two days later, it was time for Alexander's procedure to fix his tongue tie. I had no idea what to expect, but I was nervous. As we walked into the clinic room, the nurse greeted us and called us in. She asked me to sit in a chair, ready to breastfeed him right after the procedure.

"The milk will help heal the wound," she explained. James was asked to hold Alexander's head still. The whole thing lasted no more than 10 seconds…but his scream was something else. I cried.

There is nothing worse than hearing your baby cry like that. But I also knew it was for the best. It was just a tiny snip under his tongue. The nurse reassured us, "He's not in pain, he's crying more because his mouth had to be held open."

As soon as she finished, she gently handed him to me. I began feeding him right away and he instantly settled. Once he was calm, the nurse asked, "Do you mind if I hold him for a moment?" I nodded. She held him to her shoulder, giving him the warmest, most caring cuddle. Then she looked into his eyes and softly said, "I'm sorry."

It was one of the sweetest moments I've ever seen. He just looked at her calmly, like he understood.

Later that day, Alexander had a hip scan. Because of the way he was born, bum first and legs over his head, they wanted to check everything was developing normally.

"I HAVE FAILED MY BABY!"

After a few minutes, the technician said, "Good news! There are no issues with his hips." I was so glad to hear her say that.

♥♥♥

The next day, we were told we'd be heading home. James fetched the car seat… and then realised we had no idea how to use it. How tight should the straps be? Should his head be at that angle?

James watched video after video trying to figure it out. It felt like we might need a degree in engineering for this thing. We even asked a nurse, but she gave us the classic "Sorry, I'm not allowed to help with that." After countless attempts James finally figured out the car seat straps…we hoped.

By the time we got our discharge papers, it was already dark and we had a 40-minute drive home through peak traffic. We said our goodbyes to all the amazing staff. They cleared out my personal freezer drawer of frozen breast milk and then… out we went.

Two whole weeks of living in the hospital, we were finally taking our little man home.

I don't think James has *ever* driven so slowly. You could've overtaken us on a push scooter. Luckily, it was a dual carriageway, so other cars could pass us if they wanted.

I CAN'T STOP PUSHING

I sat in the back, watching Alexander like a hawk and Alexander? Slept the entire way.

Back home, my breastfeeding routine changed. I no longer had nurses for advice, but they'd said I could call. And I did…*a lot*.

People talk about having a baby, the pregnancy and birth, what they don't talk about is what happens *after* you bring the baby home. This is a whole different story.

Breastfeeding isn't glamorous… let's be honest, it's leaky, awkward, and often involves a dressing gown hanging off one shoulder and a muslin cloth thrown over the other. But it's also natural and beautiful. It is real life, and honestly, it should be more normal than it's made out to be.

If people were coming over, they needed to be prepared they were going to see a boob. Or two. There were a few people I'd cover up for, mostly to avoid that painfully awkward "where do I look?" moment… but most of the time, I just didn't have the energy to care. My baby needed feeding, and I wasn't about to run and hide to make everyone else more comfortable. Well actually, the only one that needed to be comfortable was me.

"I HAVE FAILED MY BABY!"

To survive, I had to get organised:

➢ Alarms… I set alarms for every feed. He didn't always wake me, so I couldn't risk oversleeping.

➢ Snacks… I was *starving*. I tried to stick to healthy snacks. It's so tempting to reach for sweets and chocolates, but for some reason, I preferred grapes. I could polish off an entire punnet without even realising it. You know that feeling when you're munching on a bag of chips, and suddenly you reach in and can't feel anything left? That's exactly how I felt every time I ate grapes.

➢ Entertainment… Depending on how long Alexander took to feed, I would either get really bored or fall asleep. So, I would record TV shows and save them for my night feeds, giving me something to look forward to. This also avoided late night shopping temptations.

➢ Breastfeeding station… all the essentials I needed at arm's reach. I would always have this set up in advance, especially at night. It's easy to forget things when you're half asleep.

Here's what helped me most when setting up my little breastfeeding station:

- A comfy chair (a rocking one with arms is ideal, but any seat that supports your back works)
- A travel mug with a hot drink - safety first!

I CAN'T STOP PUSHING

- A big bottle of water (breastfeeding makes you very thirsty)
- Healthy snacks… and a cheeky treat, *obviously*
- The TV remote within arm's reach
- My phone and charger (plus the landline nearby, just in case)
- A soft blanket and a few pillows to get cosy
- A footrest for extra comfort
- Lip balm and hand cream (my skin was so dry)
- Muslin cloths for inevitable spills and baby sick
- Tissues for those emotional moments
- And most importantly… a last-minute toilet trip BEFORE I sat down!

Having this little setup made those night time feeds so much easier. Even when I was tired or sore, knowing I had everything I needed right there with me, made such a difference.

♥♥♥

The other thing I really needed to get right was burping Alexander. Honestly, I struggled with it at first. Getting those tiny little burps out wasn't as easy as I thought it would be.

"I HAVE FAILED MY BABY!"

I tried every trick in the book. Rubbing or tapping his back, sitting him up on my lap, holding him over my shoulder… sometimes it worked, sometimes it didn't.

Babies are all different, and sometimes that stubborn wind just won't budge. Milk can cause wind in babies, and if you don't help them get it out, it can make them really uncomfortable or even sick.

One tip I learned that actually made a difference was the "bicycle legs" move. I would gently move his legs in circular motions, like he's pedalling a bike, then softly push his knees towards his tummy. It's a nice way to help push the wind out. And no, this didn't make him burp…it made him fart instead! But as long as it helped him, that's all that mattered.

The biggest challenge I faced was keeping myself awake. Being prepared and having plenty of distractions really helped. There were times I didn't even realise I was dozing off, but having the pillows as a safety net ensured Alexander was always safe.

Speaking of safety, being aware of your surroundings when you're half asleep is crucial - especially when navigating a dark house with a baby in your arms.

Picking up your little one from the crib is one thing, but if the kitchen hasn't been tidied up or if pathways are

I CAN'T STOP PUSHING

blocked, being extra careful about your surroundings can save you a lot of trouble. I learned this the hard way.

♥♥♥

One night at 2 a.m., Alexander had reflux. He sometimes struggled with burping after feeding. I went to the kitchen in the dark as I didn't want to blind him with the light. My eyes had somewhat adjusted to the darkness, and I knew exactly where the medicine was.

As I carefully held Alexander in one arm, I reached up to the top shelf with the other to grab the medicine… and *knocked* over a glass. *SMASH*! The sound of it shattering echoed through the entire house, and in an instant, glass was everywhere. And, of course, I was barefoot.

Before I could even register what had happened, James came flying down the stairs, completely naked. "Are you okay? What happened?"

"James, it's okay. We're fine," I said. "I just need some help, please. I dropped a glass." I thought we were being burgled." he said. "You just gave me a heart attack!" I couldn't help but laugh, and of course, Alexander was now wide awake. "I'm sorry. I didn't mean to wake you."

"I HAVE FAILED MY BABY!"

Once his mini heart attack was over, James ran back upstairs to grab some clothes before tackling the clean-up. He returned, with a dustpan and brush, and started sweeping up the larger pieces. Then, he vacuumed every inch of the floor, making sure no tiny shards were left behind. He even carefully checked my feet, vacuuming around them to ensure there wasn't a single speck of glass.

"Thank goodness you're here," I said, feeling very relieved. "I have no idea what I would've done if you weren't home tonight."

"You'd probably still be standing there," he teased.

As Alexander grew, he fed more often to boost my milk supply. Sometimes he'd just finished feeding, then want more. My nipples were so sore that feeding him became unbearable. I tried creams, used the shield, and even attempted expressing, but nothing seemed to help. Thank goodness this phase passes.

One thing that does help, is rubbing *your* milk on the wounds. I wish I knew this earlier.

Eventually, my supply increased and things got easier. But then came the leaks - always, *always* in the one shirt that shows *everything*.

I CAN'T STOP PUSHING

Leaving the house took a bit of courage, but I knew I needed to do it. It's way too easy to stay in. But getting out? Seeing actual humans? I think I would go mad if I stayed home all the time. We spent almost every day out with Ally, who I'd met at the expectant parents' course. We'd go on long walks, head to baby groups, and even visit each other's homes. It was such a relief having a friend nearby who was also a new mum.

When we were out, Alexander always had impeccable timing for the most inconvenient times to feed…like the moment my food arrived at the table or while shopping, and I needed to reach items on the bottom shelf while feeding him in the carrier. I thought I'd feel self-conscious breastfeeding in public, but I'm still waiting for someone to comment.

The next stage of my breastfeeding journey was when he started growing teeth. Need I say more? But I will. I thought the pain from cluster feeding and building my milk supply was the worst of it… but oh no, that was just the warm-up.

There were days I'd be mid-feed, thinking everything was going fine, and then… chomp. The shock. The pain. The immediate negotiation: "Please

"I HAVE FAILED MY BABY!"

don't do that again. Mummy needs those!" I became a chew toy. No one warned me that the hardest part of feeding might not be at the start, but halfway through… when your baby has teeth *and* attitude.

It wasn't perfect, and it wasn't always pretty. Yes, I cried, leaked, got bitten… but breastfeeding gave me some of the most calming, connected moments I've ever had. Just the two of us, in our own little world. Bite marks and all… I wouldn't change it.

The final stage of my breastfeeding journey was stopping altogether. Moving over to a bottle after months of breastfeeding wasn't easy… for either of us.

I also realised how easy breastfeeding was… literally milk on tap. I could feed him anywhere, anytime.

Bottles? They were a hassle. It wasn't just cleaning them. It was prepping them, making sure the temperature was just right.

That's when we discovered the prep machine. Honestly, I'm sure you've heard me say "game changer" before, but anything that makes your life easier, quickly becomes a necessity. I could wake up in the middle of the night, pop the bottle on the machine, press a button, give it a shake and just like that, milk ready at the perfect temperature.

I CAN'T STOP PUSHING

Feeding from a bottle was also much quicker. With breastfeeding, I could be feeding for an hour. Bottles? Done in half the time. But while my body slowly adjusted to producing less milk, my heart wasn't quite ready to let go. I didn't want to stop. I'd miss those moments, holding him close in my arms, just us, in our own little world.

Stopping was emotional and came with a lot more dishes than before… but, as it turned out, the cleaning was only just getting started.

Chapter 16

"THE ULTIMATE POONAMI!"

Other than breastfeeding, there are many other challenges that come with having a baby. It would take countless books to cover it all, but there are some things that definitely need to be shared.

Since Alexander had spent some time in neonatal care, we hadn't given him a bath yet. Before we left the hospital, a nurse had given us a quick demonstration, so we had a general idea of what to do. But now, we were on our own.

For his very first bath, we decided to keep it simple. Given how tiny he was, we laid him down on a soft mat on the floor, and gave him a gentle wipe-down with a damp cloth. He absolutely loved it.

For the next bath-time, I wanted to make it more special. I climbed into the bath myself, running the water so it was just deep enough for his little bum to be submerged.

James handed him to me and I sat him on my legs with my knees up. With him snuggled safely, I gently splashed some water around him. The little faces he was making were so cute. As I was enjoying this beautiful moment, I suddenly felt something warm spreading across my stomach. Yep - he had *peed*. With no nappy to save me, I ended up right in the line of fire. I stared down at the warm, yellow-tinted water and sighed. "Well, that's one way to mark your first bath," I said, laughing. James didn't even try to hide how funny he thought it was, but then lifted Alexander off me, so I could sort myself out.

Bathing was the easy part. We had not yet experienced the infamous challenge all new parents face: *the poonami*.

Now, if you're wondering what a poonami is, allow me to enlighten you. It's when your baby's poo is so extensive that no nappy stands a chance of containing it. If you're one of the lucky ones, you only experience a minor poonami that leaks up their back or slightly out the side. We encountered quite a few of these, and let me tell you, we handled them like a pro.

Okay, maybe I'm exaggerating a little - I was the one handling it while James stood at a safe distance, ready to gag at the mere sight of anything remotely resembling poo or vomit.

And there's a lot of that when you have a baby around.

"THE ULTIMATE POONAMI!"

♥♥♥

Then, there's the ultimate poonami… a fully-clothed disaster that leaks out the sides, up the back, and into places you didn't even know existed. No number of wipes or shred of sanity will save you here. There's only one solution: straight to the shower. Throw them in, clothes and all. Don't even think about removing the clothing first, as you are asking for trouble.

If you think nothing can top that, let me introduce you to the mid-nappy change ultimate poonami. Babies have a knack for peeing the moment you open their nappy.

It is almost like the fresh air activates their need for the toilet. Not a huge problem if you have a girl, but if you have a boy, you'd better grab a wipe and cover that tiny hose quickly, or you'll find yourself in the firing line. Once you have averted that crisis, you'll need to clean them up. This requires lifting their legs toward their tummy, leaving their bum exposed with full range of motion, and the freedom to fire at any time.

Oh, remember the whole bicycle legs trick for wind? Yeah, during a nappy change, that move becomes the trigger to a tiny, bare-bottomed pressure washer. You're basically asking for it. This is where your speed will become your greatest skill.

I CAN'T STOP PUSHING

The mid-nappy change ultimate poonami doesn't care about your doors, your carpets, or you. It strikes when you least expect it. If you're lucky enough to have a nappy ready, you might just be fast enough to stop it.

I had the unfortunate experience of dealing with the ultimate poonami while Alexander was fully clothed, and to make matters worse, we weren't even at home. You didn't think it could get worse, did you?

Of course, it had to happen at his very first baby singing group. He was about 5 months old at this point, so just starting to understand baby groups. I love singing as well, so I was really excited for this.

We were also meeting my friends Jen and Ally there, with their little ones. It's always more fun when you go somewhere with friends. That morning, I had dressed him in the perfect outfit. He looked absolutely adorable. I took every opportunity to dress him up.

It was a 20-minute drive to the group, giving him just enough time for a nap so he'd be happy and awake for the music. When we had arrived, parking was a nightmare. There was hardly any space, and I ended up parking quite far from the hall.

"THE ULTIMATE POONAMI!"

Luckily, I had the pram with me so I didn't have to carry both him and the baby bag. As soon as we had walked in, Jen and Ally were already there, waiting to go in.

"Hey, you made it," Jen called, running over for a cuddle.
"Hey, sorry we're late," I replied.
"He looks so cute in that outfit," Ally said. "Thanks! I couldn't resist," I laughed.

We paid our money and were just about to head in when the smell hit me. "Oh no... please don't let it be..." I muttered. I picked Alexander up and lifted his jumper. Sure enough, the poo had started making its way up his back, and stood out like a neon sign on his white vest.
Great. Just great.

"I'll catch up with you guys inside," I said to the girls. "I need to give Alexander a quick change."

I asked one of the ladies at the door where the bathroom was. "Oh, it's right behind you," she said with a smile. I spun around. "Oh, silly me. Thanks!" I said, feeling a bit flustered. I headed in, locked the door, pulled down the baby-changing table, laid out the mat and popped Alexander down. His trousers were, of course, covered in poo. I carefully removed them and saw the full extent of the mess... it had spread all the way down his legs. How did someone so small produce so much?

I CAN'T STOP PUSHING

I began the mammoth task of wiping him down. Poo was just going everywhere. Thank goodness the mat was wipe-clean. After cleaning his legs, I unbuttoned his vest… and that's when I noticed it had gone even further. Up his back, through his jumper, and all over the mat. Fantastic!

There was a knock at the door. "You okay in there?" Ally called. "I'm fine." I replied, trying to sound more confident than I felt.

Fine? Not even close.

I glanced at the sink, briefly considering washing Alexander in it, but it was far too small. I took a deep breath. I'd figure this out. Just when I had thought things couldn't get worse, I made a rookie mistake. I tried to pull his jumper and vest over his head.

Did you know that baby vests and jumpers are designed to be pulled down over their shoulders? I didn't. So, I ended up smearing more poo over his head. Brilliant!

Alexander lay there, completely naked, and now with more poo on him than before. I tossed his soiled clothes into a nappy bag - they were beyond saving today.

"THE ULTIMATE POONAMI!"

And then I heard it: that unmistakable bubbling sound. No way. He was pooing *again*. In a panic, I grabbed the nearest thing I could find: a load of toilet paper. It was more absorbent than the few wipes I had left. Thank goodness!

What a mess. I felt like I'd failed my baby...*again*.

It took me another 20 minutes and several more knocks from Jen and Ally checking in. I should have asked for help, but they had their own little ones to look after.

♥♥♥

I eventually managed to get Alexander cleaned up, changed, and bagged up the entire disaster. Feeling exhausted but relieved, I finally made my way out of the bathroom.

Jen and Ally were so relieved to see me walk out. "What happened?" Jen said. "What took so long?" Ally asked.

I took a deep breath, "the ultimate poonami," I said... and let rip with every last crappy detail.

The woman running the class overheard our conversation, and kindly offered to refund part of the fee, since I'd missed so much. So kind of her!

We finally made our way into the music class, determined to make the most of what was left. Luckily, there were still a few songs to enjoy, and Alexander bounced along to the music, giggling away.

I CAN'T STOP PUSHING

I also enjoyed a very much deserved cup of coffee.

And now… whenever I go out, I always carry a potty-training pad to place on top of the changing mat. It absorbs everything and is big enough to use as a shield as well. Trust me!

It's the only thing that can survive a true poonami.

Chapter 17

"YOU'RE BASING IT ON MY PHOTO?"

Alexander was around six months old when I noticed something unusual during one of his nappy changes. He was lying on the floor, babbling happily to himself, when I saw it…just above his groin, there was a small, swollen area, almost in the shape of an 'M'. I wasn't sure what to make of it. I hadn't seen anything like that before. "What is that?" I whispered to myself. It was definitely something new. I quickly grabbed my phone and snapped a photo, thinking, better safe than sorry. Within a few minutes, the swelling had gone, and everything seemed normal again.

A week later, we were at Alexander's six-month check-up, with the consultant. As usual, they were going through the normal checks - his weight, length, and his hips, since Alexander had been born breech. "He's doing great, growing well, and I don't see any issues here."

"That's a relief," I said. Then, I remembered the strange swelling from the other day and pulled out my phone.

"Actually, I wanted to show you something."

I CAN'T STOP PUSHING

I handed him the photo of the 'M' shaped swelling. He looked at it for a moment. "This looks like it could be a hernia," he said. "A hernia?" I repeated. I hadn't expected that. "Yes, though I can't feel anything right now," he said, gently pressing his fingers along Alexander's abdomen and groin area. "It might come and go, which is why you may not see it all the time. I'll book him in for a proper check-up, just to be sure."

"Okay, that sounds good. I'm glad I took the picture then," I said. "It's always better to have something to reference." He replied.

A few days later, a letter arrived to inform us that Alexander had been booked for surgery. My heart pounded as I read it, but I trusted the doctors, and it sounded like they knew what needed to be done.

Around this time, my mum had come to stay for a whole month. She hadn't met Alexander yet, and with my dad tied up with work, she'd made the trip on her own.

The day she arrived; I was beyond excited. I had been counting down the days. Steven was driving us to the airport since James had the car for work. It was over a two-hour drive, and because Alexander was only five

"YOU'RE BASING IT ON MY PHOTO?"

months old, we couldn't keep him in the car seat for too long. We left a little earlier so we could stop at a service station about half an hour from the airport. That way, we could get Alexander out of the seat for a while, and I could give him a feed.

Sitting there feeding him, I was so restless. The time couldn't go fast enough. I was about to see my mum.

About twenty minutes later, a message came through saying she was through customs and had her luggage. We arranged to meet in the car park to avoid the extortionate parking fees. I strapped Alexander back in, and off we went.

The moment we drove into the car park, I spotted her. Steven pulled up near a row of cars. I jumped out and ran over to give her the biggest cuddle. I popped her suitcase in the boot, and she climbed into the back seat next to Alexander. It was like love at first sight. Her very first grandchild was finally right there next to her.

♥♥♥

Her timing couldn't have been more perfect. With James working long hours, it was a huge comfort knowing she'd be there when Alexander went in for his operation.

"So, when's the surgery again?" Mum asked after dinner that night. "Next Thursday," I replied. "I'm a bit nervous, but I'm sure it'll go smoothly. They said it's a pretty common operation."

"It'll be fine. I'll be here the whole time."

"I'm so glad you're here. James has to work that day, and I don't think I could handle it all alone," I replied. "I'm also glad your mum's here, and I'll be home later that evening," James said. "That's what mums are for," she said.

♥♥♥

Alexander's surgery day came, and we had to be at Westmere General by 10 a.m. Since he'd be under anaesthesia, Alexander wasn't allowed food for hours before the operation. I could only breastfeed him until 6 a.m., then only small sips of water were allowed.

James gave me a big hug before heading out for work. "Call me as soon as it's over, okay?"

"Don't worry," I said. "We'll be fine." We packed everything, then we made our way to the hospital. Alexander, completely unaware, was happily playing with his favourite toy in the car seat. I'd packed an overnight bag, just in case, but the plan was to be home the same day. Still, I liked being prepared.

We pulled into the closest parking area to the hospital and started unpacking the car.

"YOU'RE BASING IT ON MY PHOTO?"

"We'll leave my overnight bag in the car for now," I told Mum, pulling out the pram and Alexander's backpack.

As we searched for the exit, I couldn't see any signs for an elevator. The only visible way out was through the car entrance we'd just driven through - but there was no designated path for pedestrians.

"We'll just have to risk it," I said, not wanting to waste time and potentially be late. We carefully pushed the pram through a tight gap, then headed towards the road.

We turned a corner and saw it: the steepest hill I've ever seen. My heart sank, and Mum let out a sigh beside me. We began the climb, pushing the pram slowly and stopping every few minutes to catch our breath.

"Whose idea was this again?" I asked, laughing. Mum groaned. "You'd think they'd make this easier for parents with prams."

After what felt like an eternity, we finally reached the top, sweaty and out of breath but relieved to be on flat ground again. We still had another ten-minute walk along the main road to get to the hospital. At least this road had no more hills.

When we arrived at the hospital, the nurses were so kind, making the check-in process very easy. We were then shown to our own little cubicle.

I CAN'T STOP PUSHING

There was a small space with two chairs for us and a cot bed for Alexander. A nurse came in shortly after, with the tiniest hospital gown I'd ever seen. It was covered in tugboats and lighthouses. "Oh, my goodness, look at this," I said, holding up the gown. "He's going to look so cute."

Just as I finished dressing him, the nurse came back with an update. "Alexander's operation will now be in the afternoon, so you'll be staying overnight."

Of course. *Nothing* ever goes to plan.

I couldn't feed him, and explaining that to a five-month-old was impossible. I used his favourite shows to distract him and thankfully, he was still taking a few naps during the day, which helped pass the time.

"Mum, would you mind going back to the car to grab my overnight bag?" I asked. "I don't want to leave in case the doctor comes by or they call us in suddenly."

"Oh, not that hill again." Mum said, "But yes, of course, I'll go get it." We both laughed, knowing how awful that climb was. While Mum was getting my bag, I called Steven to ask him to collect her. He was more than happy to and said he would meet her outside the hospital by the road, at 4 p.m., to avoid finding parking.

♥♥♥

"YOU'RE BASING IT ON MY PHOTO?"

When the time came for Mum to leave, I couldn't even walk her out since we still hadn't been called in. She gave us both big hugs. "I'll see you both tomorrow, alright?" she said. I hugged her again. Holding on for a moment longer. I didn't want her to leave.

"You'll be fine," she said and gave me a big smile before heading out the hospital doors.

Five minutes later, a man appeared. "Hi, I'm one of the surgeons. I've got notes about a photo. Can I see it?"

"Sure," I said, showing him. "Looks like a hernia. Can you send me the picture please?" I sent the photo to his phone as requested.

"So, for this operation, you're basing it on my photo?"

The surgeon nodded. "Yes." I was feeling a little unsettled about trusting their judgment. But he talked me through the procedure, easing my nerves a little.

"Follow me," he said. "We're going down to the operating room so you can hand Alexander over to the team." My heart immediately started pounding. Every step down that hallway felt heavier, my nerves building with each one. Alexander, blissfully unaware of what was coming, smiled up at me.

Inside, the team was waiting. One woman, the lead surgeon, came over to me and said, "Can I see this photo please?" I handed her my phone, and after a brief glance, she turned to her team. "It's a double hernia," she said confidently. "Let's prepare for a double hernia operation."

"Wait... double hernia? So, this is really all based on my photo?" I asked. "Yes, but we'll confirm once we are in. Don't worry."

I kissed Alexander's forehead and whispered, "It's going to be okay," and handed him over.

As I watched him get carried away into the operating room, I could feel my hands trembling and my heart pounding, struggling to hold back tears. I needed a distraction.

The wait was going to be long, and my nerves were getting the best of me. Maybe I should grab something to eat, I thought, trying to give myself something else to focus on. I also didn't know when I would get another chance.

♥♥♥

There was a selection of shops just across the road from the hospital, so I decided to head over and see what they had. As I stepped outside, I spotted Mum standing on the side of the road, waiting for Steven to collect her. I walked over, and she immediately opened her arms for

"YOU'RE BASING IT ON MY PHOTO?"

a hug. "You're doing great," she said. "Just take it one moment at a time."

"Thanks, Mum."

Steven arrived five minutes later. I waved goodbye and then wandered over to the shop. But my mind wasn't on food. No matter how hard I tried, I couldn't stop thinking about Alexander.

I stood in front of the shelves, staring blankly at all the food options. I needed my strength, even if every part of me was screaming that food wasn't important right now.

I forced myself to choose something, hoping that a few of my favourite things might stir my appetite. I grabbed a delicious wrap, my favourite bag of crisps, a cheeky bar of chocolate, and a strong coffee. I definitely needed these to help me stay awake and alert.

After paying, I slowly made my way back to the hospital, and I found the cubicle we had originally been waiting in. This time it was very quiet.

I sat down with my food, and unwrapped the wrap. And then the tears started. I scrolled through pictures of Alexander. That smile. That face. The fear took over. What if I didn't see him again? I tried watching a movie. Tried eating. But nothing helped. I just sat there crying quietly, wishing time would pass faster and wishing my mum hadn't gone home.

♥♥♥

Finally, after an hour, although it felt like forever, a nurse appeared. "You can go see him now." I started crying again. This time with tears of joy.

His cries echoed down the hallway. When I walked in, I noticed a nurse who was cradling him, trying to calm him down. But Alexander hated being cradled like that. He preferred to be held over my shoulder or in an upright position, and that's all I could think about. Instead of thanking her, the first thing I blurted out was,

"He doesn't like to be held that way." I instantly felt guilty. The nurse was being so sweet, and here I was, sounding ungrateful. "I'm so sorry," I quickly added. "He's just more comfortable in a different position."

She smiled and handed him over to me without hesitation. The moment I held him; I could feel him start to calm down. For the first time in hours, I felt like I could breathe again. "We'll need to get him upstairs to the room now," she said.

"Do you want to carry him, or would you prefer him on the bed?" I hesitated. I wanted to hold him, but the thought of accidentally hurting him made me nervous. "I think it's best if he stays on the bed," I said.

"YOU'RE BASING IT ON MY PHOTO?"

They took us to one of the wards. The whole walk up he was crying. He was not a happy bunny. Just as we were settling in, one of the nurses asked, "Has he had any painkillers yet?"

"No, he hasn't," another nurse replied. No wonder he was screaming! As adults, we complain about pain even with medication...imagine a five-month-old who can only express his pain through cries. Once the medicine kicked in, he finally settled, closed his eyes, and drifted off to sleep.

Later, I wanted to change his nappy, but I was terrified. I asked one of the nurses for help. "Is it safe to change his nappy? I'm so worried I'll hurt him."

"It's perfectly fine. Just change it like you normally would." Even with her reassurance, my hands shook the whole time. I carefully cleaned him, trying to avoid touching the two little lines where they operated. They were so small, each one only a centimetre long. Alexander just lay there calmly. Then came a lovely surprise. "Look," the nurse said, pulling down a bed from the wall. "You can sleep right next to him." I hadn't even noticed there was a bed there. "Thank you," I whispered.

Sleep didn't come easily. My eyes were burning because I was so tired, but my brain was on high alert. I

I CAN'T STOP PUSHING

listened for every noise. Every cry. I was ready to jump at a moment's notice. We had many night feeds and OBS checks, but although it was exhausting, I was just relieved to have him safe in my arms again.

The next morning, we woke up to good news. "Looks like you'll be going home this afternoon." One of the nurses said. "We'll get the discharge papers ready for you."

"That's wonderful. Thank you so much."

I began packing our things and a nurse came in shortly after to remove Alexander's cannula. She then turned to me. "Would you like a coffee for the road?"

"That would be amazing, thank you," I said. I got Alexander into the pram and glanced at my suitcase - a little carry-on with wheels. How was I supposed to manage both?

I thought for a moment, then noticed the sturdy exterior of Alexander's pram cot. It wasn't ideal, but it was solid enough that I could balance the suitcase on top. "Thank you for everything - and for the coffee," I said. The nurses smiled. "You are welcome. Take care now."

"YOU'RE BASING IT ON MY PHOTO?"

With Alexander settled and my coffee in hand, we made our way out of the hospital and began the 10-minute walk back to the parking lot. The sun had come out, and the fresh air felt amazing after being indoors for so long. I also called James on the walk back to update him. He was at home and I could not wait to see him. He was also so relieved it went well.

As I reached that hill, something caught my eye. It was a pedestrian walkway that looked like it went into the parking building. "Wait…is that…?" I turned the pram and made my way across the street. Sure enough, as soon as I walked up the path, there they were…elevators.

"You've got to be kidding me," I muttered. I paid for the overnight parking and took the elevator down three floors to where I had parked. After unloading the pram and putting Alexander in his car seat, I sat in the car for a quiet moment to have a few sips of my coffee, before beginning the long journey home.

♥♥♥

In the weeks that followed, I made the most of the time I had with my mum. Time was going so much faster than I thought. But while she was here, James and I decided to do something completely crazy. And as if we didn't have enough on our plates, what did we do?

I CAN'T STOP PUSHING

We got a kitten and named him Mo.

Having a kitten? Almost more demanding than a baby. Actually, worse… because they can walk.

Between feeding, playing, cleaning up accidents, and constantly trying to stop him from destroying the blinds, the cheeky behaviour was only just beginning.

Chapter 18

"STAY WHERE I CAN SEE YOU?"

Before I became a mum, I used to see all those sweet, picture-perfect moments between parents and their kids, walking hand-in-hand through the shops, playing in the park or having an ice-cream. I'd look at them and think, "I can't wait for that."

What I didn't see? The chaos happening five seconds before or after that. The screaming, the chasing, the mess and the sugar rush that made them go mental. It turns out, parenting isn't something you can understand from the outside. You have to dive in, head first, and hope for the best.

In the early days, when your baby was truly a baby - eating, sleeping, and yes, vomiting all over you, only to repeat the cycle - it's almost deceptively easy. You might think I'm joking, but trust me, this phase can be the most manageable. You're in a fog of tiredness, but at least they stay where you put them.

A cat, on the other hand? That was a whole different story. We now had Mo to keep an eye on as well.

I CAN'T STOP PUSHING

It wasn't just the blinds and the mini puddles on the carpet… it was the *'presents'* he brought in. Many mornings we'd wake up to 'parts' scattered around like some kind of horror film.

The one thing I didn't expect was that Mo would make a friend. An *actual* friend. The cat from two doors down used to meow at our front door, calling Mo out to play. We'd watch them roll around and chase each other across the garden. It was one of the cutest things I've ever seen.

♥♥♥

Then he learned to roll over. James and I were SO excited. We filmed every attempt. Each day, he practiced and practiced until, one morning, he finally rolled over. "Did you see that? He did it!" I shouted.

Next up was weaning. Alexander showed all the signs of being ready for solids at around six months. I started him off with various flavoured pouches. At first, it was all new tastes and weird textures, but once he got into it, I introduced finger foods. That's when the chaos really started. I remember placing soft bits of food in front of him and watching him squish it between his fingers with the biggest smile. It was hilarious… until it wasn't. Everything… and I mean *everything*… ended up on the floor. So, to save our sanity and protect the carpet, we bought a big wipeable mat to go under the highchair. That was a game changer.

Well... until he realised he could throw food *past* the mat. With great force, I might add. Usually at my face.

Weaning also changed one very regular thing: the *smell* of his poo. Gone was that sweet, milky scent I'd gotten used to. In its place? A full-blown, eye-watering, I can't breathe, *what-the-actual-hell-did-you-eat?* kind of smell. And no...you *never* get used to it.

♥♥♥

At eight months old things took a turn for the worst. Alexander became really unwell with a very high temperature. He didn't want to eat or do any of his usual activities. The GP sent us straight to the paediatrics unit at Westmere General Hospital. Tests showed it was a virus and he'd need IV fluids overnight.

James held him tight while they placed the cannula. His scream...that high-pitched, panicked cry I'll never forget. It felt brutal - but we knew it was to help him.

They showed us the room we'd be staying in. Then, I took a moment to step away and cry. After what I had just experienced, I needed a good cry.

I CAN'T STOP PUSHING

We then said our goodbyes to James and got comfortable for cuddles, and his favourite show on my phone, until dinner time. I was still breastfeeding, so the ward sent up a meal for me - not that he wanted any of it anyway.

Despite the drip, he was still the happiest little bunny. His bed was a huge metal cot - just like the one from his hernia op. He smiled at me through the bars and giggled away.

We had a night of endless cuddles. Then, after one feed, I paced the room as I tried to get him to burp. But he threw up everything all over the floor. The nurse was a legend, wiping it away while I cleaned us both up. Thank goodness for wipe-clean flooring.

By morning, his numbers looked good and the team gave us the all-clear to go home later that day. It took a week or so for Alexander to feel more like himself and to start eating regularly again. I am so glad I followed my gut - sometimes, you just know when something's not right.

♥♥♥

After sitting and rolling came the crawling phase - or so we thought. Alexander was just over one year old and he had other ideas. He got into the crawling position, rocked back and forth for a bit, then decided; "Nope."

Instead, he pulled himself up on the coffee table and within days he was walking. Crawling? He skipped it. Walking turned into running and suddenly, I was chasing a tiny tornado around the house. He'd disappear the moment I turned my back - under the table, behind doors, I'd even be searching the washing machine.

Oh, but if he was quiet? That silence is a very clear sign they are up to something... usually something they should not be doing. Just the other day, I was in the kitchen, putting away groceries, when I suddenly noticed how quiet it was. "Alexander?" I called. No response.

I quickly dropped the last bag of groceries and rushed through the living room. As I peeked around the corner into the hallway, there he was with a permanent marker, drawing all over the wall. It was impossible to stay mad at that little face, though. He just smiled up at me with those big, beautiful eyes and let's just say...the permanent markers, were *permanently* hidden.

Then came the talking. His first "Mummy" made me melt. But let me tell you...once they start, they *don't stop*.

"Mummy." "Mummy." "MUMMY." After the hundredth time before 9 a.m., I was like, "*I take it back.*"

I CAN'T STOP PUSHING

And then... toddlerhood. Need I say more? But I will. Toddlers are like tiny drunk people with no sense of danger and zero impulse control. One second, they're giggling, the next they're lying on the floor screaming because their banana broke in half.

A friend of mine told me once that his daughter had a full-blown meltdown in the supermarket. He tried reasoning with her, but she just screamed louder. So, what did he do? He lay down on the floor next to her and started doing the same. She stopped immediately. "Daddy, you're embarrassing me," she said. "Well, you're embarrassing *me*," he replied. She never did it again. Honestly, I'm not sure I have the guts to do what he did, but I admire his bravery.

Alexander didn't really throw tantrums in public at first. He had a different strategy…running away. He was *fast*.

Let me tell you now: if you're taking a toddler shopping, you NEED a pram or a trolley. The moment they are not securely contained, they slip out like tiny octopuses, and disappear faster than you can say, "Stay where I can see you." We tried everything - toddler reins, wrist straps, outright bribery with his favourite

"STAY WHERE I CAN SEE YOU?"

snack. Sometimes they worked, sometimes they didn't. We'd be in a shop, thinking, "We've got five minutes to grab milk and bread." Next thing, he's legged it down the aisle, squealing with laughter. James and I would be sprinting after him, dodging baskets and apologising to strangers.

Alexander, on the other hand, thought this was the best game ever. The more we chased him, the faster he ran, laughing hysterically and shouting "you can't catch me!" I will admit, it's hard not to laugh.

Maybe this is how children bring the kid out in us again. It's easy to get caught up in the seriousness of it all - after all, you're responsible for keeping this tiny human alive. But in the middle of all the stress, the mess, the shouting and the crying…there's magic.

Real, ridiculous, unforgettable magic. Because before you know it, the toddler years will be gone.

These are the days we'll miss. The little legs running, the marker-coloured walls, the chaotic dinner times, and yes…even the supermarket chases. One day, we'll look back and wish we could do it all over again.

Even the tantrums?

Maybe.

Chapter 19

"ALWAYS TRUST YOUR GUT."

Alexander was almost two years old when we first heard about COVID-19. At that point, they were saying it only affected people who had recently travelled abroad, so James and I weren't worried.

One Thursday evening, after picking Alexander up from nursery, he came down with a temperature. I figured it was just teething as he had another tooth coming through. I gave him some medicine to bring the temperature down and didn't think too much of it. By morning, though, his temperature spiked to 39°C, and he developed a cough. He still seemed happy in himself, but something just didn't seem right. So, I trusted my gut and called the doctor. "Let's bring him in just to get checked," the nurse said.

James drove us there, but waited in the car while I took Alexander in. At reception, they put us in a separate room as a precaution. His temperature had gone up again, and he was starting to shiver. I was just about to wrap him in my jumper, but when I looked at his face…

"ALWAYS TRUST YOUR GUT?"

he was turning blue. "Is it just me, or is he turning blue?" I asked the doctor as he walked in. His face changed instantly. "Go to my office, now." I gathered our things and followed him.

"I'm not happy with his colour," he said. "I'm going to put him on oxygen and call an ambulance."

I suddenly felt sick with worry. What I thought was a routine check had turned into something far scarier. As he left to make the call, I phoned James. "They're calling an ambulance and putting him on oxygen."

James came running in. Alexander hated the oxygen mask and became hysterical. James held him while I ran out to grab a few things from the car. One of the receptionists stopped me when I came back in. "Are you alright?" she asked. I nodded…then burst into tears. I was trying to be strong for Alexander in the room, but now that he could not see me, I couldn't hold back. She handed me a glass of water while I took a moment.

Not long after I returned to James and Alexander, the paramedics arrived. We followed them out to the ambulance, where they helped us climb inside. One of them suggested I lie on the bed and hold Alexander on my lap for the journey. James followed behind in the car. As the ambulance pulled away, the sirens went on.

I CAN'T STOP PUSHING

My heart was racing. The paramedic saw my face and said, "Don't worry. It just helps us get through traffic quicker."

James rang, panicked. "They've put the sirens on?"

"Just to get there faster," I explained. Alexander fell asleep on the way, but his temperature kept climbing.

When we arrived at Westmere General, the hospital ran more accurate tests and, thankfully, he didn't need oxygen. But with a temperature now over 40°C, they kept him in for observation.

After a few hours, the temperature broke and we were sent home with no clear diagnosis, but he'd improved.

We were shattered. We ordered takeaway as we had no dinner, but as it arrived around 7 p.m., Alexander's temperature shot back up again. I rang 999. When the paramedics arrived, he was sat up smiling like nothing had happened. Classic!

They checked him over and decided it was best to take him back in. After some tests, they diagnosed tonsillitis. To this day, I still think it was COVID. He had all the symptoms, right?

"ALWAYS TRUST YOUR GUT?"

The day the pandemic became real was at a friend's little girl's birthday party. We'd just gone upstairs to change Alexander's nappy, and I was checking my phone, when I saw a message in our local group. There was a case of COVID-19 at one of the local schools. This felt close.
Too close. I had a gut feeling that something big was coming.

After that, I made everyone who entered our house wash their hands immediately… yes, even Steven. He kept telling me not to worry, but I couldn't ignore that nagging feeling deep down.

A few days later, I started quietly prepping: long-life milk, frozen fruit, anything I could store in the cupboard. Just enough to make me feel a bit more in control.

Everyone had their own pandemic story. Ours kicked off with my redundancy. I'd seen it coming and, if there's such a thing, it happened in the gentlest way you can lose a job.

Then a few weeks later, just before full lockdown, I woke at 2 a.m. to Alexander crying. He was only 18 months old. I tried everything, but nothing settled him. He didn't have a temperature, but he couldn't tell me what was wrong.

I CAN'T STOP PUSHING

It's one of the hardest parts of parenting... trying to understand a toddler who can't talk yet.

I brought him downstairs and put on the TV. He calmed a little and fell asleep on me. Ten minutes later, he was crying again. By 5 a.m., I was exhausted. I woke James to take over so I could rest. By 7 a.m., James was waking me. Alexander was still crying.

I rang 111. They told me to contact the GP at 8:30 a.m. I was lucky to get through straight away. The GP rang back. "Give it a few more days," she said. Nope. I was done. I had been up since 2 a.m. with a screaming child who was now practically rolling on the floor in pain.

"I'm taking him to A&E," I said. "You might end up sending us there anyway." She agreed.

At the hospital, the nurses were amazing. Alexander was emotional, and to top it off, I was suddenly hit with a familiar sensation 'down there'...my period had just started. Perfect timing.

A nurse sat with Alexander so I could sort myself out. Once I was back, I tried everything to distract him... snacks, toys, his favourite shows on my phone...but nothing worked. Eventually, he fell asleep in my arms, exhausted from crying.

"ALWAYS TRUST YOUR GUT?"

A nurse came by offering sandwiches. "It's just for patients," she said, then added, "Would he eat this?" I shook my head. "He's too fussy." She was clearly hoping I'd take it for myself, but I didn't. I really wish I had because I had no other food with me.

As she turned to leave, she suddenly paused.

"His ear is bleeding. Did you know that?"

"No," I said, shocked. His left ear had been facing away from me. Within minutes, we were surrounded. The consultant looked at me and said, "Well, now we know why he's in so much pain. It looks like he has an ear infection."

It hadn't even crossed my mind. He didn't show any signs that the pain was coming from his ear. It just goes to show, always trust your gut, and I'm so glad we went to A&E. We stayed until his fever dropped, and they started him on antibiotics. He finally began to improve.

A month later, lockdown had started. Alexander had another ear infection. He was crying again in pain, this time with a fever and discharge coming out of his left ear. I rang the doctor…and was told he couldn't be seen.

I pushed. Eventually, they agreed as long as we stayed in the car and called when we arrived. It was pouring with rain and the doctor came out in full PPE.

I CAN'T STOP PUSHING

I got Alexander out of the car, and he was screaming uncontrollably in my arms. The doctor checked Alexander's temperature which was over 38°C and gave him a brief look.

"He doesn't need antibiotics," he said. "He's *fine*."

He was *not* fine. I was *not* impressed. Normally, I avoid antibiotics wherever possible, but this was a case where they were definitely needed.

The next day, he was still in pain and still had a fever. I couldn't take it anymore. My gut kept telling me to push for an antibiotic. I needed to get another opinion. Since it was Saturday, I called 111 to get a doctor's appointment. As luck would have it, the doctor on duty was none other than James's old family doctor, who had previously worked at our current practice. Talk about a small world.

He thoroughly examined Alexander, including checking his ears, and immediately confirmed it was an ear infection. I explained what had happened the day before, and he was horrified that we hadn't been given an antibiotic. He prescribed antibiotics immediately. I was so relieved…but more bad news was coming.

"ALWAYS TRUST YOUR GUT?"

The pandemic was a strange, lonely time. Even going shopping felt weird. One-way aisles, masked faces, the guilt Of walking backwards for something you forgot.

Steven, James's dad, who was 78 and incredibly fit (and he had climbed Kilimanjaro at 72) suddenly lost two stone in two weeks. Doctors refused to see him. "It's COVID," they kept saying. I wasn't convinced. With lockdown in place, we couldn't visit. James eventually took the risk and drove him to a COVID drive-through centre. They couldn't say for sure what was wrong. But because of this, James now had to self-isolate as a precaution.

Then Steven developed new symptoms. Turned out to be a bladder infection. He couldn't drive as he was too weak; James was self-isolating and I was looking after Alexander… so a friend collected the prescription.

The following day, we did our usual check-in call to see how he was doing. It was an earlier call at 7 a.m., but we knew he never slept in late. We were surprised to find the phone engaged. Who would he be on the phone with at this time of the morning? We tried again about ten minutes later and finally got through. He had been on the line with 111, because he had woken up very short of breath. They told him they would send a doctor to his house to check him, but hadn't given him any idea of how long they'd be.

I CAN'T STOP PUSHING

I called 111 myself to see if I could find out how long he would be waiting. They couldn't provide any idea of the wait time, as they had to wait for a doctor to become available.

I called Steven to let him know the update. Then he said, "Olivia, I'm really not good. I'm struggling to breathe." Chills ran down my spine as I heard the sound of his voice and it terrified me. Tears filled my eyes as I realised this could be the last time, I speak to him. "Call 999," I said. "I love you." And I hung up.

I stood there for a minute to compose myself, a million thoughts racing through my mind about how this could unfold. Thank goodness Alexander was asleep at that moment. I took a deep breath and remembered that James was upstairs waiting for me to update him. I called him, as he was still self-isolating, and told him what had happened.

His only response was, "I need to be there" and I replied, "I know." I heard him coming down the stairs, and we just looked at each other from across the room. I wanted more than anything to run over and hug him, but I couldn't. He looked at me with tears in his eyes, and I looked back with tears in mine.

"ALWAYS TRUST YOUR GUT?"

He told me he would keep me updated and then walked out the door. In that moment, I felt absolutely petrified for him and his dad. I called Steven's neighbour, Penny, and asked her to be outside to guide the doctor or paramedics when they arrived. Steven's house is tucked away in the back of a small complex.

James called to tell me he had arrived. He knew not to enter the house and stayed in the car, but he understandably just wanted to know what was happening.

Penny kept messaging me with updates from the doctor. The doctor who arrived had no PPE with her, but made the decision to go in anyway. That is a true hero, risking her own life to help him - not like the doctor who refused to help Alexander, or the doctors who refused to see Steven in person. She assisted Steven in walking from his lounge to his bed so he could lie down and be more comfortable. Then, she went back outside to wait for the ambulance, leaving him alone. She had no choice.

Two ambulances arrived not long after. The paramedics were briefed and put on all their PPE before entering. The one line that Penny overheard the doctor say to the paramedics was: "I don't think he's going to make it."

Just after they went in, Penny could hear them shouting his name repeatedly.

I CAN'T STOP PUSHING

Steven had now lost consciousness. I paced the house, sobbing. I couldn't sit, couldn't clean, couldn't think and Alexander slept through it all. They managed to stabilize Steven, bringing him back and getting him onto the stretcher to wheel him into the ambulance.

As they were moving him out, James approached to find out what was happening. He was told off for being there, but the ambulance crew completely understood why, and appreciated that he had kept his distance. They explained they were taking Steven to Westmere General hospital for further care and investigation, but, for now, he was stable... thank goodness.

Steven was taken to Westmere General. On oxygen. They didn't know what was wrong, but they were looking after him. James returned home and stayed upstairs, isolating. I left his dinner outside the door, crying behind my mask.

Then, at 8 p.m. ... my phone rang. It was Steven. I couldn't believe it. He was calling us! He didn't have COVID. It was an infection. One that could've been avoided if the doctors had just seen him. But because they didn't, by the time he made it to hospital, his

"ALWAYS TRUST YOUR GUT?"

kidneys were functioning at just 6%. He was *that* close to losing his life.

But the most important thing? He was going to make a full recovery. And because he didn't have COVID, James could finally come out of isolation. We hugged him and didn't let go.

Fast forward a year, I'd just started a new job, and we had some very exciting news: We were expecting baby number two.

Chapter 20

"MY BRAIN HAS TURNED TO MUSH."

At just nine weeks in, I was already showing. And I don't mean a tiny bump... I mean it was becoming impossible to hide. So, I decided it was time to share the news at work. My boss already knew James and I were hoping for another baby, so I think she was half-expecting the announcement. She was so excited for us, and telling her felt like a huge weight off my shoulders.

I had all the same symptoms as before - no morning sickness, just a little nausea here and there... and yes, all the farting. I swear, it was like my body forgot all sense of dignity the moment I got pregnant again. Even when I went to Ally's house, she'd call me out on it. "Seriously, Olivia?" she'd laugh. At least she knew what to expect by now. But I was definitely expanding faster this time. I swear, I looked five months pregnant already. Thankfully, I still had all my maternity clothes from before, so I didn't need to hunt for anything new. Between work and running after Alexander and Mo, the weeks just seemed to fly by.

"MY BRAIN HAS TURNED TO MUSH?"

The 12-week scan came around before I could blink. James and I had already talked about how many kids we wanted; he was set on two, but I always hoped for more.

"I really hope it's twins," I joked as we walked into the clinic. "Especially since you don't want any more after this one." He laughed. "Twins? Oh dear."

Just then, the nurse called our name and we followed her to the room. I made myself comfortable on the bed, and the scan began. The nurse smiled and said, "The baby is doing really well." I felt instant relief. And then… "And there's only one baby in there." I laughed and looked at James. "Well, so much for twins." James laughed back, but I knew he was relieved. At least baby was healthy. That's all that mattered.

Fast forward to the 20-week scan; this time we had decided to find out the gender, but keep it a secret between us, just like we had with Alexander. We loved having that little secret. Of course, that meant lying a bit to family and friends, but it was worth it.

As we waited for the scan, I couldn't help but hope for a girl. I'd had a girl's name picked out for as long as I could remember. The scan began… "It's a boy," the nurse said.

I CAN'T STOP PUSHING

I grinned and sighed. "Another boy," I said, turning to James. "Well, boys do give the best hugs and don't have the sass and hormones girls do." But we had no idea what we were in for with two boys.

The next challenge? Choosing another name. We went through the usual routine: jotting down our favourites, debating back and forth, and I even researched names that would pair well with Alexander. I loved that Alexander could be shortened to Alex, so I wanted something similar; strong, but with a cute nickname. After loads of back-and-forth, we finally settled on Theodore. It just felt right.

Thankfully, choosing his middle name came a little easier. Theodore Jacob. Jacob was the name of my late grandfather, and I loved the idea of honouring him this way. James agreed, and just like that, our little boy finally had a name: Theodore Jacob Bailey.

By the time October rolled around, I was seven months into my pregnancy, and things were mostly going well - except for one annoying problem. I was so uncomfortable. It felt like there was this constant pressure, right between my legs, like something was

"MY BRAIN HAS TURNED TO MUSH?"

rubbing against the bone in my groin on the left side. Every time I turned over in bed, it felt like baby's head was lodged somewhere it shouldn't be. It was unbearable.

"Is this normal?" I muttered one night, trying (and failing) to get comfortable. I felt bruised all the time, and nothing I did helped. By mid-November, I'd had enough. "I can't take this anymore," I groaned to James. I'd spoken to my midwife a few times about it, and she finally suggested, "Why don't you do a self-referral to physiotherapy?"

"Brilliant idea," I said. At least there was something I could try.

♥♥♥

I'd already taken early leave from work. After Alexander's early arrival, I knew I'd need time to rest. At the end of November, I finally sat down and filled in the physio referral - something I kept forgetting to do thanks to full-blown mummy brain.

"I can't even remember simple things anymore," I told James one evening. "It's like my brain has turned to mush."

He just laughed, "Well, you've got enough on your plate. Alexander's keeping you on your toes, and we've got another one on the way." He wasn't wrong. I finally submitted the referral and now all I had to do was wait and hope they could fix whatever was going on down there.

I CAN'T STOP PUSHING

As Christmas approached, I got caught up in the usual madness like: shopping, wrapping, cleaning, planning meals. If this baby came early, I needed everything done yesterday. I was on such a mission that I completely forgot I'd even filled out the form. I was also so worried about how Alexander would adjust to the new baby. I didn't want him to feel left out, so I bought him loads of little bits to keep him entertained.

By mid-December, I felt like Supermum. Presents wrapped. Hospital bags packed - this time with underwear, thank you very much. The house was spotless. I finally had time to just be with Alexander. We had days out, decorated the house together, and took loads of family photos. Alexander, of course, was in his element trying to help with the decorations and getting tangled in tinsel. We had some incredibly special moments, including a very small family get-together for his 3rd birthday.

Then, Christmas Day arrived, and Steven came over to join us for the festivities. Alexander was bursting with excitement. We always start off Christmas morning the same way, with coffee, of course, and opening our

"MY BRAIN HAS TURNED TO MUSH?"

Christmas stockings. James and I have a tradition where we go all out with the stockings instead of focusing on big presents. It's always fun to see how creative we can get with the small stuff.

Then came breakfast… smoked salmon and scrambled eggs on toast. And yes, we make the eggs in the microwave because, honestly, who has time to faff around on Christmas morning?

After breakfast, we finally moved on to the presents. Alexander was in his element, tearing open wrapping paper. "Look, Mummy! More cars!" he shouted. He's absolutely obsessed.

Once the chaos of presents was over, we bundled up for our usual Christmas walk before the main event - the grand Christmas feast. James handled the roast, I did the sides, and together we made enough food to feed a small army.

Within an hour, it was all gone. We collapsed onto the couch in a food coma, watching Christmas films and nibbling on chocolates we definitely didn't need. And just like that, Christmas came and went, and we made it to the New Year. Still no baby.

♥♥♥

I was so done. I mean, I love being pregnant - those baby kicks are magic - but I'd had enough.

I CAN'T STOP PUSHING

I was tired. In pain. I wanted him out now.

Sleep? Forget about it. I started researching remedies to bring on labour. Spicy food, pineapple, sex - *anything*. Nothing worked. Then, just as I was giving up hope, the phone rang. "Hello, this is Physiotherapy." I almost cried. "Thank you so much for calling me back." We started chatting and then - "Wait, did you say you're pregnant?"

"Yes," I replied. "Oh no, Olivia, I'm so sorry. We missed that in your notes. You should've been seen ages ago. Can you come in this afternoon?"

"Absolutely."

When I arrived, the physio was so apologetic. "I'm so sorry for the delay. We completely missed your pregnancy note."

"Oh, don't worry about it at all," I reassured her. She assessed my hips and said, "They're completely out of alignment." She lay me down and worked her magic… pulling, shifting, realigning. Afterwards, she stood me up again. "Much better now. It'll feel a little strange at first, but that's just your body adjusting."

"Thank you so much," I said. She booked me in for a follow-up appointment the next Friday.

"MY BRAIN HAS TURNED TO MUSH?"

That night, for the first time in weeks, I climbed into bed and turned over without any pain. It was heaven.

The following week felt more normal, other than the fact that I felt like a whale. This bump just kept getting bigger and bigger. I spent some more time with Alexander, but it was getting more challenging as he just wanted to be picked up or he wanted to climb all over me. At the follow-up, she checked everything and smiled. "All good. I'm happy for you to have this baby now."

"So am I!" I laughed.

♥♥♥

That night, James and I had a lovely, peaceful evening after Alexander fell asleep. Candlelight dinner followed by us being very lazy on the couch watching a movie. We knew we needed to enjoy the peace while it lasted.

Chapter 21

"I CAN'T STOP PUSHING."

The next day was Saturday, and it started like every other day, with our usual morning routine. The only difference today was that James had plans to go flying in the afternoon.

Oh, I don't think I've mentioned this yet - James flies a paramotor. He's definitely got the adrenaline bug. He's done it all: caving, skydiving, bungee jumping, you name it. But for him, nothing beats flying.

Lately, he's been getting in quite a bit of flying because he knows that once the baby arrives, his flying days will be fewer and far between.

So, with the weather looking amazing, he decided to take advantage and squeeze in another flight. He spent the morning with us, then made his way over to the field after lunch. Alexander and I found lots of fun games to play on the carpet to keep us busy for the afternoon.

Before we knew it, it was already 3:45 p.m. I suddenly felt a small pain in my back. It wasn't

"I CAN'T STOP PUSHING."

alarming at first – just a mild cramp. I figured it was probably from moving around so much and didn't give it much more thought. But then, a few minutes later, there was another one. And then another. Could this be it? I wasn't sure yet, but just to be safe, I grabbed my phone and opened the tracking app I had downloaded for this exact moment.

I started timing them, but they were all over the place. One was 8 minutes apart, the next was 15 minutes. They were so irregular that I couldn't tell if this was the real deal or just false labour.

While I tried to focus on tracking them, Alexander was bouncing all over me, full of energy as always. Every time a contraction hit, it wasn't excruciating, but it was uncomfortable, and his bouncing on me made it worse. "Alexander, please don't climb all over mummy," I asked. "But mummy, I want to play," he replied. "I know, baby, but mummy's feeling a little… funny right now. Just play on the carpet for a bit, okay?"

I decided it was time to give James a call, just to give him a heads-up that something might be happening. I wasn't sure if he'd answer though, so I really hoped he hadn't launched yet. As soon as he picked up, I felt so relieved… Of course, Alexander immediately tried climbing all over me again.

I CAN'T STOP PUSHING

"Hey, babe, I think I might be having contractions," I said. "Oh really?" he replied. "They're irregular but getting more frequent. Alexander keeps climbing all over me, which is becoming very uncomfortable." There was a brief pause on his end. "Alright, I'll pack up my gear and head straight home. Don't worry."

I hung up and tried to relax a bit, thinking James would be back soon. But an hour passed, and I still hadn't heard the door open. The contractions were getting more uncomfortable now, and although still irregular, they were definitely more intense.

Frustrated, I picked up the phone and called him again. "James, where are you?" I asked. "Oh... uh... I'm still here," he said. "I ran into Tom and we started talking, but I'll leave right now."

"You what?" I moaned, feeling another contraction coming on. "I'm in labour here, and you're chatting with friends?"

"I'm so sorry. I didn't realise how much time had passed. I'm coming now, I promise." I hung up, shaking my head in disbelief. How had he managed to lose track of time at a moment like this? The contractions were stronger now, closer together, but still irregular enough

"I CAN'T STOP PUSHING."

that I wasn't sure if it was time to go to the Maternity Unit yet. I was definitely feeling it, though.

♥♥♥

As soon as James finally walked through the door, he immediately switched into full daddy mode. "I'm so sorry I'm late," he said, giving me a quick kiss on the cheek before scooping up Alexander. "Right, little man, let's get you sorted for dinner."

I took a moment to breathe through another contraction slowly tightening across my belly. With Alexander distracted, I took the chance to slip upstairs. I went through our bags one last time, making sure everything was ready. The baby clothes, my nightgown, the snacks, the chargers… everything was there.

Coming back downstairs, I lowered myself onto the couch, trying to find a comfortable position. I was definitely starting to feel them now. I closed my eyes and focused on my breathing. From the bathroom, I could hear splashing water as James got Alexander into the bath. "Are you doing okay down there?" James called. "Yeah, just… breathing," I replied as another contraction started.

♥♥♥

It was around 6 p.m., and the contractions were getting more intense. I suddenly felt an urgent need to go to the loo.

I CAN'T STOP PUSHING

I ran upstairs, practically holding my bum as I rushed to make it in time. Once in the bathroom, I barely had a moment to get my knickers down before my bowels completely emptied. Well, at least I thought they did.

It's a strange feeling but not unusual - the pressure from the baby's head pushing down can do that. I cleaned myself up and as I looked down, noticed a great big red blob on the toilet paper. I couldn't believe it… I was pretty sure that was the plug, also known as the mucus plug. For those unfamiliar, it's like this protective barrier that keeps germs out of your uterus - once it's gone, well, labour is well and truly on its way.

So, I knew it was a sign that things were really starting to move. As soon as I finished relieving myself and got cleaned up, I went to speak to James. "You should probably call your dad to come over. Tell him to bring an overnight bag just in case, because at this rate, I don't think we have long before this baby decides to make an appearance." James nodded, already reaching for his phone. "Alright, I'm on it," he said.

I sat on the edge of the bed for a moment, breathing deeply, trying to focus my thoughts. Things were starting to move fast and I knew we were getting close.

"I CAN'T STOP PUSHING."

Part of me was excited - but mostly, I was trying not to panic. Alexander was happily playing in the bath, which helped me relax knowing he was content.

Within minutes, James was off the phone and Alexander was dried and dressed in his pyjamas. "Dad's on his way," he said, coming to sit beside me. "Are you okay? How are you feeling?"

"I'm okay… for now," I managed to say. "But we definitely need to get ready."

♥♥♥

Then we realised we hadn't even started making our dinner yet. Of all nights to choose the most complicated meal, of course, it had to be tonight. It wasn't something we could just toss in the oven and forget about.

No, tonight's dinner was steak, egg, and chips with a mushroom cream sauce…one of our all-time favourites, but I could barely stand through a contraction, let alone cook through one. "James, I don't think I'm going to manage dinner tonight."

"Don't worry. You just relax and keep an eye on Alexander in the lounge. I'll take care of dinner." James is actually an amazing cook, so I knew I could relax. I took a deep breath, forcing a smile at Alexander, who was happily playing with his toys.

I CAN'T STOP PUSHING

Every few minutes, another contraction hit. I kept changing position on the couch, trying to get comfortable while still trying to give Alexander attention. "I really hope your dad gets here soon, James. These contractions are getting more intense, and I'm not sure how much longer I can play with Alexander."

Just as I said that, there was a knock at the door. James's dad, Steven, had arrived. Thank goodness. "Perfect timing, Dad," James said, opening the door. Alexander couldn't get there fast enough. "Grandad," he shouted with the cutest smile on his face. "Hello. Don't worry, I'm here now. You two just focus on what you need to do. I'll take care of Alexander."

I sat at the table as James gave a five-minute warning for dinner. The contractions were getting so intense I was starting to struggle to breathe through them. I was extremely conscious that Steven was sitting on the couch across from me, while I was making extremely embarrassing sex sounding noises, as I breathed my way through each contraction. Talk about the ultimate cringe moment… and there was nothing I could do about it. Not only was it embarrassing, but it

"I CAN'T STOP PUSHING."

was also happening every few minutes. He didn't seem bothered, so I did my best to just deal with it as it really helped the contractions.

By about 7 p.m., Steven said he'd take Alexander to bed so we could eat. We had lots of cuddles and kisses goodnight, and then Alexander happily went with grandad to read some stories before bed.

Breathing through each contraction just became harder and harder. It was like I was hyperventilating, and I had to stop whatever I was doing for each one. I decided it was time to give the midwives a call to let them know what was happening. As I was talking them through what had happened so far, another contraction hit me hard, and I had to stop mid-sentence to breathe through it.

"Just breathe, take your time," the midwife said. "You're doing great." I exhaled slowly, waiting for the contraction to pass. "They're definitely getting closer together," I said.

"Give it another hour and see how you feel. If things change quickly or you want to be checked, don't hesitate to come in." she replied. "Thank you, that makes sense," I said. "Just one more question… we're having dinner now… should I even be eating?"

I CAN'T STOP PUSHING

I know, weird question, but I was cautious this time around after getting sick during my first labour with Alexander. After all, last time I threw up from just sipping water. "Absolutely. Eat what you can," she encouraged me. "You'll need your strength for later."

Then I remembered I had one more important request: "Oh, and one more thing. If possible, I would really love to have a water birth."

"No problem." she said. "We'll make sure the birthing pool is ready for you." I thanked her profusely and then continued eating my dinner after hanging up the phone.

I took small bites of my steak, egg, and chips between contractions. It was hard to focus on eating, but I knew the midwife was right - I needed the energy to keep going.

Midway through my meal, I remembered that I had a TENS machine. A friend had kindly lent it to me, swearing it made all the difference during her labour.

For anyone unfamiliar, a TENS machine is a small device that uses electrical currents to help reduce pain. I'd never used one before, but I figured it was worth a

"I CAN'T STOP PUSHING."

try. James placed the sticky pads on my lower back and switched the machine on. The sensation was... strange, to say the least. It felt like tiny electric shocks running through my back, which caught me off guard at first. But soon enough, I could tell it was helping. The contractions were still there, but the pain was noticeably more bearable. As they got stronger, I cranked up the machine to increase the current, and it felt like I had more control over the pain.

While I was focusing on my contractions and trying to keep calm, James had already finished his dinner and was finally getting the car packed. After days of reminding him to have a bag ready, he now still had that to do as well - last minute, of course. You'd think after the first time, he would've learned to pack in advance.

At around 9 p.m., I was still timing my contractions and they were now coming fast... just two minutes apart. I called the maternity unit to update them. Mid-conversation, another contraction hit, and I had to pause to breathe through it. "You're definitely ready to come in," the midwife said. "Make your way to the unit as soon as you can."

It was all happening so fast. There was no time to overthink or get nervous, and honestly, that was a blessing. I didn't feel scared - just focused.

I CAN'T STOP PUSHING

♥♥♥

I popped upstairs to gather the last few things I needed before we left. But as soon as I entered the bedroom, another contraction started. This one was so intense that I had to bend over the bed, gripping the sheets for support. Once it passed, I cranked up my TENS machine again, to ease the pain.

James appeared in the doorway, still casually pulling things together. "We need to go right now." I urged, still catching my breath. "I'm just brushing my teeth," he replied, completely unfazed. I stared at him in disbelief.

"Seriously?" I muttered. "I'm only in labour, but sure, I guess we have time for that."

"Two minutes, I promise," he replied. All I could do was shake my head, trying not to laugh - and cry - at the same time. Alexander was now fast asleep and Steven was back downstairs. This made me feel so much more relaxed knowing that Alexander was settled.

♥♥♥

We said our goodbyes and finally, we were heading out to the car. However, just as I was about to step out the front door, another contraction hit me hard.

"I CAN'T STOP PUSHING."

I had to bend over and grip the bottom of the stairs for support. I was breathing so deeply as the pain seemed to take over my entire body, making it difficult to move.

James rushed past me, glancing back. "Why are you going upstairs? We need to go." I couldn't respond. Everything in me was trying to focus on getting through the contraction. "Babe, we need to go." he repeated.
Between breaths... and moans, I just managed to say,
"I... CAN'T... TALK."

The contraction finally eased, and I didn't waste a second. I shot out the door before the next one could start. As we climbed into the car, James looked over. "Do you want me to drive fast or take it slow?" he asked, clearly trying to help but not sure what to do. "Quick... but safe," I gasped, gripping the door handle as another one was starting. "I feel like this is happening really fast."

The contractions were becoming closer and more painful with every mile. James was doing his best to keep the car steady, trying to avoid every bump and sharp turn to keep me as comfortable as possible.

"I'm sorry," he said, his hand resting on my thigh. "I just want to help." I looked at him between contractions. "I know you do. Don't worry... just get me there," I replied.

I CAN'T STOP PUSHING

The pain kept escalating, and with each contraction, I found myself lifting off the seat as if I could somehow escape it. I knew it was useless, but my body was in full fight-or-flight mode.

For a moment, the thought did cross my mind if I was going to have this baby in the car. The drive was only about 15 minutes, but it felt like an eternity. The contractions were relentless, and with every one, I gripped the seat and screamed my way through them.

Each time I screamed; I saw the panic in James's eyes. I kept reassuring him that the screaming actually helped me cope, but he still had the same worried look every time. I had never wanted anything more than to be out of that car, and safely in the hands of the midwives.

♥♥♥

Even though the COVID-19 pandemic was over, James still had to show a lateral flow test, which he had done before we left home. As we were getting closer to the maternity unit, James asked what I preferred, "Should we go in together, or should I rather go ahead to give them the test and then come back for you?"

"Go in first and let them know we've arrived." I was

"I CAN'T STOP PUSHING."

sure I'd be mid-contraction by the time we got there. I had the TENS machine intensity up to 60 by this point. I clearly hadn't read the instructions and I should have only set it to 50.

As we rounded the corner into the parking area, a big contraction hit. WOW! The TENS machine, even on full, was doing nothing. I was screaming so loud through the contractions by this point. I was so relieved we had arrived.

James parked the car as close as possible to the front door and ran inside. While I waited for him, I suddenly felt an intense pressure below. My trousers felt like they were bulging in my groin area. Oh no! Is this it? Am I going to have this baby in the car?

Within minutes, James was back at the car, opening my door. I raised my hand as if to ask for a second. "Do you need a wheelchair?" he asked. But then, just as suddenly, the pressure began to subside. Phew, that was close.

I shook my head, got out of the car, and saw Sally and Charmaine, the on-duty midwives, waiting by the entrance. They were holding the door open for me to get in quickly. Charmaine grabbed my hand and guided me to the birthing room, knowing I needed to get there before another contraction started. James and Sharon followed quickly behind. James still had to wear a mask.

I CAN'T STOP PUSHING

I thought I had better ask if I needed to wear a mask as well. "I think we can make an exception on this occasion." Charmaine said smiling. Thank goodness. I couldn't imagine trying to breathe through these contractions with a mask on.

♥♥♥

They'd already prepared the birthing pool that I'd requested on the call with them earlier. We were clocked into the room at 9:50 p.m. I sat down on the bed, with James right next to me in a chair. Sharon needed to go over a few questions and confirm some details while Charmaine left the room to grab supplies.

Mid-conversation, another contraction hit. This time, the TENS machine gave me a sudden shock - not once, not twice, but continuously. It startled me so much that I ripped the cable out of the machine and told James and Sharon that I needed something else for the pain.

Note to self: Always read the full instructions before using anything that involves sending electric currents through my body.

Charmaine rushed back in with the gas and air. Thank goodness! I remembered how amazing it was the last time. I grabbed it and started using it immediately.

"I CAN'T STOP PUSHING."

But I hadn't even been using it for two minutes when an overwhelming urge to PUSH hit me. The pushing sensation kept building and building. And then... every woman's worst nightmare - my bowels emptied. I was still fully clothed, sitting on the bed, and I was shitting myself.

Panicked, I shouted, tilting my whole body to the side, "My bowels are going!" Sharon quickly came over, trying to reassure me, saying it was just the baby's head starting to come down. My response? "It's not stopping!"

As if things couldn't get worse, my waters broke. The embarrassment and discomfort I felt in that exact moment were overwhelming... and I was very wrong thinking it couldn't get worse. I felt an overwhelming need to lie on the bed. Sharon asked, "Do you need to push?"

Trying to keep up with the gas and air (even though I knew it wouldn't kick in fast enough), I shouted, "YES." Which, of course, meant my trousers had to come off.

Off they went, and I could feel them trying to clean me up. Then Sharon looked up and said, "I can see his head. Stop pushing! Breathe the gas and air slowly and blow the head out."

Um, *NOT POSSIBLE!* My body felt like it was ejecting him at a tremendous speed, and no matter how hard I tried, I couldn't stop.

I CAN'T STOP PUSHING

"I CAN'T STOP PUSHING," I shouted. They kept telling me to keep using the gas and air, but I kept pushing it away. It was doing nothing for me and there was no time for it to kick in.

No pain relief and now I was trying to push out what felt like a watermelon. All I could think was…this would pass. I was pushing so hard that I honestly thought I was going to push out my insides too. I could feel everything. Incredible yet painful all at the same time.

Between arguing that the gas and air wouldn't work, trying to push, scream, and then blow, while listening to the midwives (and James relaying their instructions), it happened. "Look down. Your baby is here," Sharon said.

Wow! It all happened in about 20 seconds. Normally, they'd note the time his head came out, but he practically flew out. Sharon and Charmaine confirmed his birth time: 9:58 p.m. Just eight minutes after entering the room, and only two hours and two minutes from his due date. If we had driven any slower, he would've been born in the car park. James's first response: "WOW. Did that just happen?"

"I CAN'T STOP PUSHING."

♥♥♥

And then they placed him on my tummy. This gorgeous little face, with his tiny black eyes, staring up at me. I suddenly realised we hadn't confirmed the gender. I asked Sharon, who then confirmed it was indeed a boy.

ANOTHER BOY.

Well, looks like I'm not getting that little girl I was secretly hoping for, but the more I looked at this little man the more the idea of a girl faded. Boy, was this little man cute.

Chapter 22

"A WATERMELON THROUGH A LEMON."

Baby had arrived, but I was still happily puffing away at the gas and air. I'd completely forgotten to stop... that stuff really is *so* good. Baby started to wriggle... and a burning, 'oh-my-word, that hurts' feeling down there started. Honestly, it hurt more than the labour I'd just got through.

"I've never heard you scream like that before," James said. I stared at him. "You try pushing a watermelon through a lemon and see how *quiet* you are." "Fair point," he said.

I kept repeating that the burning sensation wasn't stopping. I continued breathing the gas and air, hoping it would help the discomfort. Sharon told me she would have a look, but the cord needed to be cut first. James was thrilled as he'd missed that moment last time. The cord, however, was stubborn. "It's like cutting a massive piece of calamari," Sharon joked to James. The moment he managed to cut it was the exact moment the burning sensation finally stopped.

"A WATERMELON THROUGH A LEMON."

Sharon now took a look to see what was wrong and said, "Ah, that explains it. You've got a graze."

"A graze?" I replied. "*Down there?*" A graze anywhere on the body is painful, but down there? I still get chills thinking about it. "I noticed when he was coming out that he had his hand right next to his cheek. His nails must have scratched you then," she said. OUCH!

♥♥♥

Now came the next fun part - the placenta. This experience was definitely different from the first time around. Sharon warned I'd get mini-contractions while delivering the placenta. So, back to the gas and air I went... and then, with a *plop*, the placenta kind of oozed out in one big blob. Weirdly satisfying, not half as painful. It was over! I had done it - no painkillers, just pure willpower!

Sharon then inspected my placenta, which felt a bit strange, but also fascinating. She explained to us how much she loved seeing how it had formed, saying it was one of her favourite parts of the process. Charmaine then came over with a large rubbish bag. "I'm afraid I don't think we're going to be able to save your leggings," she said. We both laughed, agreeing there was no point in even trying, nor did we want to see the state they were in.

I CAN'T STOP PUSHING

So, there I was, still lying on the bed, covered in a variety of fluids (to put it nicely), when the midwives suggested I rest and only get up whenever I felt ready. But lying there naked, wet, and sticky in my own biofluids wasn't exactly my idea of relaxing, so I decided to get up.

The first task? The dreaded 'first wee.' I had to do it into a bowl so that Sharon could check it. To my surprise, it was much easier than I thought. Although, it just kept going… I had no idea I'd drunk that much water. The bowl overflowed and then fell into the toilet. Luckily, Sharon was watching and saw everything just in time. A quick shower, then into the bath they'd run earlier to actually relax. "Remember," Sharon smiled, "you're not pregnant any more. You can have it *boiling* if you want."

YES! Just what I needed to hear. I told her to keep it going, and soon enough, I was in absolute heaven - a hot bath at last. While I soaked, James enjoyed skin-to-skin cuddles. Sharon then asked if we had a name. I glanced at James; he nodded. "Yes, his name is Theodore Jacob Bailey," I replied. She loved it. I leaned back into the warm water, feeling such relief that

"A WATERMELON THROUGH A LEMON."

everything was over and Theodore was out safely. But before I knew it, it was time to get out of the bath and finally have a proper cuddle with my little man. Holding a newborn in my arms again felt surreal. Starting again felt strange, but the instant feeling of love at first sight made any doubts disappear.

I breastfed him and it all came back to me. I had missed breastfeeding so much. Then Sharon reminded us how to swaddle him, so he could get some sleep after such an exhausting day. Since it was already 3 a.m., and there weren't any other rooms available until later, Sharon made up the bed right there in the birthing room. James and I didn't mind that it was just a single bed as we were too tired to care.

With only one night-feed a few hours later, I managed to get about four hours of sleep in total.

Waking up the next morning felt a little strange, as if we hadn't quite adjusted to the idea that our little guy had finally arrived. Even though the room didn't have much, luckily, there *was* a small kettle and coffee supplies, because coffee was definitely needed. While sipping our coffee, we decided it was time to start surprising family with the news. We started with my parents.

I CAN'T STOP PUSHING

"Why didn't you call during the night?" Mum asked. "Mum, I had just delivered a watermelon. I needed to sleep." She laughed. "Okay, okay."
"Plus, it was 2 a.m. your time," I added, "so calling in the middle of the night didn't seem like the best idea."

Once they heard that, they agreed and were, of course, thrilled to finally welcome a second grandchild into the family. And just like everyone else, they absolutely loved his name.

We both showered before the duty midwife came in to give us the good news: one of the corner rooms with an en-suite bathroom had become available, and it was ours if we wanted to stay longer. This was exactly what we had hoped for. Having Alexander at home constantly wanting mummy would make things a lot more challenging. I missed him so much already, but I knew I needed to rest and get used to feeding again.

Off we went to this lovely little room with a big bed and my own bathroom. It really was the perfect place for some much-needed quiet time. The room even had a name: the "OAK" room. After doing a bit of research, I found that the symbolic meaning of "OAK" is

"A WATERMELON THROUGH A LEMON."

longevity, strength, stability, endurance, power, and honesty. It was the perfect room. We got settled in, and they kindly brought us some breakfast. I never thought I'd be so excited to see jam on toast...I was *starving*.

After breakfast, and feeling like I had a bit more energy, we decided to dress little man in his first outfit. I'd packed four sizes; three were too small (he had giant feet!) and one massively big. "Oh great," I sighed. "He's too big for everything I brought. How did I get it this wrong?"

"Uh oh...Rookie mistake." Charmaine said. You can never be 100% sure though until they're born. But I suddenly felt out of my comfort zone. James promised he'd bring more clothes when he went home later. At least this time we were only 20 minutes from home, instead of 40 minutes, when I was in hospital with Alexander.

I settled into the room and decided to have a nap before lunch. After a wonderful rest, I woke up to Theodore protesting, ready for milk. The adjustable bed was brilliant for feeds and so comfortable. However, I struggled a bit with getting him to latch. Having gone through this with Alexander, who had tongue-tie, I wondered if the same thing might be happening with Theodore.

I CAN'T STOP PUSHING

I asked the midwife, who had just brought in my lunch, what she thought. She agreed it would be worth getting it checked. Once Theodore finished feeding and drifted off to sleep, I finally enjoyed my lunch. With my earphones in, I started watching a movie on my phone. It was lovely to have the peace and quiet, but at the same time, I really began to miss Alexander.

Before James headed back with clothes for Theodore, he video-called so I could say hello to Alexander. To my relief, he was happily relaxing with grandad and didn't seem upset that I was staying away for a couple of days. We said our goodbyes so James could pack up and headed back to the maternity unit to be with us.

As soon as James arrived, I had a nice long shower while James watched Theodore. After becoming a parent, having a shower feels like a luxury. Once I finished drying my hair and getting dressed, I decided to check out the clothes James had brought. Thankfully, we now had more sensible sizes. I also asked him to bring extra nappies. The hospital had provided them for us when Alexander was born, however, in the maternity unit, they don't provide them.

"A WATERMELON THROUGH A LEMON."

♥♥♥

One thing I had not experienced before was this unbelievable cramping pain in my stomach while breastfeeding Theodore. It almost felt like contractions. The midwives explained this was caused by my uterus shrinking back down to normal size… and I thought the pain was over. Thank *goodness* it only happened during breastfeeding and not continuously throughout the day.

As the day went on, I started to miss home. Staying in the maternity unit was great for bonding with Theodore and getting the rest I needed, but I missed being at home with James and Alexander. I decided I would stay one more night, and then on Monday afternoon, James could collect us to surprise Alexander at nursery. He urged me to think it over, reminding me that I wouldn't get the same rest at home. But my heart was set - I was ready to go.

First thing Monday morning, I spoke with the midwives. I was so emotional (thanks hormones), but they were lovely and prepared all the paperwork as quickly as they could. After lunch, I managed to take a photo of the two amazing midwives, Sally and Charmaine, cuddling Theodore. Yep, the same lovely ladies who delivered him.

I CAN'T STOP PUSHING

Around 4 p.m., James arrived to help me pack up so we would not be late collecting Alexander. We said our goodbyes and made our way to the car for Theodore's very first journey. Having a baby in the car felt calmer this time, compared to last time, when we were both absolutely terrified.

I was so excited to see Alexander and introduce him to his new brother. I also felt nervous about how the moment would go, as I'm sure any parent would be. I played the scenario over and over in my head. Alexander didn't seem like the jealous type; if anything, I thought he would be more helpful than anything else.

Finally, we arrived at the nursery, and James went to collect Alexander so I could surprise him. As soon as he saw me, his little eyes lit up. He couldn't wait to give me a cuddle. I opened the door and wrapped my arms around him, giving him the biggest hug ever. I literally cried as I held him close.

There's something about the love for a child; even being away for just a couple of nights is so difficult. Of course, there are those moments when they scream and shout at you, and you just want to walk away. But I would rather endure the screaming and shouting

"A WATERMELON THROUGH A LEMON."

every day… than have another moment without him.

Once Alexander got into the car, he couldn't help but peek at his new baby brother, who was sound asleep in his car seat. James got him all buckled in, and we made our way back home.

I found it strange coming back home after being in the hospital with both of them. It felt almost surreal, and it took me a few minutes to feel at home again. It was like I had been gone for so long.

When we got inside, I laid a mat on the floor and took Theodore out of his car-seat, which of course woke him up.

I quickly changed Theodore's nappy; it had been quite a long drive. Alexander did not leave my side the whole time. Then I turned to him and said, "Alexander. Do you want to hold your baby brother?" He nodded; his eyes wide with excitement. "Yes, please mummy." We sat Alexander on the couch, and I carefully placed Theodore into his arms, still supporting him. "He's tiny," Alexander whispered. It really was love at first sight.

Chapter 23

"OF COURSE, I'LL GIVE YOU CUDDLES."

Two weeks after Theodore was born, things took an unexpected turn. I was breastfeeding him when I noticed he felt a little too warm. I grabbed the thermometer and it showed 38°C. A baby that young with a fever is a giant red flag. I tried not to panic and called our GP just to be safe. "Is his temperature still 38°C?" he asked. I checked again and it had dropped back to normal. "It's down now," I replied. "Okay," he said, "Keep an eye on him. If the fever comes back or anything else seems off, let me know."

I thanked him and hung up, feeling slightly reassured… until my phone rang five minutes later. It was the doctor. "I've been thinking," he said, "I decided to call the paediatric ward at Westmere General hospital to get a second opinion. The head of paediatrics strongly recommends that you bring Theodore in for a check-up. It's probably nothing, but with a baby so young, we don't want to take any chances."

"OF COURSE, I'LL GIVE YOU CUDDLES."

"Thank you. I'll head over right away," I said. I rushed to pack a bag of essentials for Theodore and myself then hurried out the door. The hospital was a 40-minute drive.

♥♥♥

When we finally arrived, the staff quickly took us straight in to check Theodore's OBS. Everything seemed normal, but the nurse said they weren't taking any chances. She showed us into a side-room to wait for the consultant. While I was waiting, I couldn't stop wishing James was with me. I felt so scared as it was, and now I was doing it all on my own.

The head paediatrician entered the room, his expression was serious but calm. "We're treating this very carefully," he explained. "A baby under three months shouldn't have a temperature of 38°C. We'd rather be overly cautious than miss something important." He checked Theodore's vitals ... still normal. As he continued his examination, I started second-guessing myself. Did I really see the temperature correctly? So far, I was the only one who had. Maybe I'd overreacted?

Then he led me into another room where a few of his colleagues were waiting. They tried to put in a cannula, which Theodore absolutely hated. His cry was ear-piercing, and it broke my heart.

I CAN'T STOP PUSHING

The head paediatrician then turned to me and said, "We need to run more tests just to be sure. I'll need to check for infection, which means doing a lumbar puncture."

"What is that?" I asked. "We need to get some fluid from his spine. You might want to step out for this - it's not something you'll want to see."

"From his spine?" I asked. He nodded. "It's the best way to check for infections like meningitis. He will be fine and won't remember it." Maybe he won't... but I certainly will!

My legs felt like jelly as I stood up. I kissed Theodore's tiny forehead, trying to reassure myself more than him. As I walked toward the door, I made the mistake of glancing back. The nurses were already positioning him on the table, trying to hold him still.

I ran out of the room as a flood of emotions hit me all at once. My chest tightened, tears streamed down my face, and I felt like I was gasping for air. The thought of what he was going through played over and over in my head, and I was terrified I might never see him alive again. I had a sudden surge of energy, and I practically speed-walked to the hospital café. I needed to do something... *anything*... to distract myself.

"OF COURSE, I'LL GIVE YOU CUDDLES."

I ordered a coffee (not that I needed more caffeine right then) … I just craved something warm and familiar. But what I really needed was to talk to someone. I called Mum, and the moment she answered, I burst into tears again. "Mum, they have Theodore right now, and I'm just so scared," I cried. "I can't get hold of James as he's still at work."

"Oh, sweetheart, I'm so sorry. He's in good hands, though. Try to take a deep breath. I am here if you need me." she said.

They said I needed to give it an hour and that hour crawled by. I rushed back upstairs and asked the first nurse I saw, "Where's Theodore Bailey?" She smiled. "He's in the ward with one of the nurses, resting. Follow me."

The nurse was holding him when we arrived. "He was crying a little while ago, but finally fell asleep," she said, handing him over. She explained they had struggled to get the spinal fluid and eventually gave up.

"But we did manage a blood test, and it looks like he has a virus," she said. "He'll need to stay on a drip overnight, but that should do the trick."

Feeling so much more relieved and just so happy to have him back in my arms, the nurse led us to the room we'd be staying in for the night. *I couldn't believe it*!

I CAN'T STOP PUSHING

It was the exact same room I'd stayed in with Alexander when he had that virus at eight months old. Talk about déjà vu.

I curled up on the pull-out chair, stroking Theodore's hand while the drip dripped. Not exactly how I'd pictured week two of new-born life, but he was safe and that's all that mattered. After that, he fully recovered and we had no further temperatures to worry about. Thank heavens.

Six months later, Theodore and I were getting out and about regularly while Alexander was in nursery. We attended a few of the local baby groups, which was great to meet new people.

James and I were slowly starting to work out how different Theodore and Alexander were. One of the things, that was significantly different, was that Theodore seemed to have a thing about men. If I handed him to James, he'd cry. If Grandad held him, he'd cry. But if I gave him to a complete stranger, who happened to be a woman, he was absolutely fine. This of course meant that he was permanently attached to me, and if I left the room, he would scream. I couldn't get a break from him.

"OF COURSE, I'LL GIVE YOU CUDDLES."

One Saturday morning, we were preparing for our very first family outing as a family of four, heading to a friend's birthday party. Coincidentally, the birthday boy's name was also Alexander. His dad, Joe, and James used to work together.

The party was two hours away, and we wanted to make sure we arrived on time, so we planned to leave right after breakfast. James and I took turns getting ourselves ready while the boys finished their food. James called up from downstairs, "We need to leave soon if we want to beat the traffic. Are you ready?"

"Almost," I replied. "Just make sure the boys are ready, and I'll be down in a minute." Once I was ready, I double-checked the bag, making sure we had everything: nappies, snacks, changes of clothes for the boys, and, of course, the gift for the birthday boy.

James grabbed the keys, and we herded the boys into the car. As we were buckling them in, Alexander asked, "Do you think the other Alexander likes cars like I do?"

"Maybe," James answered. "You'll have to ask him when you get there." With the boys safely secured in their car seats and the boot packed full of essentials, we were finally on our way.

I CAN'T STOP PUSHING

The drive was filled with sing-along songs, endless rounds of 'I Spy,' and, of course, the inevitable "Are we there yet?" question asked a few hundred times. Alexander was so excited about this birthday party; however, Theodore didn't really know any different as he was only six months old. Both boys fell asleep during the drive, giving James and I a much-needed break to enjoy our own music for a change, instead of the usual nursery rhymes on repeat.

We finally arrived at a beautiful countryside town hall in the middle of nowhere. Since we got there early, we found a great parking spot and helped with the party setup. Soon enough, other children started arriving, and the party was in full swing. Inside, there was a table filled with snacks and drinks, while outside, a bouncy castle had been set up on the lawn. Theodore was content playing on the mat I'd brought for him, and Alexander was having a blast bouncing around with the other kids.

After about an hour, lunchtime rolled around, and the children were eagerly ready to eat. While everyone was settling down for lunch, I took the opportunity to breastfeed Theodore before offering him a little

"OF COURSE, I'LL GIVE YOU CUDDLES."

something to snack on.

After lunch, we sang "Happy Birthday" to Alexander, and then it was time for cake. As expected, the kids got a huge burst of energy and went absolutely wild. Thankfully, the bouncy castle was still up, so they had somewhere to burn it off.

♥♥♥

Since we had travelled such a long way, we weren't in any rush to leave. Once most of the guests had gone, we stayed behind to help tidy up. The kids formed a kind of pass-it-along line, to get everything into Joe's car. With Theodore in my arms, I was carrying a few last things to our car when suddenly, I heard a cry behind me. I turned to see James rushing over to Joe, who was kneeling beside Alexander.

All I could make out was that Alexander had hit his head badly. When Alexander turned toward me, I saw blood streaming down his face, and he was sobbing uncontrollably. Panic washed over me, and for a moment, I felt weak at the knees. But then, a surge of energy kicked in, and I rushed over to help. One of Joe's friends, who was training to be a nurse, immediately ran over to help as well. Joe grabbed a medical kit from his car, and they started working to stop the bleeding.

I CAN'T STOP PUSHING

Meanwhile, I was knelt beside Alexander, trying to comfort him and reassure him that we were doing everything to help. It was hard not being able to do much with Theodore still in my arms.

Joe then came over and asked, "Do you want me to take Theodore for you?" As I mentioned, Alexander hated men. But I decided to chance it, because Alexander needed me more. He needed both his mum and dad, and I couldn't imagine what must have been going through his little head. I didn't hesitate and handed Theodore to Joe.

Adrenaline surged through me, and I focused completely on helping Alexander. The nurse-in-training was trying to wrap bandages around his head, but it was turning into a bit of a mess. I was following her lead, but James later said, "If she'd just used the bandage with the big pad on it, we could've stopped the bleeding quicker by applying pressure."

In the chaos of Alexander screaming and everyone talking at once, that message didn't get through. While we were dealing with this, Joe called 999 to get an ambulance. Alexander was losing a lot of blood, and we didn't want to wait any longer for help.

"OF COURSE, I'LL GIVE YOU CUDDLES."

As we finished securing the bandage, Alexander looked up at me and asked, "Can I have cuddles with you?" James, who had been holding him the whole time while we bandaged his head, also needed a break. Alexander, understandably terrified, had been trying to wriggle free. Without hesitation, I swapped places with James. "Of course, I'll give you cuddles." I said to Alexander. As I wrapped my arms around Alexander, I suddenly remembered that Joe was still holding Theodore. Thankfully, Theodore was completely calm with him.

At that moment, all I wanted was to comfort Alexander. James came to tell us an ambulance will be on the way as soon as possible. Because of Alexander's age, he was considered an emergency, so the first available ambulance would be dispatched to us.

I decided to take Alexander inside where it was quieter and more comfortable. He became very quiet at this point, so I monitored him closely. After a while, he started chatting again, which was a good sign. Since the ambulance was still a distance away, they sent a first response paramedic who happened to be nearby. He arrived within 15 minutes and came straight inside to check on Alexander. When he saw him, he seemed relieved and gave Alexander a big smile.

I CAN'T STOP PUSHING

The paramedic examined him and reassured us that Alexander was doing well. He explained that the cut on his head was actually quite small, and that head wounds tend to bleed a lot more, which can make them look worse than they really are.

While we were sitting inside, Joe came in to check on us. I asked him what had actually happened since I hadn't seen it. He explained that the kids had formed a line to pass presents out to the car, and Alexander was at the bottom of the steps. Alexander had simply turned around, tripped over his own feet, and hit his head on the edge of a concrete step. He wasn't even running; he just turned and fell. How on earth do kids manage to do that? I thanked Joe for his help.

By this point, James had taken Theodore back to the car. We hadn't come particularly well-prepared for a trip to hospital. I had a few changes of clothes and only so many nappies, but we knew we'd figure it out. Right now, the most important thing was making sure Alexander was okay.

Joe's mum kindly offered for James and Theodore to stay at her house since I was heading to the hospital with Alexander. He just wanted mummy, and James was fine with that.

"OF COURSE, I'LL GIVE YOU CUDDLES."

It's a thing with kids: when they're hurt, they want mummy, but when it's time to play, they go straight to daddy. That seems to be the trend in our household.

The paramedic came back in to check on Alexander. Considering how much blood there was, the cut was no bigger than a 50-pence piece. He was incredibly lucky. The paramedic said Alexander had likely gone into shock because he had become very quiet, as though the adrenaline had worn off. He checked his vitals, and thankfully, everything was fine.

♥♥♥

They then told us the ambulance had arrived, and they needed to take Alexander in to hospital to get him checked properly. The ambulance crew consisted of two lovely lady paramedics, who were very friendly and even showed the ambulance lights to both boys. This really helped Alexander, who was a little nervous. We all went inside the ambulance, and the paramedics began strapping Alexander in. I realised this was the perfect moment to grab a few things from the car. I didn't know how long we'd be at the hospital or when I'd see James again, so I rushed to get whatever essentials I could.

The one thing we hadn't packed was a phone charger, but luckily, James had one that was plugged into the car.

I CAN'T STOP PUSHING

His phone could charge, while mine still had enough battery life, thank goodness. At least I could play some videos, or let Alexander play games, to keep him distracted while we were in the hospital. Once we boarded the ambulance, the paramedics said, "You won't be able to lie on the bed with Alexander. Our rules have changed and he'll need to be strapped in on his own."

"That's alright, I completely understand. At least I can still hold his hand," I replied. He seemed happy enough to go on his own, as long as I could stay close and hold his hand. It was definitely the safer option. As they struggled to secure the straps, I couldn't help but think…what if this had been a more serious emergency? They'd need to get him strapped in a lot quicker. The paramedics shared a little laugh about it between themselves, and eventually managed to get everything in place.

The paramedic who first arrived turned to me. "Are you alright, Mum? You've been through a lot." It took me a second to process. No one had asked me that yet, and I realised I hadn't even thought about it. "I'm fine," I said, still not really *knowing*. I was so focused on

"OF COURSE, I'LL GIVE YOU CUDDLES."

Alexander that my own needs weren't even a consideration.

I gave James a big hug goodbye. Luckily, I had just fed Theodore before we left, so I wasn't too worried about being away from him for a little while. I didn't have a breast pump with me, but we'd figure it out.

Finally, we were off to the hospital - a strange feeling, knowing we were two hours away from home, heading to a place we'd never been before. I felt completely unprepared. But whoever prepares for a sudden hospital visit?

When we arrived, the paramedics handed Alexander over to the nurses, and we thanked them profusely before they left. James arrived, with Theodore, a few minutes after us. I was so relieved to have him there. One of the nurses came up to us and asked, "Has Alexander had any pain relief yet?" James and I exchanged surprised looks. "No, he actually hasn't," I replied, suddenly realizing how odd that was. Despite everything that had happened, no one had thought to give him pain relief - not even the paramedics. The nurse looked at us with sympathy and said, "This poor child... but considering how calm he's been, I can see why it wasn't the first thing anyone thought of." She went to get him some pain medication, then showed us to a waiting room. "Only one of you is allowed to stay with him, I'm afraid," she said, which complicated things.

I CAN'T STOP PUSHING

The waiting room was small, and although there wasn't much space for anyone else, it was empty. I turned to James. "You should go get something to eat," I told him. "We don't know how long this will take, and you're the one driving."

He handed me Theodore, and thankfully, we had the pram with us, so I could settle him while I waited. The nurses came around with tea, coffee, and biscuits, which thrilled Alexander. He munched on biscuits to his heart's content, while I sipped on coffee, trying to stay awake. To keep Alexander distracted, we video called my parents in South Africa. He proudly showed them his bandaged head. He even enjoyed showing off his "battle scar," which helped keep his spirits up.

Luckily, we didn't have to wait long before we were called in. The doctor took a close look at Alexander's head and said, "His vitals are all fine. He's very lucky. It's an easy fix." He asked Alexander to lie on the bed, and I braced myself, wondering if he was going to need stitches. But instead, the doctor said, "We're going to glue the wound closed. It should heal nicely, and there probably won't be a scar at all." I was baffled.

"You can glue a wound closed?" I asked. He smiled. "It's a great alternative for situations like this."

"OF COURSE, I'LL GIVE YOU CUDDLES."

After he finished, we thanked the doctor and nurses. I called James to let him know we were ready to leave. "I'm just finishing up dinner," he said. "I'll be there soon." When he arrived, I couldn't help but smile when he told me he'd found fish and chips for dinner. "Of all things," I laughed, "I thought you'd grab something from a drive-thru." He grinned. "Sometimes, sitting down for a proper meal makes all the difference." We loaded up the car, and then I realised I hadn't eaten yet. It wasn't too late, only about 8 p.m., so we stopped quickly at a drive-thru so I could grab something. We also got Alexander a little treat because he had been such a trooper through everything. On the drive home, both boys fell asleep. I was exhausted but managed to stay awake the entire ride. By Monday, Alexander was perfectly fine and back at nursery.

Two weeks passed without any incidents, but then one Tuesday, I got a call from the nursery. Alexander had fallen and split his wound open. He had been running, tripped, and hit his head on a tire. At least it wasn't concrete this time. I rushed to pick him up and took him to minor injuries. The nurses couldn't help but giggle at the fact that he had injured himself in the exact same spot. Once again, they just glued it back together, and he was good as new.

Chapter 24

"NO MORE BRUSHING IT OFF."

One thing you quickly learn, when you have kids, is just how much sickness they bring home. When Alexander first started nursery, it felt like he was constantly unwell. He was off so often that they even suggested it might be better for us to pull him out completely, until his immune system was strong enough for him to attend regularly.

The frustrating thing about nursery is that even if your child is sick, you still have to pay for the session. So, with him off more than he was actually going, we were essentially paying for countless sessions he wasn't even there for. Just a complete waste of our money. It was also taking a toll on James and me, constantly having to take time off work.

But at the end of the day, no amount of money matters when your child is unwell. I would gladly take unpaid leave every single day if it meant I could be home with Alexander or Theodore…taking care of them and giving them all the cuddles they need.

"NO MORE BRUSHING IT OFF."

We decided to stick it out for a few more weeks, and slowly but surely, his immune system started to improve. Before we knew it, he was going more regularly, and we were hopeful that by the time he started school, he wouldn't be picking up quite as many bugs. But the thing we forget is - when they get sick… we get sick too.

Now, I'm not someone who gives in to illness easily. I tend to power through, tell myself I don't have time to be sick, and just keep going. James, on the other hand, always seems to catch whatever the boys bring home. And I'm sorry, but let's just talk about *man flu* for a second. I swear, they act like it's worse than labour. Honestly, you'd think they were dying.

I remember once having the proper flu - like, barely able to focus - but I still managed to plan a birthday party around Christmas, do all the Christmas shopping and wrapping, cook meals, run Alexander to nursery, and do all the other day-to-day stuff. *No* time off. *No* break. Meanwhile, when James caught the same bug…he was in bed for a week. Something feels a bit off about that, doesn't it? But that's life. I've just learned to roll with it.

Then one day, Alexander came home with something different. He started complaining of a sore throat.

I CAN'T STOP PUSHING

I gave him some medicine and hoped it would pass. But then he went off his food - which is very unlike him. He didn't want to eat, didn't want to drink, and he just wasn't himself.

So, I did what we all do: a bit of online research. Every symptom pointed to *Scarlet Fever*. I'd honestly never heard of it before, but it sounded awful. Then we had a message from nursery saying there had been a confirmed case of Scarlet Fever. That just added to my suspicions. But he didn't have a rash or high fever yet.

I decided to trust my gut and call the doctor. Call it mother's instinct... something just didn't feel right. They weren't overly concerned and didn't think it was Scarlet Fever, as he didn't have all the symptoms associated with it. I carried on giving him medicine, kept him hydrated as best I could, and watched his temperature closely.

A few days later, when his fever spiked, he came out with a rash and he still wasn't improving, so I called the doctor again. This time, they agreed it was Scarlet Fever. Finally, they listened - and he got the antibiotics he needed. Within a couple of days, he was so much better.

♥♥♥

"NO MORE BRUSHING IT OFF."

A couple of weeks later, my throat started to hurt, and I just remember thinking, *"Oh no, please don't let this be what Alexander had."*

I was still breastfeeding Theodore at the time. He refused to take a bottle, and we were up multiple times a night, so I didn't exactly have the luxury of bedrest while being unwell. Thankfully, James happened to be home during that time, which made things a little easier, as he could at least do the housework and help sort Alexander.

I carried on with our usual night-time routine: fed Theodore while watching my favourite show in the background, took a bit of medicine to ease my throat, and then tried to get some sleep.

My breastfeeding journey with Theodore was slightly different compared to Alexander because I was sleeping on the couch every night.

Not because James kicked me out, or anything like that, but because it was genuinely easier. Getting up and walking downstairs every time he woke up just felt like more hassle than it was worth and it was just exhausting.

The couch was right next to my unbelievably comfy rocking feeding chair. It made those middle-of-the-night feeds simpler.

And honestly, the setup worked perfectly for us.

I CAN'T STOP PUSHING

But that night, something felt off. I woke up with a throat that felt like it was lined with razor blades. I had never experienced pain like it in my entire life. I dragged myself up, took some painkillers, sipped some water, and hoped that by morning it would have settled. *It hadn't.*

In fact, by the next day, it was worse - *so much worse*. I couldn't even swallow. And let me tell you, you don't realise how many times a day you swallow until *every single one* feels like you're swallowing knives. I tried everything to stop myself from doing it, holding my breath, clenching my jaw, but it's impossible. And it hurt every single time. I tried to eat honey to help soothe my throat, but it only worked for a minute, maybe two if I was lucky. Still, I had Theodore to feed. I pushed through the feeds, but I was starting to really struggle. My whole body felt off.

♥♥♥

The next night, I woke up feeling incredibly nauseous and lightheaded. I was so hot, and I was sure I had a temperature. I knew I needed to get to the bathroom. Somehow. I slowly got up and started walking, willing myself not to pass out. As soon as I reached the bathroom, the nausea suddenly lifted - but

"NO MORE BRUSHING IT OFF."

it was replaced with this overwhelming wave of dizziness. I felt like I was about to collapse. The only thing I could do in that moment was lie down - right there on the cold laminate floor. And so, I did.

I just lay there, not knowing how long I'd be there, but feeling so grateful for the chill of the floor and - more importantly - that Theodore was still asleep. I remember lying there in the dark, thinking to myself, *"What am I going to do? I don't think I can just 'power through' this one."*

In that moment, I was worn out, on my own, and honestly… I didn't know how much more I could take. I didn't have my phone to call James, and I didn't want to shout out and wake the whole house. Eventually, after a few minutes of lying there and feeling like I had a little bit of energy, I managed to pull myself up and crawl back to the living room, where I stayed curled up on the sofa. I grabbed the thermometer I'd luckily left beside me, and my temperature was 41 degrees Celsius. All I could think was: "If this is what it is now, I can't even imagine what it was before I went to the bathroom."

I just wanted to sleep but couldn't fall back asleep. My throat was still on fire, my body was shaking, and I was now starting to feel genuinely worried. Something didn't feel right. By morning, I knew I had to get help.

I CAN'T STOP PUSHING

No more brushing it off. No more just pushing through. I couldn't keep going like this. As soon as I woke up, I could feel the rash. It was all over my face and chest. It was an incredibly unpleasant burning sensation, with heat radiating off my skin. And then it hit me. The utmost sympathy for what Alexander had gone through. We see our children unwell, but until we experience what they are going through, we can never fully understand. The pain he must have been in… and even though I was giving him all the love and cuddles I could, I hadn't really grasped how awful he must have felt. That realisation brought with it a heavy wave of guilt. The kind we carry as parents every single day, but this time, it hit especially hard.

I'm not usually one to wish days away, but I couldn't wait for each one to end, just to feel a little closer to recovery. I went through bottle after bottle of honey and finally got my antibiotics. But even those quiet moments feeding Theodore - that just him and me time - were ruined by the pain and exhaustion. All I wanted to do was sleep. After what felt like the longest week, I finally began to feel more like myself again. We often forget how important it is to look after ourselves…until something forces us to stop.

"NO MORE BRUSHING IT OFF."

I assumed that once I was better, life would go back to normal. I was wrong.

♥♥♥

Unlike when I had Alexander, I didn't have any close friends nearby with babies. That made everything feel harder. I wasn't getting out as much, and staying at home all day became the easier option - TV on, sleep when I could.

People always say, "Sleep when the baby sleeps," and while that advice is meant to be helpful, staying in constantly can take a real toll on your mental health. It's amazing how quickly isolation can creep in, especially when you're not talking to anyone outside of your household.

I started crying almost daily, often silently, and most of the time I didn't even tell James. I didn't want to worry him. He was already dealing with the pressure of work. I was 'just' at home feeding a baby - this was meant to be the easier job. I never truly understood that parenting could be the harder one. To this day, I wish I'd spoken to him sooner.

♥♥♥

Eventually, my tears came even when James was home and, of course, he noticed. He did everything he could to support me, but by then, I was already deep in it. I was beyond the kind of help a hug or reassurance could offer.

I CAN'T STOP PUSHING

I want to be clear - I was never a danger to myself. But I became consumed with worry. I worried constantly. About Alexander getting hurt at nursery. About not being able to reach James and worrying if something had happened to him? I even began dreaming that he was seeing someone else. Deep down, I knew it wasn't true, but the dreams felt so real, I'd wake up in tears. It reached a point where I knew I had to get help.

But the thought of making that call terrified me. James offered to do it. He spoke to someone first, explained what I was going through, and then passed the phone to me. The moment I started speaking, I broke down in tears. Each call with the lovely woman on the other end made me feel a little more like myself again. It wasn't even the weekly exercises she gave me - it was simply the fact that she was listening.

After just a few weeks of phone calls, I felt like a new person. I started going out more which made such a big difference.

I'm so glad I found the courage to reach out.

Chapter 25

"WE NEED NEW BATTERIES."

Having children takes up so much time and energy. Before kids, I imagined nappies and night feeds… I didn't picture having roughly one percent of the day left for me. I need to feed Alexander and Theodore, wash them, keep them vaguely entertained… then tackle the laundry (that never-ending cycle… spin… repeat). Add bins, recycling, cooking, dishes, grocery runs, the odd shower, and, if I'm lucky, something vaguely resembling lunch. None of this gets done while I'm breastfeeding Theodore, since I need to sit down for that, which means I have even less time.

Meanwhile James somehow finds forty-five minutes for a loo break (but we won't get into that). At least he *is* helpful when it comes to housework. He's very thorough, and always has a go at me if something isn't cleaned or if the dishwasher isn't loaded properly. So, what do I do? I leave it to him!

Let's not forget the cat. Between cleaning his litter tray, playing with him, feeding him, and trying to stop him from destroying the blinds, we've got our hands full.

I CAN'T STOP PUSHING

Mo keeps us incredibly busy. By the time I finish everything on my to-do list at the end of the day, I'm utterly exhausted and just want to crawl into bed. James, on the other hand, has other ideas. He wants to enjoy the one thing I haven't mentioned yet: mummy and daddy time, or more commonly known as sex.

They say that sex goes out the window when you get married, oh no, it really goes out the window when you have children. The only way we manage to find the time is by planning for it. How crazy does that sound? But it's true. We schedule a date and time, and then the next challenge is hoping we actually have the energy to go through with it. Something that's not always guaranteed.

Fast forward about six months, and Alexander and Theodore are now sleeping through the night, which means I can too, apart from the couple of night time feeds I need to do. With a bit more energy, I finally have some extra time to enjoy that much-needed mummy and daddy time. The next hurdle, however, is simply remembering to make it happen, as it's usually the last thing on my mind. The times to attempt this are when the boys are asleep, ofcourse.

"WE NEED NEW BATTERIES."

Depending on my energy levels, it could be a quickie, or if James is lucky, I might feel adventurous.

♥♥♥

On one of those rare occasions, after a delicious dinner and a few drinks, I suddenly had a burst of energy. No idea how this happened; must be the wine.

Feeling adventurous, I decided to dress up to surprise James. I went all out with a stunning black and red corset-style outfit, fishnet stockings, lace gloves, big curly hair, and just the right touch of makeup and perfume for effect.

I lit loads of candles and put on the perfect music to set the scene. I was feeling pretty good. This was the last thing James would have expected.

I heard the dishwasher go on, and then, suddenly, the sound of him coming up the stairs. I quickly lay down on my tummy, facing the door, my heart racing with excitement. As soon as he opened the door, our eyes met, and a smile spread across his face.

He paused for a moment, taking it all in, and the only word that came out was, "WOW." I could see the excitement in his eyes… it felt like it was our first time all over again. With a playful grin, I said, "I was feeling adventurous, so I thought I'd surprise you."

I CAN'T STOP PUSHING

Without hesitation, he immediately started pulling off his clothes. I sat up on the bed as he walked over and kissed me passionately. He pulled back for a moment, taking a long look at my outfit, and then, looking into my eyes, said, "You look incredible." He kissed me again, then gently pushed me down and climbed on top of me. Smiling, he whispered, "How adventurous are you feeling?"

"What do you have in mind?" I responded curiously. He reached into his drawer and pulled out... yes, you guessed it - a DILDO.

Now, I've never really been into sex toys, even though he'd suggested it in the past. But since we were being adventurous, I thought...*why not?*

With a grin from ear to ear, he took it out of the box, pressed the button...and nothing happened. This took longer than I thought. I don't know about you, but if I wait too long, the feeling just disappears completely - and then it takes forever to build it all back up again. James tried again to get it working. "Don't tell me we need new batteries?" I asked. He jumped up, saying, "We do, don't move," and ran downstairs to grab some. A few minutes later, he came back with the bad news: we didn't have any spares.

"WE NEED NEW BATTERIES."

Of course, we didn't - because I kept forgetting to buy those exact ones. The one night we finally get some time together, and I'm actually in the mood to be adventurous... we need bloody batteries.

If there's one thing I've learned as a parent, it's to always have a lifetime supply of batteries - for everything from noisy toys to thermometers. And now, who would've thought I'd need to add a dildo into the mix.

Luckily, James didn't wait too long, and we still managed to enjoy our 'mummy and daddy' time with something new to laugh about.

♥♥♥

A few weeks later, just as we were getting into bed, we found ourselves in the mood again. This time, it was spontaneous - no toys or outfits, just us. James pulled the covers over us and leaned down to kiss me when suddenly, I heard a noise. I stopped him and pulled the covers down, checking the baby monitor beside me, but the screen was still off. Then, I turned to my right…I got such a fright!

I sat up so fast that I nearly head-butted James. Standing right next to the bed was Alexander, just staring at us. I assume the noise I heard was him coming into the room, but I have no idea how long he had been standing there. Thank goodness we were still fully clothed, and he hadn't

I CAN'T STOP PUSHING

witnessed the 'main event'. He was still young enough not to understand and simply said, "Mummy and Daddy cuddle." We both gave him a big cuddle before I took him back to bed. Meanwhile, James sorted himself out. After that scare, though, I think it's safe to say we both weren't in the mood anymore.

Those spontaneous moments are always great fun, but now I find myself constantly checking the door every now and then, just in case. And don't even get me started on these moments when you have a pet. Mo, the cat, would just sit and stare - or worse, decide he wants cuddles and rub himself against me, purring away. Thank goodness cats can't open doors and we made sure to keep the door closed just in case.

Things only got worse a few weeks later. I was downstairs preparing lunch, and James was working away from home that day. Grandad was over, spending time with the boys.

While I was busy in the kitchen, I didn't realise that Theodore had wandered upstairs to explore our bedroom. Suddenly, he came running down the stairs and went straight into the lounge. "Grandad, look what I found." Theodore shouted. Not thinking much of it,

"WE NEED NEW BATTERIES."

since he was always finding random things to show Grandad, I carried on making lunch.

Moments later, Theodore came running into the kitchen. "Mummy, look what I found." he said excitedly. I glanced down - and my heart stopped. He was holding the dildo. I tried to keep calm, even though I was screaming inside.

"Wow, that's cool," I said, forcing a smile. Then I quickly took it from him and rushed back upstairs to hide it on the highest shelf in the cupboard.

Why had James left that in his bedside drawer where Theodore or Alexander could easily get to it? To be fair, it had probably never crossed our minds that they would find it. But now they are at that age where they are very curious.

I avoided the lounge for as long as possible, dreading what Grandad might say. After finishing lunch, I finally walked in, trying my best not to make eye contact with Grandad. My face felt like it was glowing red with embarrassment. I handed him his lunch and waited to see if he would say anything. To my relief, the entire afternoon passed by with us chatting, and he never mentioned it. Neither did I. I can only hope that he was too distracted with Alexander to notice what Theodore had been waving around. To this day, I still don't know if Steven saw it or was just graciously pretending not to.

I CAN'T STOP PUSHING

When James got home, I told him the whole story. He looked just as embarrassed as I felt.

"What were you thinking, leaving that in the bedside drawer?" I asked. "I guess I didn't think they'd go through our stuff," he replied.

This was a huge wake-up call for both of us - we needed to be way more careful. My mum always said you have to raise your standard of living by a metre, or two, when you have kids. Now, we know why.

Chapter 26

"I THOUGHT THAT MIGHT BE THE CASE."

We blinked, and Alexander started big school! It didn't take long for him to settle in. His teacher, Mrs. Thompson, was amazing, and having nursery friends in his class really helped.

Meanwhile, Theodore had started what he sweetly called "little school" for two days a week… and I wasn't sure who cried more in those first few weeks. As you know, he was *so* attached to me. Drop and run was the only way. The longer I stayed, the louder he cried. But apparently, the second the toys came out, he forgot all about me.

♥♥♥

By the first week of October, just as we were getting used to our new routine, James came home with some bad news: he'd been made redundant. As if that wasn't enough, a letter arrived the same week that our mortgage would double in February. With me at home looking after Theodore for most of the week, James's salary was our only income. He took a week off to clear his head… another blessing in disguise.

I CAN'T STOP PUSHING

During this break, he had the opportunity to now spend more time with the boys, like on the Saturday afternoon, when we took Alexander and Theodore to the park. James pushed Alexander on the swing, while I followed Theodore, who decided to explore every corner of the playground. James kept smiling over at us. It was such a relief to see him actually smiling. In the evenings, we would sit together on the couch, watching our favourite shows. "It's nice having you around more," I said, snuggling close to him. "I didn't realise how much I needed this," he replied, wrapping his arm around me.

Every morning, James would scan job listings and send out applications, but he also made time to relax and go paramotoring. As you know, he loves it, and goes as often as he possibly can. He says that when he's up there, it's just quiet - no screaming children, no busy life, just calm and peaceful. The perfect place to think. By the end of the week, James seemed more like himself, so we decided to make some plans for the weekend. On Saturday, we took the boys for their much-needed haircuts. It's always a gamble, though - we never quite knew how they'll react.

"I THOUGHT THAT MIGHT BE THE CASE."

Sometimes, they sat quietly and tolerated it, while other times, it's a full-on protest.

Today, I was hoping for the best as we walked into the barber shop, which, thankfully, had a little red car for kids to sit in during their haircut. The boys absolutely love cars, so this usually works in our favour. "Look, Alexander." I pointed at the car as we entered. His eyes lit up, and he immediately ran over to it. "Can I drive it, Mum?" he asked excitedly. "Of course. But you have to let him cut your hair, okay?" He nodded, and started beeping the horn and steering the wheel.

The barber started with a number two around the back and sides. Alexander sat still, as the clippers buzzed gently around his ears. "You're doing great, my babes." I said, giving him a thumb-up. After finishing Alexander's haircut with a good trim on top, it was Theodore's turn. This was always the wild card moment.

Theodore stood beside the car, arms crossed, looking suspiciously at the barber. "Theodore, do you want to sit in the car like your brother?" I asked. He shook his head. "No, I don't like haircuts." he said. The barber had dealt with reluctant kids before and had a trick up his sleeve. "Hey, Theodore, how about this? If you sit in the car and let me cut your hair, you can have a lollypop afterwards.

I CAN'T STOP PUSHING

What do you say?" He eyed the barber and then the lollies. "Okay," he finally agreed and hopped into the car. "Good choice." the barber said, getting to work quickly before Theodore changed his mind. With the haircuts done, the boys received their lollies. They both looked incredibly cute with their new haircuts. As we made our way out, the boys were happily munching on their sweets, getting nice and sticky.

For Sunday, we went on a picnic with Ally, and her son Ben, at a farm trail she loves. The sun was shining, there was a wonderful breeze, and the children were full of energy pointing out every animal they saw. We took our time following the path. It was incredibly peaceful and the only sounds were the birds and sheep in the distance - aside from the kids' excited screams and shouts, of course.

After a while, we found a perfect spot for our picnic. A small clearing with a stunning view of the fields. We spread out a blanket and unpacked our food. The children didn't hesitate to fill their faces with snacks and sweets. It was so lovely to be outside and we all just felt so relaxed, especially after everything that had happened in the last couple of weeks.

"I THOUGHT THAT MIGHT BE THE CASE."

We thought things couldn't get any worse than they already were. We were wrong.

That evening, I realised I hadn't done the food shop for the week. I quickly went online to see if I could schedule a food delivery. To my relief, there was one available slot for the next day. But I clearly wasn't paying attention and didn't notice that the slot was for 10 p.m. instead of 10 a.m. I completed my order and took advantage of getting some sleep.

♥♥♥

The next day started off like any other. James was at home, job-hunting, and Theodore and I took Alexander to school. I would usually take Theodore to a baby group on a Monday morning, but I decided to head straight home, to be there for our food delivery. At 10:15 a.m., I checked my phone to see how far away the order was. The orders do have an hour slot for delivery, but you are able to track them. This is when I realised my mistake. *Oh no*! James noticed my frustration. "What's wrong?"

"I booked our food delivery for 10 p.m. instead of 10 a.m.!"

He laughed. "Oh well, there is not much you can do about that. At least it is coming today."

"I guess you're right," I said. "I'll find something to keep myself busy until it arrives."

I CAN'T STOP PUSHING

As baby group was now almost finished, Theodore and I spent the morning playing with his toys and reading his favourite books. After lunch we went for a walk around the neighbourhood, collected Alexander from school, had a nice easy dinner, a relaxing bubble bath and in no time they were asleep. *What is this witchcraft?*

With the boys finally asleep, I headed to my bedroom to get my own pyjamas on, and then I was going to start with the kitchen and laundry, to keep myself busy until our delivery arrived. Just as I walked into my bedroom, my phone rang. It was my friend, Jen, whom I hadn't spoken to in ages. "Hello Jen." I answered. "Hey. It's been so long." Jen said. "I saw on social media about James being made redundant and wanted to check in on you."

"Thanks for calling. It's been a bit tough."

"I can imagine," she said. "How are you holding up?"

"We're taking it one day at a time," I replied. "James is job-hunting, and I'm trying to keep things normal for the boys." We continued chatting for a while, catching up on each other's news. It felt so good to speak to her again.

"I THOUGHT THAT MIGHT BE THE CASE."

Suddenly, James walked in. He climbed into bed without a word. "Are you okay?" I asked. "I'm not feeling well," he replied, pulled the covers over himself and then immediately went to sleep. "Hello? Are you still there?" Jen asked, noticing I had suddenly become very quiet.

"Yeah, sorry," I replied. "James just came in, climbed into bed and went straight to sleep. It's only 8 p.m., and he said he wasn't feeling well. It's just very strange."

"That is strange," she agreed. "Maybe he's just exhausted from everything that's been going on?"
"Maybe," I said. "Hopefully a good night's sleep will help. I better get going as I have a lot to do before my food order arrives. Thanks for checking in. It means a lot."

"Let's not wait so long to talk next time. And please let me know how James is in the morning."
"I will. Speak soon." I promised. "Bye," she said.

After hanging up, I turned off the lights and made my way downstairs. I had a mountain of laundry to fold and another load running in the machine. After folding the clothes and cleaning the kitchen, I decided to check on James, who was still fast asleep. He looked peaceful and didn't have a temperature, so I left him to rest.

Just as I was coming downstairs, I heard a knock at the door. The delivery is finally here. The delivery guy was very happy and chatty considering it was already 10 p.m. I told him all about my time mix up and he found this hilarious.

After bringing the groceries inside and putting them away, I realised I hadn't hung the next load of laundry from the machine. I decided to treat myself to a very well-deserved glass of wine, and a movie on in the background, to enjoy while hanging the clothes. Why not? Before I knew it, it was almost midnight and I needed to sleep. Who knows what time the boys will be up in the morning? I went upstairs and found James awake, complaining of stomach pains and feeling really nauseous.

"You don't look good," I said. "Maybe call 111 for advice." He groaned, "You're being ridiculous. I don't need to do that." I was definitely worried and decided to look online at what his symptoms might mean.

"Can you show me where the pain is?" I asked. He pointed just below his belly button. This set off alarm bells and my immediate thought was his appendix.

"James, this reminds me of what your dad went through when his appendix ruptured… same spot, same symptoms."

"I THOUGHT THAT MIGHT BE THE CASE."

"But this is different. I'm sure it's nothing," he replied. "I would recommend that you call 111 and ask them. You don't want to wake up in the morning and have an even bigger problem," I said. James started to get annoyed with me and told me to stop worrying so much and just leave it alone.

My gut was telling me something was very wrong, and I was only trying to help. I told him I knew exactly how this was going to go, and I was going to take this opportunity to get some sleep, so I was well rested and ready for anything. I told him to wake me if he needed, put my ear plugs in, gave him a kiss goodnight and went straight to sleep.

♥♥♥

At 5 a.m., I felt James stirring next to me. I turned around just as he tried to stand up, but he struggled and sat back down again. I sat up and took out my ear plugs. "James, how are you feeling?"

"The pain has gotten significantly worse," he admitted. "Are you finally ready to give in and call 111 please?" He finally agreed. "Yes, I think it might be a good idea now."

Seeing how much pain he was in, I told him I would make the initial call. It took a while to get through, but finally, someone answered. "Hello, I'm calling about my husband, James. He's in a lot of pain," I explained.

I CAN'T STOP PUSHING

They asked the usual questions and then I handed the phone over to James to explain his symptoms. The pain had literally come out of nowhere. He had no symptoms before this at all. I was struggling to process it all. Thank goodness it was still early, and the boys were still sleeping. After speaking with 111, they advised that a clinician would be calling him back within two hours. I gave him some painkillers, but it was clear pretty quickly they weren't working and he was only getting worse. I decided to ring 111 again to let them know, hoping it might speed

things up and someone would call him back sooner.

"He can't wait any longer," I said. "His pain is getting worse." Then suddenly the home phone rang. I asked the agent to give me a minute, to check if it was the clinician, and it was. I apologised to the agent and ended the call. "The clinician is on the phone, I am coming up now," I told James as I made my way up the stairs and passed the phone to James. "Hello," James said. "The pain is below my belly button, and it's getting worse." While James was speaking to the clinician, I started packing a bag for him and prepared the boys bags as well.

"I THOUGHT THAT MIGHT BE THE CASE."

If we needed to get to the hospital quickly, I wanted everything ready. As you know, I love to be prepared. I would also need to get Alexander to school later. I didn't know exactly how I was going to manage it, but I was determined to try. I then made breakfast packs for each of the boys to eat in the car. Normally, I'm not a fan of letting them do this, but keeping them happy and calm was the priority. Having everything ready also stopped me from just sitting and worrying.

James finished on the phone just as I walked back in the room. "He suggested I go straight to A&E as soon as possible."

"I thought that might be the case," I said. "I'm almost ready. Just give me two minutes to get changed, then I'll get the boys in the car." Alexander and Theodore were still asleep, which was such a relief as this allowed me to concentrate on getting everything ready.

After getting dressed, it was around 6:45 a.m. I gently woke the boys so they could use the bathroom before we left. "Boys, time to wake up," I said. "We need to get ready to go."

While they woke up, something told me to check on James. I found him lying on the bed on his stomach, breathing heavily, almost as if he were in labour. His pain had become much worse. "James, are you okay?" I asked.

"I don't know how I'm going to sit in the car all the way to A&E," he said. "I'm in so much pain."

"Do you want me to call an ambulance?" I asked. "Don't be silly. We don't need to call an ambulance. Just give me a minute," he insisted hoping the pain would ease. "James, let me rephrase the question. Are you feeling guilty about calling an ambulance?" I asked. He hesitated for a moment and then responded with, "Yes."

I decided to trust my instincts. "I'm calling an ambulance," I said. "My gut tells me that this is serious, and it will be less stressful for the boys as well."

The boys were now downstairs, happily playing with their toys. I gave them a snack and a drink, then put on their favourite show to keep them occupied while I called 999. I spoke to a very kind lady on the line. "Can you tell me exactly what's happening?" she asked. I explained, "My husband is in severe abdominal pain. It started suddenly and has gotten much worse. He's having a hard time finding a comfortable position.

"I THOUGHT THAT MIGHT BE THE CASE."

We spoke to 111 who told us to head straight to A&E but as he is having to lay down, I don't know how I am going to transport him in the car."

"I understand", she replied, "I need to ask a few more questions. Please can you also give him some aspirin, just in case he is having a heart attack."

"The pain is definitely in his abdomen, not his chest. But of course, I will give him aspirin just in case."

"Okay," she said. "An ambulance is on the way and will get to you as quickly as possible. Just keep an eye on him and call us back if his symptoms get any worse."

♥♥♥

While waiting for the ambulance, I quickly called James's dad. "Hi, it's me. James is in a lot of pain, and I've called an ambulance. Can you come over to help?"

Without hesitation, he replied, "I'm on my way. I'll be there as soon as I can."

Back upstairs, James was struggling. He hadn't moved from the bed and was trying every possible position to relieve the pain. His breathing was almost like he was panting, as he tried to tolerate the discomfort. I decided to call 999 again to check on the ambulance.

"Hi, I'm calling to see if there's any update on the ambulance. My husband is in severe pain and struggling."

I CAN'T STOP PUSHING

The operator assured me, "He's at the top of the list. The only thing that could delay them further would be if there's a cardiac arrest. They're on their way and should arrive soon." After an hour I could finally hear the sound of an ambulance siren. The relief that help had arrived, literally made me cry. Given how busy they usually are, we were so fortunate to have only waited an hour.

I guided the paramedics up to our bedroom. "This way," I said, leading them to James. "He's in here." I left the paramedics to take over and I hurried downstairs to check on the boys. They were being little superstars, completely absorbed in their TV show. I don't think they even noticed the paramedics arrive.

I stood at the bottom of the stairs trying to overhear what the paramedics were saying as they assessed James. They seemed unable to pinpoint the issue, which only made me more anxious.

They asked him a load of questions, but as James was in so much pain, he was struggling to talk. I made my way upstairs to help him answer where I could.

"Could this be caused by stress? We've been through so much lately. James was made redundant one week ago, and our mortgage is about to double.

"I THOUGHT THAT MIGHT BE THE CASE."

We've been struggling with money, and I'm worried it's all just too much for him." The paramedic nodded. "It's hard to say for sure", but then made some notes so they had that on file for the doctors. One of the paramedics then turned to James. "Are you okay with making your own way to A&E?" he asked. James, clearly in discomfort, replied, "I will try."

I was taken aback. If the paramedics had seen my expression, they would have instantly known what I thought of that suggestion. This was absurd - James was in so much pain, and they expected him to get himself to the hospital?

"I have two very young children downstairs," I explained, "and they're completely unaware of how much pain their father is in right now. If you could take him, it would be a huge help. I really don't see how he could manage sitting in a car when he can barely get comfortable lying down." The paramedics exchanged glances, and I could see they were weighing their options. "We understand your concern," one of them said, "but we need to ensure it's necessary for him to go by ambulance."

Trying to push my frustration aside, I continued. "I just don't want to take any chances," I insisted, looking over at James, who was clearly in so much pain. The paramedic finally gave in. "All right, we'll take him." I was so relieved.

I CAN'T STOP PUSHING

I grabbed James's things and they helped James down the stairs. I gave James the biggest cuddle at the door, not knowing when or even if I was going to see him again. "Thank you," I said to them, feeling so grateful.

I did my best to stay strong for the boys as they gave him a cuddle goodbye. As we closed the door, I took the boys upstairs so that they could see the ambulance. I didn't want them going outside as the paramedics needed to help James without these little monkeys getting in the way.

We sat at my bedroom window so the boys could take a picture and watch the ambulance for a moment. That's when Steven, James's dad, arrived. The boys were so excited to see him and made their way downstairs. I explained the story to Steven so he knew what was happening and then he went straight in to the lounge to take care of the boys and give me a minute.

♥♥♥

Just as he made his way into the lounge, I looked out the kitchen window to find the ambulance was gone.

I later found out that before heading to the hospital, the paramedic had given James some morphine to help

"I THOUGHT THAT MIGHT BE THE CASE."

manage the pain. That's why it took a bit longer for the ambulance to leave.

But even with the medication, the pain must've been unbearable, because somewhere on the way there, James lost consciousness in the back of that ambulance.

A few hours after arriving at the hospital, he was sent for a scan. Then came the wait. They brought him back to the waiting area, gave him more pain relief, and eventually found him a bed so he could finally lie down.

That first night, him in hospital, me at home with two sleeping boys and no answers… was one of the longest nights of my life. I kept checking my phone way more than was healthy, hoping for news and dreading it all at once.

At 9 a.m. the next morning he called me. Whatever I thought it might be… I wasn't ready for what it actually was.

Chapter 27

"I THOUGHT YOU MIGHT BE WORRYING."

"It's not good news," he said. "They found a mass on my bowels, and they think it's cancer." My heart sank. I started pacing the pavement by the car. I had just dropped Alexander at school and Steven was at home with Theodore. I needed a moment to process this conversation.

"Cancer?" I whispered, starting to tear up. "Yeah," James continued, "they said the mass ruptured my bowels, which explains the pain. They need to operate, but they're not sure yet if it's life-threatening."

"Can we come and see you? And what can I bring for you?" I asked. "Of course, you can. I'll send you a list," he replied. I rushed home, packed everything James had asked for, sorted a bag for Theodore, and we headed straight to the hospital.

Seeing him was harder than I expected. He looked so fragile. But when we walked into the room, he smiled. "Hey," he said. I sat beside him and took his hand. "How are you holding up?" I asked.

"I THOUGHT YOU MIGHT BE WORRYING."

"As comfortable as I can be. It's just a waiting game now. Thanks for bringing my bag. They're planning to operate this afternoon." He hesitated. "Could you ask the nurse about my antibiotics? I was supposed to get them yesterday, but nothing's come. And my cannula needs to be changed. It's so uncomfortable."

"Of course," I said and headed straight out. I could feel myself getting wound up as I headed down the hallway. He'd been waiting all night in pain. I spotted two staff members sitting by the computers outside the ward. "Excuse me, could I get some help please?" A woman turned in her chair. "Of course. What can I help with?"

"My husband, James Bailey, was supposed to get antibiotics yesterday. He also needs his cannula changed." I explained. "I'm actually one of the surgeons. He hasn't had them yet? That's not good. Let's sort it now," she said. Definitely the right person to ask. We walked straight back to James's cubicle. She reintroduced herself, Dr. Robinson, as they had met already and James explained everything. She was clearly annoyed. "You were supposed to be on antibiotics for at least 24 hours before surgery to reduce the swelling. I'm so sorry. I'll make sure it's sorted immediately." Minutes later, a nurse appeared, replaced the cannula, and finally got his antibiotics going.

I CAN'T STOP PUSHING

"Thanks for sorting that out," James said. "Hopefully, I'll be a bit more comfortable now."

♥♥♥

His surgery was scheduled for 3:15 p.m. We suddenly realised the clothes I'd packed weren't exactly hospital-friendly. Trousers and shorts? Really? He'd be spending most of the time in a gown, especially with bowel surgery ahead. "I don't know what I was thinking," James laughed. "Yeah, I probably should have questioned that." I giggled.

Then a woman walked in. "Hi, I'm Gemma," she said. "I'm part of the oncology team, and I just wanted to check in with you both." James and I exchanged a quick glance and realised what her visit likely meant. She pulled up a chair and started asking questions about the past few days, our family, *everything*. Then she gently said, "If it is cancer, you'll be stuck with me. I'll be with you every step of the way." James nodded. "If it is, I'm glad it'll be you."

"I know this isn't what anyone wants to hear, but I'm here to help you through whatever comes next. We'll take it one step at a time." She was so lovely. And although the possibility of cancer was terrifying, at least we knew we would be getting a lot of support.

"I THOUGHT YOU MIGHT BE WORRYING."

As she left, I looked over at James, and we both sighed. "I guess we'll just have to wait and see," I said.

♥♥♥

Theodore was getting restless. I wasn't surprised. We'd kept him in his pram with snacks and a movie on my phone, but even an endless supply of distractions only goes so far for a little one. Steven noticed and stood up. "I'll take him for a walk," he offered. "To give you some time."

"Thanks, Steven, that would be great."

We spent the next half an hour holding hands and just chatting. Both of us did not want this time to end. All I wanted to do was cry, but at the same time I just wanted to be strong for him, so I fought back the tears as best I could so he didn't notice.

At 1:30 p.m. I knew we had to go. We had to pick up Alexander from school by 3:15 p.m. and we still had a 40-minute drive. I gave James a kiss goodbye and found Steven and Theodore by the lifts, playing a guessing game of which door would open next.

That's one way to keep him entertained.

♥♥♥

I was hoping the usual after-school chaos would be a good distraction - but no such luck. James was still all I could think about. I told Steven to head home.

I CAN'T STOP PUSHING

It was no use him hanging around. I thanked him for his help and said I would keep him updated.

By 7 p.m. the boys were *supposed* to be winding down for bed, but they were still full of energy and practically bouncing off the walls. I didn't realise it at the time, but this was a blessing in disguise, as it definitely took my mind off James. Just as I was about to settle them for a story, my phone rang. I hesitated, not recognising the number, but something in my gut told me to answer it. "Hello?" I stepped into my bedroom, closing the door behind me, to block out the noise from the boys' room. "This is Dr. Stevens, the surgeon." I immediately felt scared. I thought he was calling with bad news. "Oh…hello. I wasn't expecting to hear anything tonight." I replied. "Not everyone calls, but I like to personally update families. The operation went very well. James is doing okay."

"I am so relieved to hear that. Thank you. That's so kind of you." Then came the next part. "We were able to remove the entire tumour. As far as we can tell, we got it all. But… it felt cancerous." He said. "You think it's cancer?" I asked. "We won't know for sure until the biopsy results are back, but based on my experience, it felt like a cancerous tumour. I wanted to prepare you."

"I THOUGHT YOU MIGHT BE WORRYING."

We'd researched this surgeon. One of the top surgeons in the country. Hearing *him* say the word "cancer" …in that moment it felt like my whole world started falling apart.

He continued. The tumour had ruptured James's bowel; they had to remove his entire left colon. A stoma might be needed, but there was no guarantee how long he would need it. It could be temporary or permanent. It all depends on how his body will heal after surgery. I thanked him profusely and hung up.

♥♥♥

I stood still for a moment, then took a deep breath. The boys were still making noise, but I knew I had to push it aside. They needed me. We read a story and eventually, they fell asleep. I crept out, and the moment their bedroom door clicked shut, I sank to the floor and finally let go. I broke. Silent tears streamed down my face. I'd held it together all day, but I just couldn't anymore. I wanted to be with James. But I needed to be here. Once I calmed myself, I reached for my phone to call Steven.

Just as I was about to dial, it rang. It was the same number. My whole body tensed. "Hello?" A soft voice replied on the other end. "Hi, this is one of the nurses at the hospital. I just wanted to let you know that James is awake. Would you like to speak to him?"

I CAN'T STOP PUSHING

"Yes, please." I said, almost crying again. A few seconds later, I heard his voice. "Hey. I thought you might be worrying. I just wanted you to know I'm awake, I'm okay, and they're looking after me." I smiled through tears, feeling so happy for the first time all day.

"That's all I needed to hear." I didn't tell him about the surgeon's call. He needed to rest. Afterwards, I phoned Steven. He was devastated by the news, but relieved to know James had made it through surgery and was awake.

I hadn't cried in months. But in the past 24 hours, I'd cried more than I thought possible. We'd already been through so much - my redundancy during the pandemic, the chaos of raising young kids, the medical neglect when we nearly lost Steven during COVID - it was overwhelming to say the least. And just a week ago, James lost his job and our mortgage is doubling.

It's been one hit after another. They say things happen in threes: the mortgage, the job, and now the surgery. Surely this was our three.

"I THOUGHT YOU MIGHT BE WORRYING."

Seeing James after the surgery was one of the scariest moments of my life. I walked into the room with Steven and Theodore, my heart racing. He smiled as soon as he saw us.

"Hey, you," I said, kissing his forehead. "How are you feeling?"

"In a lot of pain, but the Morphine helps. I'll get through it." He was trying to stay strong. I didn't want to push. "We won't stay long," I said. "We just wanted to check in."

"Thanks for coming. I needed this." As soon as he started moving uncomfortably, I stood up.

"We'll let you rest," I said. "We'll be back soon, okay?"

"Love you."

"Love you too," I whispered and walked out, holding it all in once again.

Chapter 28

"I DON'T WANT THIS."

I spent the next few days in pieces - crying more than I ever have. Money, the house, the car… all the stuff that once felt huge, simply had vanished from my mind. All I could think about were the boys and James. What if it really was cancer? What if he missed graduations, weddings, all those milestones?

One afternoon I sat on the sofa, staring out of the window while the boys played. Every memory we had shared together suddenly felt fragile… family holidays, working on the ships, walking through the shops, spontaneous date nights. What if that was all we got? I couldn't hold back the tears. Alexander noticed:
"Mummy, are you okay?"
"I'm fine, baby… just thinking about Daddy." He
hugged me tightly. "It's going to be okay, Mummy."
I wanted to believe him so badly.

All those material things didn't matter anymore. I would give it all up just to have James healthy and back home. Nothing else was important. Not without him.

"I DON'T WANT THIS."

One night, after the boys had finally fallen asleep, Steven stayed a bit later than usual. I was very restless and could not decide whether to sit on the floor or the sofa.

We talked through everything, and he started telling me about the days when James's mum had cancer: her daily routine and all the medicine she needed. As he spoke, I just felt scared.

The thought of James going through something similar made me cry again. I put my head into my hands. "I don't want this."

Steven paused for a moment, searching for the right thing to say. Then gently said: "I know it's not nice." There was nothing else to say. After he left, the house felt too quiet.

Every night after that when the boys went asleep, I found myself sitting on the lounge floor, praying with everything I had. "It's not cancer, don't let it be cancer. Please, let him be okay."

♥♥♥

Hospital visits with Theodore were not easy. He has so much energy and just wanted to run. Thank goodness Steven was there to help. He took Theodore for walks so I could help James. James was so fragile and barely able to move after the surgery.

I CAN'T STOP PUSHING

His cannula needed changing, he was out of water, and he needed help to get into a more comfortable position.

His entire torso was bound by staples running from just below his chest all the way down to his belly button.

"Shall we count them?" he asked, smiling. I nodded and gently traced along the staples. "Forty-eight," I said, smiling. "This scar will be a brilliant addition for Halloween," he joked. We laughed, then we stared at each other... last Monday, he'd been chasing the boys around the lounge, Tuesday he was in an ambulance. It's unbelievable how fast life can change.

♥♥♥

That weekend, I managed to sort out childcare so I could spend two full days at the hospital with James. Steven looked after Theodore, while Jen and Ally kindly took turns watching Alexander between the Saturday and Sunday.

James had told me the air conditioning in his ward was not working and he still couldn't shower, which was making him feel even worse. So, I packed up everything I thought might help... a handheld fan, some wet wipes, a cooling spray... anything to make him feel a little more human.

"I DON'T WANT THIS."

♥♥♥

As I made my way to the hospital on Saturday, I cried the entire way. When I walked into his room, I could see how much he was struggling. The cannula was causing him discomfort *again*, and he had just had a load of morphine which made him feel *very* out of it for a while. I sat in silence, put my headphones on, and watched something on my phone. I was just happy to be near him.

When he finally opened his eyes he said, "Okay, I'm back." I looked at him confused. "It's the effect of the morphine. It just knocks me," he explained. We both just laughed.

"Could you help me have a wash? I want to feel human."

"Absolutely," I said. I helped him with a wipe-down, and a shave, which he had not had in almost a week.

Later, we decided to go for a short walk to let James stretch his legs and get some fresh air. He couldn't take the morphine with him, so he had a dose before we left. We made our way out of his ward in search of a wheelchair. As much as he needed to walk, he got tired very quickly. The hospital wheelchairs are different from the regular ones you see every day. These things are massive, heavy, metal contraptions and to make them more confusing… you pull them backwards.

I CAN'T STOP PUSHING

We grabbed a couple of vanilla iced coffees from the hospital café. James was still only allowed liquids and just wanted something tasty. We then made our way outside for some 'fresh-air'… except smokers had ignored the sign.

"Excuse me, this is a no smoking area," I said to them. One of them was annoyed, but reluctantly extinguished their cigarette, the others seemed completely uninterested in listening. "It's okay, babe. Let's just move a bit further away," he suggested.

I sighed, frustrated but knowing he was right. We relocated to a quieter, *cleaner* spot, a little further from the entrance where the air felt fresher. "Much better," I said, glancing over at James.

He took a deep breath, his face relaxed just a little. "Thanks for this," he said. I smiled, placing my hands on his shoulders, and kissed him gently on the cheek. For the next half-hour, we just sat there, enjoying the quiet… a moment of calm where we felt a bit more like ourselves again.

It reminded me of those strange, still moments during the COVID-19 pandemic. The whole situation felt oddly surreal, almost alien.

"I DON'T WANT THIS."

All I wanted was for things to go back to how they were. But we both knew that wasn't going to happen, well at least not for now - so instead, we did our best to hold on to a feeling of normal, even if just for a while. But soon, the time came to head back inside.

"We should probably go back now," I said, standing up reluctantly. James nodded. "I am starting to get uncomfortable and will need some morphine soon."

♥♥♥

After helping him settle back into his bed, I spent some time making sure he had everything he needed…phone charging, fresh water in his water bottle and his table set up next to him with easy access to everything.

Before I knew it, it was time to make my way home. Saying goodbye hurt all over again. He still had a long way to go and there was so much uncertainty hanging in the air.

I held his hand a moment longer and gave him a kiss goodbye. I gave him one last smile, before walking out, even though I was aching inside. I made my way back to the car and started the long drive home. I cried the entire way.

Later that evening, after I'd settled the boys for bed, Steven forwarded an email a lab contact had sent, asking for James's results to be rushed.

I CAN'T STOP PUSHING

Hi Mark,

Sorry to lean on your good nature, but a friend of mine's son, James Bailey, has just had emergency surgery for a mass. The surgeon, Dr. Stevens, felt the mass was likely cancerous. The patient is a young man with two very young children and was just made redundant a couple of weeks ago. I'd be extremely grateful if you would do what you can to ensure there is no delay with the pathology.

All the best,

Tom

As soon as I received the email, I forwarded it to James. Later, he told me that the whole time he'd been in the hospital, he hadn't fully grasped how serious everything was until he read that email. The weight of it hit him, and he broke down in tears. Nurses rushed over to calm him down, and even though the last thing I wanted was upset him, he said it was a wake-up call he needed. He realised, now more than ever, how important it was to get better and come home to his family.

♥♥♥

One thing I really felt through all of this was the overwhelming support from friends and family. The messages, the phone calls, unexpected meals, surprise

"I DON'T WANT THIS."

gifts, even a friend with a cleaning company came and cleaned the house. It was incredible.

The most unexpected support came from James' company, the one that had just made him redundant. Not only did they send a gift for me and the boys, but they also extended his redundancy date until Christmas, knowing he wasn't in any condition to work or even search for a new job.

Sunday couldn't come soon enough. I couldn't wait to see him again, and although I knew the drive would be emotional, as it always was, I found some release in crying before I reached the hospital. By the time I saw James, I felt so much happier. He looked so much stronger, more alert, and he was sitting up more than yesterday.

We spent the day in the ward, except for a small walk I took to grab us another cheeky iced coffee. James had made friends with the other patients in his ward. It was fascinating to listen to their stories and despite everything, there were a few jokes as well. The only thing that really bothered James now was the heat. The air conditioning was still out, and he was so uncomfortable. But we had some good news. One of the patients in the ward, who had a window, was being discharged that day. "I'm going to talk to the nurses," I said. "You need that window."

I CAN'T STOP PUSHING

"That would be amazing," he said. I wasted no time. As soon as the other patient left, I went straight to the nurses and asked if we could move James. They didn't hesitate, and within the hour, we were shifting his things over. The relief on his face was instant as he settled by the window, finally feeling a cool breeze. "This is so much better! Thank you." he said. "You don't need to thank me," I said, sitting beside him. "I just want you to be as comfortable as possible."

The day passed too quickly. Saying goodbye did not get any easier and I found myself driving home through another flood of tears.

♥♥♥

Two days later, I received the call I'd been waiting for…James was coming home. Theodore and I collected Alexander from school then headed straight to James. Alexander was the only one who hadn't seen James in the hospital yet.

As soon as Alexander saw him, his face lit up, and he sprinted toward him for a hug. We all shouted, "Gentle!" just in time, before he launched himself at James. It had been nearly two weeks since they'd seen each other, so his excitement was understandable.

"I DON'T WANT THIS."

After packing up the last few things and thanking the amazing staff, we were finally on our way home. I knew having James home was going to be tough, there was a long recovery ahead, but I was just relieved to have him back.

When James walked through the door of our house, he stopped for a moment. "This feels so strange," he said. I knew exactly what he meant; I'd felt the same after coming home from the hospital with Alexander and Theodore. It's like walking into your own house, but somehow not.

James didn't waste any time. "I need to lie down," he said. He headed straight upstairs, climbing into bed. "That drive home was rough. Every bump felt like torture." I sat beside him as he settled in, and he began explaining his medication schedule. Mo, our cat, came to join us, and he did not leave James's side.

"I'll need to do an injection every day," he said. "It's to prevent blood clots. It's not a big deal, just something I'll have to get used to." I did not want to be present for those. As you know, I hate needles.

"I've also got a follow-up with Dr. Stevens next Thursday. He'll have the lab results by then, and they'll check how everything's healing."

♥♥♥

I CAN'T STOP PUSHING

The following days James mostly stayed in bed, resting. The boys would pop in and see him, always excited to be near him, but we had to keep reminding them, "Don't climb on Daddy." They weren't happy about it, but they listened. I tried my best to stay strong, hiding my own emotions. James had enough on his plate without worrying about me.

Over the weekend, I took the boys out as much as possible, giving James peace and quiet. In the evenings, after the boys were asleep, it was just the two of us. Sex was out of the question, of course, but cuddles were essential. Just having him there was all I needed. As the days went on James was walking around more, *slowly*, but seeing him on his feet again was so reassuring.

Before he went into hospital, James had agreed to start bereavement counselling. Something he'd never done after his mum passed away. He hadn't made it to any sessions before being admitted, but now that he was feeling a little stronger, he was finally able to go. Unexpectedly, they also helped him start processing the fact that he might have cancer…especially with his mum having gone through it too. It just made everything hit a bit harder.

♥♥♥

"I DON'T WANT THIS."

On Tuesday afternoon, the following week, Theodore was napping and Alexander was at school. I was upstairs folding laundry, just trying to keep busy. Then I heard James' phone ring. I wasn't really paying attention...until I heard him say: "Hello, Dr. Stevens." I dropped everything and walked straight into the room. I didn't say anything... I just stood there, watching James. My heart beating so fast, and my head already racing. Was this it? Why was the surgeon calling? Was something wrong? James didn't say much at first, just listened, quietly. I couldn't read his face at all, and that just made me more anxious. Then he said it, "So...it's not cancer?"

I think my mouth would have hit the floor if that were actually possible. I stared at him; eyes wide. Then James gave me one nod. That was all I needed. The tears just poured, and I couldn't stand still... bouncing on the balls of my feet, hand over my mouth, trying to keep quiet so he could finish the call.

He thanked Dr. Stevens, hung up, and looked at me - both of us in shock. I wrapped my arms around him and he pulled me in just as tightly. We just stood there, holding on. No words. Just relief. "Why are you crying? It's good news." I wiped my face, trying to compose myself for just a moment. "I'm just so happy." All he could do was smile.

I CAN'T STOP PUSHING

I then asked him about the conversation with Dr. Stevens. "He called as soon as he got the results," James explained. "He was just as shocked as we were. He really didn't think it would turn out this way."

Then James' expression changed. "He had operated on three men that day. I was the oldest of them, and the only one benign. He was so relieved to give someone good news." The room was quiet for a moment. We were so grateful for those results, but also devastated the others hadn't been so fortunate.

Steven had been coming over every day to help me. As soon as he arrived that afternoon, I couldn't wait to give him the news. I heard him at the door and went to greet him. He hadn't even made it through the door when I said, "You won't believe what we've just been told?" He looked at me, and I didn't waste another moment, "it's not cancer." At first, he could not believe it and then I could see the tears of joy and relief in his eyes. I gave him the biggest cuddle and he went straight upstairs to go see James.

No one was expecting this news.

By the time Saturday rolled around, James' pain had noticeably increased. The doctors were closed, so we

"I DON'T WANT THIS."

went to plan B. "I really think you should call 111. Maybe they can help get you stronger pain relief." I insisted. James sighed. "I guess you're right. This is getting unbearable." After a conversation with a clinician, James said, "They want me to go to the hospital. I'll need a prescription from a doctor if I need stronger medication."

"Of course," I replied. "Which hospital?"

"Not Westmere General, where I had my surgery, unfortunately," James said. "They're sending us to another one called Southwick Cross Hospital which is in the opposite direction." We packed up and made our way to the hospital, leaving Alexander and Theodore with Steven.

When we arrived, it was immediately clear it was busy! "It's about a four-hour wait to see a doctor." a nurse said. Four hours? I thought. We definitely hadn't prepared for that. "I didn't expect this to take so long," I said, looking at James. "We may as well stay now that we're here." James glanced around, trying to find a place to sit. We eventually found a couple of chairs, but it quickly became so busy that people, who weren't patients, had to give up their seats. So, I made myself comfortable on the floor.

♥♥♥

Neither of us had eaten lunch since we hadn't expected this long wait. James kept saying, "Let's just grab dinner when we're home. Don't worry about getting lunch."

"I've got some biscuits and sweets I packed before we left," I said, pulling them out of my bag. He smiled. "Oh, go on then."

As time dragged on, nearly two hours passed before they called him in to get his OBS checked. It wasn't even to see the doctor yet. We were so bored and couldn't even use our phones, as we didn't have a charger.

After two more hours, James' name was finally called. He went in on his own and after 15 minutes, he returned. "The doctor's gone to get some advice from her colleague. She's not sure if I need a different treatment, but I should be called back in soon." Just as we sat down again, the same doctor reappeared. She waved us over. "I've spoken to the surgical team," she said, "and I think it's best we get a second opinion. Come with me, I'll take you to see one of the surgeons."

This is not what we expected. At least now we were finally getting somewhere. We were taken upstairs to a different area of the hospital, where at least the waiting chairs were more comfortable - big, single sofa chairs that let you stretch out and put your feet up. James was so happy when he saw them… so was I!

"I DON'T WANT THIS."

I suddenly glanced at my phone. "It's 7 p.m. already." James frowned. "We really didn't expect this. Good thing my dad has the boys. I'm glad he's there to handle dinner and bedtime."

"Yeah, at least that's one less thing to worry about," I said. James was soon called in for a blood test to figure out what might be causing his pain. Afterwards, we returned to our chairs for what felt like another endless wait. Hours ticked by - three, in fact - before I decided to head over to the hospital reception. My phone battery was running very low, and I had no idea how much longer we'd be here. "Can you charge my phone, please?" I asked the receptionist. "I don't want to risk running out of battery." She took my phone, and I returned to sit with James, rubbing my eyes. I was so ready for bed right now and these chairs were not helping.

Finally, after what felt like forever, James was called to speak with the surgeon. "We've found a problem," the surgeon said to James. "We need to send you for a scan in the morning to investigate further." A heavy silence filled the room. "So, does that mean I need to stay overnight?" James asked. "Yes," the surgeon replied. "We'll need to admit you tonight so we can get you in for the scan first thing tomorrow."

I CAN'T STOP PUSHING

This was supposed to be a quick visit. I thought we were past all of this, yet here we were again, facing another hospital stay.

♥♥♥

Luckily, James didn't need much for now - just a charger. The staff assured us they'd make sure his phone got charged. "We're really busy at the moment, but we'll get you into a bed as soon as we can," the surgeon said. "Just wait in the waiting room, and someone will come and get you when one's available." We thanked him profusely and headed back to our chairs. It was nearly midnight and I was shattered. "As you are staying, I may as well head home. But I'll come back first thing in the morning with some stuff for you." James nodded. "I'll be fine. Just… get home safe." I gave him a big cuddle and made my way back to the car.

The drive home was brutal. It was one of the most difficult I'd ever done, even worse than the emotional ones from weeks ago. I was so tired. I cranked up the music and rolled down all the windows, blasting cold night air on my face just to keep myself awake and somehow, I made it. By the time I got home, it was nearly 1 a.m. Steven had fallen asleep on the couch but woke up as soon as I opened the door. We had already

"I DON'T WANT THIS."

called and updated him with everything, so he headed straight home. I collapsed onto the bed. I still couldn't believe how everything had played out. I just prayed tomorrow would bring better news. I was wrong.

♥♥♥

Alexander and Theodore were up at 05:30 a.m., as usual. I honestly felt like a zombie trying to get their breakfast snacks and milk ready for them. My eyes stung from lack of sleep, and I was sure I needed coffee through an IV drip just to function. "Here you go," I said, putting their bowls in front of them. As I was about to collapse into a chair with my own coffee, my phone rang. It was James. "Hey," I answered quickly. "They did the scan," he said. "Turns out I have a blood clot."

"But… you've been doing the injections to prevent that."

"Yeah, well, apparently I was supposed to be doing two injections, not one," he replied. I couldn't believe it.

"*What?* How did they not tell you that? How could they miss something like that?" James paused. "Seems they got the dose wrong. They're going to transfer me back to Westmere General Hospital for treatment."

"Did they say how long that'll take?" I asked. "They're waiting to send my paperwork over first to make sure Westmere General is expecting me, then they need to find an available ambulance," James explained. "I offered to get myself there, but they won't let me. It has to be an ambulance, just to be safe."

"Thank goodness we stayed last night and didn't just go home. Imagine if we had left…"

"I know," James said. "It could've been really bad."

"Alright, I'm coming over to bring you some more of your things, I'll see you later."

Steven came over again to look after the boys and I made my way back to the hospital. I had a little giggle when I found James. He'd been given a bed, thankfully, but it was in the tiniest, most awkward corner of the ward. I wouldn't even call it a proper cubicle. To make matters worse, the door to the ward kept hitting his bed every time someone came through. "Well, at least I got a bed. It's better than nothing," he laughed.

"So…they've got the ambulance sorted?" I asked.

"They're still waiting for the paperwork to go over," James said. "I just want to get this over with and get back to Westmere General."

"I know," I said, giving him a cuddle. I stayed for a few hours with James, but as much as I wanted to stay longer, I couldn't keep taking advantage of Steven.

"I DON'T WANT THIS."

He had been so helpful over the past few weeks, looking after the boys, and I didn't want to take advantage.

Before I left, I said, "I'll check in on you later, alright? Steven's been amazing, but I need to get back to help with the boys." James gave me a tired smile. "I'll keep you updated. Don't worry."

Throughout the day, I kept my phone close, anxiously waiting for updates. Every message was the same: no progress. At 8:44 p.m., James messaged: *In the ambulance now.* Finally! It was a difficult journey. Almost every main road was closed, forcing the ambulance to take detours down side streets, trying to find an open route. It added an extra hour to their journey. At 10:44 p.m., another message came through: *Finally arrived at Westmere General. They didn't even know I was coming. Because they're so busy, I've had to sit in the ambulance for 10 hours until a bed becomes available.* I couldn't believe it. I quickly typed: *What do you mean they didn't know you were coming?* His reply came back: *Apparently Southwick Cross didn't send over the paperwork.*

♥♥♥

After a few hours of waiting, they managed to find James a tiny bed in another ward, just for the night. I was fuming. The whole point of transferring him then, was because Westmere General was *ready*. Apparently not. He had a blood clot. This wasn't something that should be delayed… and yet here we were. Still a bed is a bed. At least he wasn't stuck in the back of an ambulance anymore. By 10 a.m. the next morning, I called James to check in. "Nope," he said. "Westmere General still hasn't received any of the paperwork." That was beyond ridiculous. Without hesitating, I called Dr. Stevens. He had told us to call if we had any problems, and I figured this was as good a reason as any.

"Hi, Dr. Stevens? It's Olivia. I'm calling about James Bailey. He's been transferred back to Westmere General with a blood clot, but none of the paperwork has arrived from Southwick Cross Hospital. He's been waiting since last night. Nothing's happened."

Dr. Stevens was horrified. "That's completely unacceptable. Leave it with me. I'll sort this out right away." And true to his word, he did. Less than an hour later, he called back. "I've spoken to the hospital and made sure everything is being handled. And Olivia, it's a very good thing they caught the clot when they did."

Even with Dr. Stevens intervening, it still took until the *following evening* for James to finally get the medication he needed. It was unbelievable… but at least

"I DON'T WANT THIS."

he was being treated.

The next day, he was discharged. "I can't believe it took three days to sort all of that," I said as we walked out of the hospital together. "But I'm just so glad you're finally going home." James smiled. "Me too."

That night, James tucked the boys into bed. Nothing fancy. Just a story, and a kiss, and I watched from the hallway. A few weeks ago, I didn't know if we'd ever have this moment again.

And Christmas… wasn't the one I'd imagined… it was so much better.

Chapter 29

"GOODBYE, MY DARLING."

Fast forward a few years and I feel like I just blinked. How did I already have a two-year-old and a five-year-old? Life was full-on! Our days were packed with laughter, and plenty of screaming and shouting. Someone was always throwing something - usually a toy car, sometimes food, and sometimes both. After everything we'd been through, it was such a relief to finally have some normality.

Our cat, Mo, was just as affectionate and cuddly as ever, even if he did still bring in mice and birds. Not the nicest thing to wake up to in the morning. One evening, we were all snuggled on the sofa. Mo was curled up beside me, fast asleep, while James and I watched the boys play, laughing as they argued over the same toy… again. "Why do they keep doing that?" James asked, shaking his head. "We have how many toys?" I laughed. "And you boys fight over the same one every time."

"Why can't they be like you, Mo? So chilled." I added, stroking his head. The boys climbed up beside

"GOODBYE, MY DARLING."

us, still full of energy. "Can we watch a Christmas movie?" Alexander asked. "Christmas was months ago... but why not," I smiled, reaching for the remote. These were the moments I treasured most. I knew they wouldn't last forever, so I soaked up every second.

♥♥♥

The following day was Saturday. We headed out to do some shopping and then rushed home to get ready for some friends coming over for snacks and drinks. It was freezing, so the kids stayed inside while we chatted and caught up, completely unaware of what was coming.

Later that afternoon, after our friends said their goodbyes, James headed to the garage to take out some rubbish. We were planning to go for a walk soon after. Just as he came back inside and closed the door, there was a knock. "James, can you get that, please?" I called while getting the boys to help me tidy up. James opened the door to an elderly man. "I'm so sorry to disturb you," he said. James stepped outside and closed the door behind him. I couldn't hear the conversation, so I carried on tidying.

A few minutes later, James came rushing back in, panic all over his face. "Olivia, is Mo home?"

"I'll go look," I said. I ran upstairs, checking all his favourite hiding spots. I called his name. Nothing. When I

I CAN'T STOP PUSHING

came back down, I shook my head.

"He's not home. What's going on?" James looked terrified. "I think we have found him." I looked at him, feeling slightly confused, yet worried at the same time. "Found him? Where? What do you mean?" I asked. "The man at the door is a neighbour from round the corner. They found a cat that looks like Mo, lying behind our back wall." My whole body started shaking. "Found him? As in...?" James hesitated, his voice trembling, "Olivia, I'm not 100% sure. He doesn't have his collar anymore, and... I just don't know if it's really him." I tried to stay calm, but my heart was breaking. "I'm his mum," I said quietly. "I'll know."

Preparing myself for the worst, I walked round to our back wall. There he was, lying lifeless. I knelt down and in a split second I knew, it was definitely him. I dropped to my knees, tears streaming down my face. "Oh, Mo... I love you so much," I whispered.

I went to knock on the neighbour's door, just to let them know we'd found him. Their back gate was right next to where we found Mo. They were lovely and already aware of the situation. "Take your time," they said. "Let us know if you need anything."

Back at our front door, I simply nodded to James,

"GOODBYE, MY DARLING."

confirming what he feared. His eyes filled with tears too.

While this was all happening, the boys were playing happily in the lounge, unaware of the heartbreak unfolding. I gave them a snack, and tried my best to hold it together for them. In that moment, it felt like my whole world was crumbling. James held me close. "We'll give him a proper goodbye."

"It feels like losing a child," I whispered. James nodded. "I know what you mean."

♥♥♥

After I finally calmed down, I asked James, "What do we do now?"

"We need to confirm it's him by getting his chip scanned." James called the vet to get us booked in while I started making dinner for the boys.

After a few minutes, he came off the phone, looking frustrated. "The local vet is unexpectedly closing for the day. I'll have to drive to their other branch, which is 40 minutes away. It's the last thing I want to do right now," he said. "Alright, let me see if Nick is home. Maybe he can watch the boys so I can help you with Mo."

I popped over to our neighbour's house and knocked on the door. When Nick answered, I explained the situation and asked if he could look after the boys, so I could help James

I CAN'T STOP PUSHING

get Mo into his cat box.

Without hesitation, he said, "Of course. I'll come over right away." Nick followed me back and immediately went into full babysitting mode, setting up the train set to keep the boys distracted. "Thanks so much, Nick," I said, feeling so grateful for his help. "No problem at all," he replied. "You guys take as long as you need." I went out to the garage with James to get Mo's cat box for the very last time. He put a towel in there and added his favourite blanket to make it as comfortable as we possibly could. As we walked around the corner, I couldn't hold back the tears; every step made the reality of the situation more painful.

We sat there for a moment, allowing ourselves to say goodbye. I gave him one last gentle rub on his ears and whispered, "Goodbye, my darling." We opened the box and carefully lifted him into it. Then we put the cover over and sealed the cat box. We cried the whole way back to the car. James was holding my hand so tightly, and I didn't want him to let go. He put Mo in the car and then gave me a great big cuddle before he got in. I stood there watching them drive away while trying to fight back the tears.

"GOODBYE, MY DARLING."

Before going in the house, I took a moment to breathe. Thank goodness Nick was still happily playing with the boys, who hadn't even noticed what was going on. Since they were still occupied, I decided to carry on with their dinner. I thought it best to get that sorted while Nick was here, saving me from running in and out of the living room to check on them while being an emotional wreck. Luckily, I had a nice easy dinner planned for the boys - pizza and chips. At least I knew they would eat it, and I could sit down with a glass of wine, which I definitely needed right now.

Dinner was ready, and the boys were happy. I told Nick he could head home if he wanted to. "If there's anything else you need, just let me know," Nick said. "Thank you, Nick. Really, I appreciate it so much," I replied.

I poured a glass of wine, and sat on the sofa, doing my best not to fall apart. Thank goodness the boys were happy. I really needed this time.

About 20 minutes later, James finally called me with the news I already knew. It was confirmed… it was Mo. He'd suffered head trauma, likely from a car. I could hear in James's voice that he was struggling to speak. "I talked to Dad," James said. "He's agreed to bury Mo at his place, but it won't be until tomorrow. He'll have to stay in the shed

I CAN'T STOP PUSHING

overnight." That thought broke me.

"Just focus on driving safely and get home when you can." Even though I was at home, overwhelmed by everything that had happened, it was James who had taken Mo to the vet, seen him again, and now had to drop him off at his dad's. I knew how much harder that was, and I was truly grateful for his strength.

When James got home, the boys were asleep. He walked through the door and burst into tears. I ran over to him and hugged him, not letting go. We didn't eat that night; instead, we sat on the sofa with a drink. I was on my third glass of wine by this point and hadn't stopped crying. "I miss him so much," James whispered. "I know," I said, crying again. "Thank you for everything you've done today." He kissed my forehead. We talked about Mo. How gentle he was, how he never left our side when we were sick, how much the boys adored him. We laughed and cried until we finally went to bed and fell asleep in each other's arms, tears still in our eyes. There are hard times in life… but this was one we just weren't ready for.

♥♥♥

The next morning, I felt emotionally drained and exhausted. The boys, as always, were up early, full of

"GOODBYE, MY DARLING."

energy. James and I made our way downstairs, put the kettle on, and made ourselves a very much-needed cup of coffee. We shared a long, comforting hug, trying our best to hold back our tears. We knew we had to have a difficult conversation with the boys to explain that Mo wasn't coming back. We sat the boys down on the sofa. James took a deep breath and began gently, "Boys, we need to talk about something important."

"What is it, Daddy?" asked Alexander. James squeezed my hand, and I continued, "Mo isn't coming back home, boys. He has gone to heaven. He's very happy there doing everything he loves to do."

"Why did he go to heaven?" asked Alexander. "Mo had an accident," James said softly. "Will we ever see him again?" asked Alexander. I pulled him into a hug, tears streaming down my face. "We won't see him here, sweetheart, but he's always in our hearts. And we can remember all the happy times we had with him." Alexander seemed okay. He gave us a cuddle and carried on playing with his toys.

♥♥♥

This news came at the start of the school Easter holidays, which meant I would have the boys at home for the next two weeks. I couldn't quite decide if this was a good thing or a bad thing, given the emotional rollercoaster

I CAN'T STOP PUSHING

we were on.

James then pulled me into the kitchen and said, "Once we're ready, we need to go to my dad's place. I need to help him bury Mo." Everything in me resisted the idea of going, but I also knew it wasn't fair to leave James's dad to handle it on his own. Wiping away my tears, I thought I would chance it. "What we really need today is a distraction. Maybe we could go to a wildlife park or a soft play to get the boys out and help us take our minds off things." James nodded. "That's a great idea. I'll call my dad and explain." James called Steven and told him what we would like to do. After listening, his dad quickly responded, "Of course, that's not a problem at all. I completely understand. Being here with the boys right now would be too difficult. You all need this break."

Steven had known Mo from when he was a kitten, just like we did. He had also buried many pets before, and because of this he was more than happy to handle it all, so we could have a day out. James hung up the phone and looked at me with relief. "Dads got it covered. He understands and wants us to take the boys out for the day." I felt so relieved. "Thank goodness. I can't stop crying, and I think getting out will really

"GOODBYE, MY DARLING."

help."

We packed our bags and prepared a picnic lunch. Soon we were off for a day out at the wildlife park. The drive was filled with excited chatter from Alexander and Theodore, who had no idea where we were going and how much we needed this distraction. We explored all the animals, played on climbing frames, bounced on trampolines, and even enjoyed tractor rides. There was so much to do to keep us busy. It was the perfect way to momentarily escape. We even treated ourselves to ice cream.

After lunch, James took the boys up one of the big climbing frames while I stayed below with the pram. As I stood at the bottom, alone, waiting for them to come down, I suddenly stopped for a moment. I looked up and felt peace.

I knew Mo was now at rest, no longer in the shed, and he was happy. Despite the tears that still came, I knew I would miss him terribly, but I also knew that he had a wonderful life, filled with so much love. He had been spoiled and cherished, and for any animal, that is the best life they could hope for.

James and the boys came down, laughing and excited from their adventure. James looked at me. "Are you okay?" he asked, wrapping an arm around me. I nodded, wiping away a tear. "Yeah, I think so. I know Mo is happy now.

I CAN'T STOP PUSHING

He had a great life with us."

James smiled, pulling me close. "He did. He was a lucky cat." We thanked Steven profusely, knowing how much it meant that he had taken care of everything.

One day after they return to school, Alexander came home and asked, "Mummy, when is Mo coming back?" That feeling of absolute heartbreak came back. I tried to explain again, gently. "Mo has gone to heaven, sweetheart." He looked up at me with wide eyes and asked, "Mummy, what happened?" I took a deep breath and decided to be honest with him. "Mo was hit by a car," I said softly. Alexander's eyes welled up. "Mummy, was the car driving too fast?" I nodded, feeling a lump in my throat. "Yes, I think so. We don't know exactly what happened, though." I replied. "Why not?" He asked. "Because we were all inside." I explained. "We couldn't see what happened." Alexander was quiet for a moment, processing this. "I miss Mo, Mummy," he whispered.

"I miss him too, sweetheart," I replied, kissing the top of his head. "I hope he's happy." Alexander added.

"I know he is," I said. "Mo's in heaven now, chasing all the birds and mice, eating all the food he wants, and

"GOODBYE, MY DARLING."

sleeping in the sun… all the things he loves to do." This seemed to put a smile on Alexander's face.

One of the hardest things for me, that I cannot get out of my head, is knowing he tried to get home. The wall is behind our house and the road is in front. He would have had to run around to the wall, but because the wall is too high, he wasn't strong enough to jump over it and was alone.

Alexander then asked, "Mummy, do you have a picture of Mo that I can have?" My heart sank at this sweet request, and I remembered the perfect picture I had seen a few weeks before, one I completely forgot I had printed. It was a beautiful moment when Alexander was about one years old, sitting next to Mo on the bathroom floor. I pulled the picture out and handed it to him. Alexander's face lit up when he saw it. "Can I take it to school to show my teachers and friends?" he asked. "Of course, that's a great idea."

♥♥♥

I made sure to speak to his teacher as well, explaining that Alexander had been asking about Mo and showing her the picture that he wanted to bring. The teacher reassured me that they would keep an eye on him and support him if he needed it. Alexander went off to school the next day, proudly carrying the picture of Mo.

I CAN'T STOP PUSHING

As the weeks went on, the pain in our hearts slowly eased. Bit by bit, we began to remove Mo's things from our home. First, we put away his food and his scratch post. It took me about two months before I could finally give away his toys, his bag of food, and a few other bits and pieces that had belonged to him. Each item I picked up brought back so many memories.

One day, as I held his favourite toy mouse, Alexander came up to me and asked, "Mummy, can I keep this one? It was his favourite, and it makes me feel like he's still here."

"Of course, sweetheart. We can keep it as a reminder of all the fun times we had with Mo." James joined us, wrapping his arms around us both. "We'll never forget him." Mo was so loved. He always will be.

Chapter 30

"TURN ON YOUR LISTENING EARS."

Parenting is beautiful… and confusing… and SLOW at the worst possible moments. There's a level of patience I never knew existed, and it's tested every single day. Every day is a blessing, and I wouldn't trade them, but catch me in one of those 'I'm-about-to-lose-it' moments and I might have a very different answer. Some days just drag on, especially during school holidays. Other days, I blink and it's bedtime. You know that rule book for parenting that doesn't exist? Well, it definitely skipped the chapter on *time*.

Kids are the ultimate timewasters. Things we as adults do on autopilot… eating, brushing teeth, leaving the house… become incredibly complicated once children are involved. And the topics James and I talk about now. Poo. Lots of poo. "What colour was it?" and "How many poos today?" It's amazing how a topic that once felt incredibly awkward to discuss at the dinner table, now feels completely normal. Then there are the nursery rhymes that are permanently lodged in my brain. I am sure you have quite a few songs now popping into your head, that you

I CAN'T STOP PUSHING

have heard one too many times.

That one thing I miss? Walking out the front door with ease. This one you will never do again, whilst you have young children, at least, just forget about it and move on with life. I was always on time - if anything, I was five minutes early. I was never, ever late.

Now, I'm never on time. I can set multiple alarms, to keep track of the time, before we need to leave, and we will still end up being late. I used to just put on my shoes, grab my bag and water bottle, and walk out. Now, every time we leave the house, it feels like planning a military operation... nappies, wipes, spare clothes, first-aid kit, sunscreen, hats, toys, snacks... for the love of snacks, don't forget the snacks.

People who aren't parents don't get it. Why would they? They have all the time in the world. How is it that these few simple tasks, can easily consume an entire day for a child? And dare I mention they become more difficult as time goes on. The whole time, the kids are flat-out refusing to listen, James and I end up taking our frustrations out on each other. Before we know it, we're in the car, simmering in awkward silence. Don't tell me this hasn't happened to you at least once.

"TURN ON YOUR LISTENING EARS."

♥♥♥

The one thing we haven't discussed is a day in the life of having children. Well, one example at least. So, let's start nice and early in the morning. 2 a.m. to be exact. Alexander was calling out to me from the other room, "Mummy, I need a cuddle."

"I'm coming baby," I said, jumping out of bed as fast as possible, as I did not want him to wake Theodore. I walked into his room to find him standing at the bottom of his bunk bed. "I want you," he said, wrapping his arms around me.

"Alright, let's have a quick cuddle, then it's back to sleep." I replied. After getting him tucked back in, he was asleep in no time, and I made my way back to bed.

Just as my head hit the pillow, Theodore came running into the room and tried to climb into our bed. I climbed out of bed, *again*, to pick him up before he woke James. He wrapped his arms around me, rubbed his eyes and then fell asleep on my shoulder. I carried him back to bed and luckily, he didn't wake up when I put him down.

By the time I finally settled back into my own bed, it was almost 3 a.m. James is such a deep sleeper and sleeps through absolutely everything. Lucky him. Honestly, I want to make the most of all the cuddles I can, before they stop wanting them.

I CAN'T STOP PUSHING

But sleep is also a basic human right... and kind of essential if I'm going to survive the day. I felt like I barely closed my eyes and they were ready to get up. Before having children, I imagined gentle cuddles and kisses waking me up. The reality? I'm usually getting whacked or kicked in the head. James, on the other hand, has... different body parts to worry about, if you know what I mean.

"Mummy, I'm hungry." Alexander said. "Mummy, I want milk." Theodore said. I could barely open my eyes - it was so bright...they'd turned the big light on. I mean...why? I squint at the clock. "It's 5 a.m. Every other house on the street is still asleep. Why are you awake? Can we please wait until 6 a.m.?"

"Snack, snack, snack." They start shouting together. You will learn very quickly how much you hate the word 'snack'. I usually try to wait until at least 6 a.m. because, seriously, 5 a.m. is just too damn early... but I gave in at 5:30 a.m. to shut them up. "Alright, alright," I moaned. "Let's get you both something to eat."

Before we had kids, James and I agreed we were going to limit screen time to the bare minimum. That went out the window pretty quickly. Alexander and Theodore aren't too bad and are usually happy to play

"TURN ON YOUR LISTENING EARS."

instead of staying glued to the TV... but let's be honest, TV means peace, and I don't get much of that... so here we are.

♥♥♥

Snacks and drinks are served, and this means I can sit down for a few minutes to have a cup of coffee. By 'a few minutes', I mean if I don't gulp down my coffee quickly, it'll be ice-cold before I drink it again, because as soon as I sit down, someone generally needs me for something.

Then as quickly as I sat down, I'm up and moving again - one load of laundry in, the dishwasher cleared, and now it's time to make their breakfast.

Alexander and Theodore are obsessed with what they call a 'snacky breakfast'. Basically, it's a mix of things served on one of those plates with all the little compartments. I try to mix it up so it's not always exactly the same...usually a variety of fruit like strawberries, blueberries, or grapes, depending on what's in season, and what they haven't turned their noses up at lately. I'll add a snack bar or a yogurt, some toast, and, of course, their daily vitamins, which they devour like they're sweets.

Every morning, without fail, they tell me they want a 'snacky breakfast'. I don't know why they bother telling me anymore - they ask for the same thing every single day.

I CAN'T STOP PUSHING

While making them breakfast, I am constantly running into the lounge, to break up yet another argument, because someone's stolen a toy - *again*. I feel out of breath, and it's only 7 a.m. If James is around, one of us keeps an eye on them while the other handles the kitchen duties. But when James is away for work, my pace and multitasking skills really kick into high gear.

Breakfast is served and there is silence for about 5 minutes. If I am feeling super lazy, which is most mornings, I will take advantage of another cheeky coffee. Five minutes go by, and this amazing breakfast I've spent the last half hour making (sometimes even longer, thanks to running in and out of the room) is only half eaten and they've already gone back to playing with their toys.

♥♥♥

I clear up the lounge, and with them happily distracted, I decide this is as good a time as any to attempt a bit of personal toilet time. Though let's be honest... there's absolutely nothing personal about it. I have to leave the door open, especially when I'm alone, so I can keep an eye on them. Luckily, we have a downstairs toilet, and from there I can just see into the

"TURN ON YOUR LISTENING EARS."

lounge to monitor what they're doing. Inevitably, they use this as the perfect time to start an argument.

I end up spending most of my time, leaning sideways on the toilet, shouting down the hallway, "leave each other alone." To make matters worse, the toilet is right next to the front door. And thanks to the extractor fan on the outside wall, anyone walking past can hear *everything* I'm saying.

And if that wasn't enough, one of them, usually Theodore, comes and sits in the bathroom for a full-blown conversation, while I'm sat on the loo. I don't really feel like sitting and talking while I'm on the toilet, doing my own personal business but clearly, this doesn't seem to bother him. Then Theodore asks, "Mummy, are you doing a poo?" I sigh, "Yes, Theodore, I am." Then Alexander shouts from the lounge, "Mummy I need you."

"Alexander, I am on the toilet, can you come here please or wait a few minutes?", I reply. "Never mind." Alexander shouts.

"Mummy, can I see?" Theodore then asked. "No, Theodore, I'm sorry, but you are not looking into the toilet." Then he follows with, "Mummy, can I wipe your bum for you?" At this point, my head is in my hands. "No, Theodore, you are not wiping my bum for me." I can't believe I'm having this conversation with my two-year-old.

I CAN'T STOP PUSHING

He then goes running outside the bathroom, leaving me a moment to check a message that came through on my phone.

Next thing I hear the front door creaking open, which of course is right next to the bathroom. Theodore starts shouting, "Hello, Mr. Mailman." I leap up, pulling my knickers up so fast that I'm still untucking and tying my robe as I rush around the corner to see the mailman, handing the boys some parcels. The mailman laughed, "Good morning. Looks like you've got some eager helpers today." He said smiling. "Yes, they're always full of surprises," I reply. "Thanks for the parcels, I didn't even hear the doorbell go."

After he leaves, I turn to the boys. "Alright, no more opening the door by yourselves, please?" They nod and run off to play. Thank goodness it was just the mail man. You'll be happy to know I have since added an extra lock, to ensure they can't open the door without me. Especially Theodore.

♥♥♥

I made my way back to the toilet to sort myself out, as I of course, had not yet finished. Dramatic toilet experience finally over and I headed into the kitchen to tidy up. After I'd finally finished cleaning the kitchen, I

"TURN ON YOUR LISTENING EARS."

thought I'd take a few minutes to play with the boys. Playing with your children is supposed to be this joyful, heart-warming experience, right?

Their little faces lighting up when you pull out the toys. "Look, Mummy built you a train track." I announced. The boys looked at the track, their eyes wide with excitement. For a moment, I thought, this is going to be great. But before I could even finish my thought, they swooped in like tiny tornados. Alexander grabbed the track and yanked one of the pieces away. Theodore, not wanting to be left out, pulled the rest apart in about five seconds flat.

"Wait. No, no, no. I just built that." I groaned, watching my carefully made train set, crumble before my eyes. They looked up at me, innocent as ever, as if they hadn't just destroyed the very thing, I spent fifteen minutes building. All I could do was sigh. It's not like I didn't have other things to do - laundry was still piled up, the house was a mess, and I hadn't even managed to squeeze in a shower yet. And here I was, trying to play with them, only to see all that effort literally ripped apart in seconds.

"Okay, boys," I said. "Let's try again… but maybe this time we leave the track together for more than five seconds?" They just giggled. Clearly, this wasn't going to end well. I may as well give up and begin the wonderful

I CAN'T STOP PUSHING

task of trying to get them dressed. Getting them dressed really depends on whether we're going out or staying home. If the weather's awful and we're not leaving the house, I honestly can't be bothered. The arguments just aren't worth it. But if we're going out, well, where should I begin? Today, I thought I'd take them to the park. It was a beautiful day, and they'd have loads to keep them busy. I then spent the next *hour* repeatedly asking them to get dressed.

"Come on, boys, let's get dressed," I said. I even offered to help them, but of course, they thought it was game time and ran off. "Come get me, Mummy." Theodore shouts, giggling as he runs around. Making it a game *sometimes* works, especially when I say, "Who's going to be the winner?" They're both ridiculously competitive, so that usually speeds things up. If not, I move on to Plan B: confiscating toys and switching off the TV. But instead of just getting dressed, they'd rather waste more time being angry… usually by launching a variety of toys at me. Still trying to keep the mood positive, I used one of our little tricks. "Turn on your listening ears, please," I say to them. They both put their hands to their ears and pretend to twist them. I always find it makes me smile when they play along. "Click,

"TURN ON YOUR LISTENING EARS."

click, click." they both said at the same time. "Alright, let's see if those listening ears are working," I laughed. "Please get dressed so we can get going."

I'm not entirely convinced the ears actually get switched on anymore... but it's worth a shot.

They *said* they'd get dressed, so while I waited for them to follow through, I dashed upstairs for a quick wipe-down.

I got myself dressed and brushed my teeth - all while keeping one eye on the camera feed from the lounge on my phone.

Feeling slightly less like a zombie and more like I could actually tackle the day, I headed back downstairs. To my relief, Alexander was already dressed. I took the opportunity to get Theodore sorted while he was glued to the TV and it actually worked. Mission accomplished.

Just as I was pulling Theodore's top over his head, Alexander shouted, "Mummy, I'm starving. I need a snack!"

"You've just had breakfast," I replied. "You didn't even finish it. If you're still hungry, you can have what's left." He folded his arms. "But I don't want that, Mummy. I want something else. Can I have a biscuit?" I tried not to laugh. "A biscuit? How about finishing your breakfast first?" "No, I don't want that," Theodore added. "I want a biscuit

too." What *is* it with kids and biscuits? I go through a pack every few days. They're obsessed. After the begging, pleading and mini tantrums, I gave in. "Alright, alright.
Fine. One biscuit each."

Now it was time to brush their teeth. Honestly, any kind of physical training would help, but running definitely gives you an advantage. Chasing them down is only the first part. Then you've actually got to brush their teeth. I'll admit I've skipped this step before… don't judge me, I swear it's not often. Alexander's pretty good when he remembers, though I always do an extra scrub just in case we missed the last one. Theodore on the other hand insists on brushing his teeth by himself. I try the 'give mummy a turn' trick, but 99% of the time it just turns into an argument. We go back and forth like this for what feels like forever - him clinging to his independence, me just trying to make sure his teeth aren't growing moss.

♥♥♥

Eventually, with both boys' teeth *somewhat* brushed (and my sanity just about intact), we make it to the front door. I ask Alexander, again, if he needs the toilet. "No." Of course not. Naturally, this is the moment they

"TURN ON YOUR LISTENING EARS."

remember they need to bring toys. Not just one. Multiple. Why can't they just pick one each so we can leave the house like semi-normal humans? "Okay," I said. "You can each pick two toys and no more."

As they made this very serious decision, I spotted that the shoes I'd neatly lined up by the door had been flung across the living room. And the bag I'd packed earlier?

Now unpacked and spread across the kitchen floor. I closed my eyes. Deep breath. Then knelt down and quietly started sorting it out, doing everything I could, to hold onto the last bit of patience I had left.

Finally, with the bag repacked and shoes located, I looked up to see that the boys had started playing a game in the lounge. There were toys everywhere. My heart sank. I'd just cleaned the lounge so it wouldn't be a disaster when we got home. I stood there, speechless.

♥♥♥

"Boys, I thought we were going to the park. You've been talking about it all morning." Alexander barely looked up. "We're playing right now, Mummy." Theodore nodded. "Go away, Mummy." I felt slightly annoyed… and also couldn't help laughing. After all that effort, now they didn't want to go? Of course.

I CAN'T STOP PUSHING

About half an hour later, they decided they were ready.

Which, of course, was *exactly* when I'd finally sat down with a cup of coffee. It was 11:30 a.m., and I knew as soon as we got to the park, they'd say they were starving. So, I made lunch before we left, a quick sandwich, a few crisps,

and five whole minutes of peace. And did they finish it? Of course not.

"Alright," I said. "Let's finish up. If we're going to the park today, we need to leave soon." With lunch over, I changed Theodore's nappy and once again asked Alexander to try and use the toilet. He refused. Naturally.

Then came the shoes. I asked them nicely - calmly - about ten times. Nothing. Eventually, I cracked. "Please. Just put your shoes on." Parents, you know that moment. When you've been talking to a brick wall and finally lose it a bit? Yeah. That. "I can't do it!" and "I need your help!" are the usual replies I get. "They're just wellies, boys," I said. "Just stick your foot in." I helped them both because at this point, honestly, I didn't have the energy to argue.

"TURN ON YOUR LISTENING EARS."

Since the park's so close, we usually walk. But Theodore, the little monkey, loves to run off, so I always bring the pram. I got him strapped in and finally, *finally*, we headed outside. As we stepped out, Alexander looked up at me and said, "Mummy, you still have your slippers on." I glanced down. Yep. There they were. "Good catch, Alexander," I laughed, and back inside we went.

As I put my shoes on, I decided to make myself a quick takeaway coffee. I definitely needed the caffeine boost to survive the day. I grab my coffee, glance at the clock. It's 1:30 p.m. We're dressed, fed (sort of), and finally out the door. Four hours of trying to leave… I don't even care where we're going anymore… I'm just happy to be out of the damn house.

Chapter 31

"ALL RIGHT, ONE MORE."

As we walked down the path, I asked the boys the same question I do every time we head out: "What are the three things we need to turn on today?" The boys shouted excitedly, "Our listening ears!" and put their hands to their ears, making clicking sounds. "And?" I continued. "Our kind hands and kind words," they said together. "Perfect," I said, smiling. Of course, I knew this might not last beyond the end of the street, but at least I could say I tried.

Alexander had developed an obsession with stones of all sizes. Every time we went for a walk he asked, "Mummy, can we find special stones?"

"Of course," I replied, searching as we walked. Every thirty seconds he asked, "Mummy, did you see any yet?"

"I'm looking," I assured him. He looked up at me. "You're not actually looking, are you?" He wasn't wrong... sometimes I wasn't. But I nodded anyway.

"ALL RIGHT, ONE MORE."

"I am, I promise. How about this one?" I said, picking up a colourful little stone by the wall. Alexander had a good look at it and then said, "Yes, Mummy, that's a really good one." Five stones later, he was finally happy enough to just walk and chat again.

The other highlight of any walk? Cars. Both boys are completely car-obsessed. They wave at every passing car. Alexander is all about racing and rally cars...he always hopes to spot one. Supercars are a good backup option as well. Theodore, meanwhile, loves buses... but honestly, he'll jump up and down waving at anything with wheels. Sometimes we get a friendly beep or wave from a driver and that makes their entire day. Other times, drivers are completely oblivious to their surroundings.

♥♥♥

As we continue our walk, Alexander starts pulling on my hand. "Mummy, I need the toilet." he announces, bouncing around. "Really, Alexander? Why didn't you go before we left?" He shrugs his shoulders. "I didn't have to go then." There's no toilet at the park, and he's too desperate to wait until we get home. "Alright, let's find a spot," I said, searching for a bush hidden away somewhere. I finally find a good spot and position the pram for him to hide behind.

I CAN'T STOP PUSHING

"Okay, let's do this quickly." Alexander stands behind the pram. "Is anyone watching, Mummy?"

"Nope, you're all clear," I assure him. After a moment, he relaxes and does his business.

"Done." I laughed shaking my head. "Alright, let's get going. Next time, try to go before we leave the house, okay?" I asked. "Okay, Mummy," Alexander promises. We all know that won't happen.

After what feels like forever, we finally reach the other side of town and find ourselves facing the dreaded pedestrian crossing. If you want to cause an argument between your kids, just dare to forget who last pushed the button. I've even had to cross back over again before, just so the other one could have a turn to push the bloody thing. Honestly!

"Mummy, *I* want to press the button!" Alexander shouts. "No! *My* turn! You did it last time!" Theodore argues. "Alright, boys, let's not argue," I said. "How about this: Alexander can press it now, and on the way back, it's Theodore's turn. Deal?" They both grumble but eventually agree. Crisis (barely) averted.

We make it to the park, and they are off. Alexander always likes to find a child to play with... whether the

"ALL RIGHT, ONE MORE."

other child likes it or not. Luckily, today the little boy is more than happy to play. Feeling relieved that he was happy, I turn my attention to Theodore, who's halfway up the slide. "Be careful, Theodore!" I called.

♥♥♥

I wish I could just relax on a park bench with a hot coffee and watch them play, but it's not that simple. It's more like a 2-hour panic attack with them constantly disappearing in different directions.

"Where's Alexander?" I say to myself, searching the playground for his familiar cap. There he is on the climbing frame. "Where's Theodore…?" Ah, behind the slide. "Theodore! Stay where I can see you, please!" I shout.

Just when I start to feel a bit more at ease, the inevitable happens. After only ten minutes of play, they come rushing over. "Mummy, we're starving." Alexander shouts. I laugh, shaking my head. "Didn't you two just have lunch before we left?"

"But we didn't finish it, and now we're really, really hungry," Alexander pleads. "Alright, alright…" I said, reaching into my bag. "Luckily, I came prepared." I hand each of them a small packet of biscuits and some rice cakes.

I CAN'T STOP PUSHING

"Here you go. This should keep you happy until dinner. I hope." They excitedly grab the snacks and sit down together to eat them. "Thanks, Mummy." They both said together as they finish. With mouths covered in biscuit crumbs, off they run again.

♥♥♥

After a good hour and a half of running around, it's almost time to head back home. I start the countdown.

"10 more minutes, boys!" As expected, they completely ignore me. "Five more minutes, okay?" Then the 3-minute, 2-minute, and finally 1-minute warnings. But of course, they show absolutely no sign of leaving any time soon. I now have to resort to the ultimate bargaining tool: dessert.

They absolutely *love* dessert. Snacks…yes, I know you have heard this word before many, *many* times…has an allocated, never-ending stomach and the same goes for dessert. "Okay, boys, if you leave now, there's a special treat waiting for you at home…" Alexander practically skids to a stop. "What kind of treat?" "How about some ice cream? Or maybe jelly?" Theodore runs over, covered in dirt. "Yes please." I smile and giggle to myself. Success. I have finally got their attention.

"ALL RIGHT, ONE MORE."

"Brilliant. But only if you finish your dinner first." I make sure to emphasize the fact that they need to 'finish dinner', knowing that without it, they'll ask for dessert the moment we walk through the door. They finally agree, and we make our way home.

Before you ask, I did make sure that Theodore had his turn to push the bloody button at the pedestrian crossing. I did not need that argument all the way home.

♥♥♥

Once we're back, I pop on the TV to keep them still for five minutes while I sort dinner.

Dinner time is my final uphill battle every single day. Breakfast and lunch are fine…cereal, toast, even a snacky breakfast… but dinner? Vegetables? Forget it. I will admit that on days that we've been out and I'm just too tired to negotiate, I sometimes give in and serve cereal or porridge… not snacks, just to be clear. I mean it is food, right? At least they are eating. Most kids love pasta. Not mine. Even the sneaky tomato sauce trick doesn't work. Theodore would live on yoghurt and milk if he could. I try though. Every night, I try.

As I prepare the meal, I hear them giggling in the living room, a sound that normally means they are up to mischief.

I CAN'T STOP PUSHING

I peek into the lounge… and they have emptied every toy box and scattered them all over the floor. I could have reacted in many different ways in that moment, but you know what… I turned around, walked out, went back into the kitchen and poured myself a glass of wine. I had a few sips for a moment and then continued with their dinner.

"We're starving!" they shout. "Nearly ready!" I shout back.

Dinner is chicken pieces, peas and sweetcorn (still frozen, the only way they'll eat them), plus sweet potato wedges…it's worth a shot. While their dinner is cooling down, I wander back into the lounge, to clear a space on the floor to put down their mat. They love having a picnic meal.

"Dinner is served!" I announce, placing down their plates. At first, they are excited. Then? "I don't like it!" Alexander shouts. "You haven't even tasted it yet," I reply. "It looks yucky, Mummy," Theodore adds.

I sigh, while having another sip of my wine, knowing this battle all too well. I don't think there is a single dish I have served that got a different response. As parents, we all find ways to get our children to eat, and, admittedly, it often involves more bribery.

"ALL RIGHT, ONE MORE."

If you're a parent, tell me if this sounds familiar:

Me: "If you finish dinner, there's dessert."

Alexander: "YES! I'm going to eat it all!" (Takes one bite) "Mmm, yummy!" One minute later: "Mummy, I don't like it anymore."

Me: "But you just said you did. And remember, you'll grow big and strong like Daddy."

Alexander: Flexes arms "I'm so strong!"

Me: "Exactly."

Alexander: "Mummy, I need a wee."

Me: "Go on then."

Alexander: "But I need you."

Me: "I'll be there in a minute. Just let me finish helping Theodore."

A moment later, "MUMMY. I'VE DONE A POO!"

I assist, obviously.

Back on the mat: "Mummy, I'm not hungry."

Me: "But you were starving. No dinner, no dessert."

Alexander: Divides his plate into what he will and will not eat. "I'll just have this bit."

Me: "No dessert unless you finish."

Alexander: Takes two bites, "I'm finished. Can I have dessert now?"

I CAN'T STOP PUSHING

Me: "But you didn't finish your dinner."
Alexander: "But I don't like it."
Theodore has completely deserted his dinner and is now playing with his toys again.
Me: "Nope. Two more bites of chicken, that pile of peas, and five wedges, then dessert."
Alexander: "But I'm not hungry. Can I have my dessert now?"
Me: Screams into a pillow. And gives them a piece of toast.

♥♥♥

It's about 6:45 p.m., and after finally clearing the dinner plates, I now needed to get the boys upstairs for a bath. A lovely, relaxing bubble bath *should* be the perfect way to wind down before bed. Throw in a little bit of fun with bath toys, and who wouldn't want that?

Every time I ask Alexander if he wants to have a bath, the answer is always "No!" I cannot understand why. "Come on, Alexander, a bubble bath is fun."
"I don't want to." Alexander insists, crossing his arms.

Now for the backup plan, I make it a game. "How about we have a race up the stairs? Beat me and you can watch something on my phone" I suggest. "I'm going to win." he shouts.

"ALL RIGHT, ONE MORE."

Finally in the bathroom: "Let's get undressed…"

"No!" he shouts. "What if you bring slime in the bath?" He hesitates. "And you can watch your show."

"YAY!" Finally, he takes his clothes off. Meanwhile, Theodore is already naked, yelling, "Woo-hoo! Bubbles!"

I always ask before they get in the bath if they need the toilet. "Do you need a wee or poo before you get in?" I ask. "No." they both reply.

Once they're finally in the bath, they happily start playing with their toys. I pop their favourite show on my phone, as promised, and place it at a safe distance from the bath… I know exactly how bath times usually turn out.

♥♥♥

Two minutes later, "Mummy, I need a wee." Alexander announces. "Alright, out you come," I said, helping him climb out the bath. I give him a quick dry so he can use the toilet. Alexander sits on the toilet for a moment, swinging his legs. Then he looks up at me. "Mummy, I don't need a wee anymore." I roll my eyes. "Okay, let's get you back in the bath, then."

Just as I'm about to help Alexander back into the bath, Theodore looks at me. "Mummy, I just weed in the bath." I stop for a moment, trying to find the words.

I CAN'T STOP PUSHING

"Oh, Theodore," I sigh, shaking my head. "Sorry, Mummy," Theodore said. "It's alright, accidents happen," I assure him, even though I'm screaming inside. "Let's drain this water and try again."

Back in the bath, I give the boys a bit more playtime. Of course, not a moment later, Theodore sits on the plug and lets the water out. And he keeps doing it. It's one of those plugs you push down to open or close, so every time he sits on it, it pops open and the water drains away. "Theodore, you're letting all the water out again. Try not to sit on it, my love," I remind him. "Oops," Theodore replies, pressing the plug down again...on purpose. By this point, my patience with bath time is wearing thin.

"Alright, boys, time to get out and get ready for bed," I announce. "But I don't want to get out of the bath, Mummy," they reply. "First you don't want to get in the bath... now you don't want to get out. What a surprise." I sigh. "Nooo!" they shout, launching water everywhere... the floor, walls, even the ceiling. "Stop it, you two - you're getting water everywhere," I say firmly. But they just keep laughing, like it's the funniest thing ever.

"ALL RIGHT, ONE MORE."

"Alright, that's enough," I say, pulling them both out of the bath and letting the water drain away. "You've soaked everything - including me."

"Sorry, Mummy," Alexander says.

"Yeah, sorry," Theodore adds. I take a deep breath. "Alright, let's get this mess cleaned up. You're going to help me dry this floor, okay?" They nod, looking a bit more serious now, and help me mop up the mess with towels. "Next time, please keep the water in the bath?" I say, smiling. "Okay, Mummy," they both reply, doing their best to help.

Pyjamas on… although I did need to help Alexander turn his pyjamas the right way around. "Okay, boys, let's brush those teeth," I call out, grabbing their toothbrushes. As expected, they run off in opposite directions.

Finally, they give in and make their way to the bathroom. "Nice job, Alexander," I say, watching him. "Just remember to get those back teeth too." He nods. "Like this, Mummy?" he asks, showing me. "Exactly. But let me give them a quick scrub too, just to make sure we get rid of all those germs and get them nice and clean." Alexander opens his mouth wide, letting me give his teeth an extra scrub. Theodore, on the other hand, is a different story.

I CAN'T STOP PUSHING

He insists on brushing his teeth by himself. After a bit of back and forth - which may or may not involve a full-on hostage situation - his teeth are finally clean. After brushing their teeth, Alexander and Theodore race to pick out their bedtime stories. Theodore will usually find a bus story, and Alexander grabs his favourite book about racing cars. They always pick the same stories every night. What's the point of having so many books?

Once they're settled on my bed, I sit between them and open Alexander's book. But just as we begin to read, Theodore asks, "One more story, please." He gives me a cheeky grin, knowing full well this tactic has worked many times before. "One more?" I ask. "Just one more, Mummy. Pleeease?" they both insist. "All right, one more," I say, already knowing it will inevitably turn into a few more.

The next story is a dinosaur one. We get halfway through when Theodore suddenly jumps up with a surge of energy. "I'm a dinosaur - RAWR!" he yells. Before I know it, both boys are bouncing on the bed. "Hey, you two - bedtime, remember?" I remind them. Theodore bolts out of the room. I put the book down to see what he's up to. "Where are you going, Theodore?" I call, following him to his room.

"ALL RIGHT, ONE MORE."

I pop my head through the door, and he's already emptying shoes and nappies from the cupboard, scattering them everywhere. "Tada!" he exclaims, leaping out and pointing proudly at the chaos he's made. *Am I supposed to be celebrating this?* I think.

"You're making quite a mess, aren't you?" I say with a sigh. He just looks at me and smiles. At this point, I decide to walk away. Bad idea. Now the puzzles are being thrown out of drawers, game boxes tipped out, and… as if that's not enough… they start hurling teddies into the hallway and down the stairs.

I sit on the bed, heart racing. I just want to scream. "Just breathe," I tell myself. "This will pass. This will pass." Just when I think it can't get worse, they both charge in and start using me as a human punching bag.

And then it hits me: I can't hold it in any longer. I've reached the point of no return. "Go to bed. Right now!" I shout, immediately feeling guilty. And what do they do? They look at me… and burst out laughing.

I can't win. I give up. Then I remember: I only have about twelve years with them before they'll be off living their own lives. How do I want to remember these nights… as a battle, or as a time when they had fun?

I CAN'T STOP PUSHING

So, we clear up the mess (after a few failed attempts), share loads of cuddles and kisses, and they're asleep in no time. I stand in the doorway, watching them for a moment, and I can't help but smile. They're so wonderful like this, I think to myself. I can't believe what we've been through so far - and to think it all started with someone announcing we were engaged and expecting a baby. So much has changed since then.

Quietly, I close their door and make my way downstairs, where James is finally home, and is already setting the table for dinner. He pulls me into a big cuddle and simply says, "Well done."

That's all I need to hear to make me smile. I take a moment to breathe, glass of wine in hand. I made it through another day. How can two little ones be so draining?

Will there be a baby number three?

Who knows… only time will tell. And that's okay.

We have time… because I'm still here.

Still pushing.

Acknowledgements

Writing this book was never on my to-do list… but life had other plans. And I definitely couldn't have done it without the incredible people around me.

Firstly, Chris, thank you for letting me share *our* story, and for the adventure of a lifetime so far. Thank you for your love, your patience, and for showing up every day. Life wouldn't be the same without you. And even when the boys have driven us completely mad and we're screaming at each other, I know that no matter what, we're in this together. I love you more than words (and clearly, I've used a lot of them).

To my beautiful boys, Thomas and William. You are my world and my greatest adventure. Every day with you is new and exciting and exhausting and magical. No matter how bumpy the ride gets, I love you to the moon and back.

Mum (and Dad, of course), thank you for being my rock. Through every meltdown (usually mine), and those moments when I genuinely didn't think I could do it. Your love and support have carried me more times than you'll ever know. I still don't know how you made it look so easy, but I hope I'm even half the mum to my boys that you've

I CAN'T STOP PUSHING

been to me. I love you so much.

Colin, what would I have done without you? From late-night chats to last-minute babysitting, you showed up, again and again. I'll never forget it and I cannot thank you enough.

To my amazing family and friends, thank you for the hugs, the wine, the messages, the "you've got this" pep talks when I really didn't feel like I did. For showing up, checking in, making me laugh when I wanted to cry. You held me together in more ways than you probably realise.

To every reader who's picked up this book… thank you for sticking with me through all of it. If even one page made you feel seen, a little less alone, or a little more human, then I've done what I came here to do.

And finally, to the person reading this thinking… *how am I supposed to keep going?* You already are. Keep pushing through.

www.ingramcontent.com/pod-product-compliance
Lightning Source LLC
Chambersburg PA
CBHW020339010526
44119CB00048B/528